UNDERSTANDING AND REDUCING PERSISTENT POVERTY IN AFRICA

Prior work has shown that there is a significant amount of turnover amongst the African poor as households exit and enter poverty. Some of this mobility can be attributed to regular movement back and forth in response to exogenous variability in climate, prices, health, etc. (''churning''). Other crossings of the poverty line reflect permanent shifts in long-term well-being associated with gains or losses of productive assets or permanent changes in asset productivity due, for example, to adoption of improved technologies or access to new, higher-value markets.

Distinguishing true structural mobility from simple churning is important because it clarifies the factors that facilitate such important structural change. Conversely, it also helps identify the constraints that may leave other households caught in a trap of persistent, structural poverty. This volume represents an interdisciplinary effort by leading anthropologists, economists, political scientists and sociologists with longstanding research programs on poverty in rural Africa. The chapters in this book help to distinguish the types of poverty and to deepen understanding of the structural features and constraints that create poverty traps. Such an understanding allows communities, local governments and donors to take proactive, effective steps to combat persistent poverty in Africa.

This book was previously published as a special issue of the *Journal of Development Studies*.

Christopher B. Barrett is International Professor in the Department of Applied Economics and Management and Co-Director of the African Food Security and Natural Resources Management Program at Cornell University and Editor of the American Journal of Agricultural Economics.

Michael R. Carter is Professor in the Department of Agricultural and Applied Economics at the University of Wisconsin – Madison, Director of the BASIS Collaborative Research Program, and Associate Editor (microeconomics) for World Development.

Peter D. Little is Professor and Chair, Department of Anthropology at the University of Kentucky.

UNDERSTANDING AND REDUCING PERSISTENT POVERTY IN AFRICA

Edited by
Christopher B. Barrett, Michael R. Carter
and Peter D. Little

LONDON AND NEW YORK

First published 2008 by Routledge
2 Park Square, Milton Park, Abingdon, Oxon, OX14 4RN

Simultaneously published in the USA and Canada
by Routledge
270 Madison Avenue, New York, NY 10016

Routledge is an imprint of the Taylor & Francis Group, an informa business

Typeset in Times New Roman by KnowledgeWorks Global Limited,
Southampton, UK
Printed and bound in Great Britain by MPG Books Ltd, Bodmin, Cornwall

British Library Cataloguing in Publication Data
A catalogue record for this book is available
from the British Library

Library of Congress Cataloging in Publication Data
A catalog record has been requested

ISBN 10: 0-415-41138-6 (Hbk)
ISBN 13: 978-0415-41138-7 (Hbk)

CONTENTS

CHAPTERS

Understanding and Reducing Persistent Poverty in Africa: Introduction to a Special Issue

CHRISTOPHER B. BARRETT, MICHAEL R. CARTER, &
PETER D. LITTLE

I. The Magnitude of Poverty in Africa and the Need for New Approaches

That the majority of Africans are materially poor is hardly disputable, nor very surprising. After all, the continent has been dealt a very unfavourable historical hand. A devastating and cruel global slave trade, long periods of colonial occupation, and a series of European-backed commercial ventures to exploit Africa's considerable natural wealth provided little institutional, infrastructural, and human capital when African countries began to achieve independence during the past century (Illife, 1987). More recently, cold war and post-cold war politics, prolonged conflicts, a series of structural adjustment experiments, and the HIV/AIDS pandemic have left large parts of the region poorer than even 20 years ago. Unlike East Asia, which has enjoyed a dramatic reduction in the absolute number of people living in poverty over the last 15 years, or South Asia, which has seen a sharp decline in the percentage of its population that is poor, sub-Saharan Africa has seen dramatic increases in both the total number of poor people and the fraction of its population that is poor (World Bank, 2000).

This reality has not gone unnoticed, and world leaders have rhetorically at least placed poverty reduction in Africa at the centre of global development efforts, as embodied in the United Nations Millennium Task Force report (UN, 2005). Yet the task is daunting. The most up-to-date figures available from the World Bank (2005) imply a population-weighted poverty gap of 42 per cent for sub-Saharan Africa as a whole (including the Republic of South Africa) relative to the $2 per-day per capita international poverty line.[1] Summed together, a poverty gap of this magnitude adds up to a shortfall of more than $200 billion per year to bring all sub-Saharan Africans up to the modest $2 per day standard of living.[2] Equal to two-thirds of the region's gross annual income and nearly ten times current global aid flows to Africa, this staggering sum underscores the need for a rigorous, strategic focus on how to propel self-reinforcing growth among the poor.

There is a general sense that past approaches, perhaps especially those predicated on simply getting the macro economy and prices 'right' – the preoccupation of donor agencies in the 1980s and 1990s – have failed to generate the broadly based economic growth needed for sustainable poverty reduction (for example, see Williamson, 2003). This recognition has in turn motivated a search for better understanding of the micro- and meso-level constraints that limit economic growth and poverty reduction.

This special issue represents an interdisciplinary attempt at advancing such an understanding, at helping shed light on how and why some African households have managed to escape or avoid persistent poverty, while others have not. This focus necessarily highlights the heterogeneity of the poor, distinguishing between different categories of poverty, the variety of structural constraints faced by distinct groups of poor peoples, and alternative growth trajectories. Such a disaggregated, dynamic approach is necessary in order to establish how donors, governments and non-governmental organisations (NGOs) might most effectively stimulate self-reinforcing growth among the poor.

The remainder of this introductory essay is organised as follows. Section II highlights novel perspectives and methods offered by the contributions to this special issue. Section III places the contributions to this issue in the context of the evolving understanding of poverty in Africa. Section IV summarises the studies' primary empirical findings on persistent poverty. Section V concludes with reflections on the nature and design of persistent poverty reduction strategies.

II. Novel Perspectives and Methods

Several features distinguish the set of studies in this issue from previous work in this area. First, each of the papers employs longitudinal data that permit the authors to identify those households and individuals who are getting ahead from those who are not, distinguishing transitory poverty caused by predictable life cycle effects and external events (for example, drought) from more enduring impoverishment related to the structural constraints of economies that do not work for their poorest members. While prior work has used longitudinal data to establish that a subset of the poor enter and exit 'transitory' poverty with some frequency,[3] the papers in this special issue focus on the non-transitory poverty of structurally poor households. The goal is to distinguish who amongst the structurally poor is positioned to move ahead over time within the existing structure, who is not, and what structural modifications or other interventions are needed to nudge the latter subpopulation onto a pathway out of poverty. In the terminology of the Carter and Barrett paper, this set of papers tries to move beyond familiar, first and second generation poverty analysis, to third and fourth generation approaches that bring into focus the structural determinants of poverty and the dynamics of those underlying structural positions.

A second novel feature of the studies presented here is that they share an asset-based approach to the study of poverty dynamics. Economists typically analyse poverty with reference to flow variables, income or expenditures reflecting budget constraints and consumption choices, respectively. However, flow measures tend to be more subject to considerable measurement error than stock variables, even in well-run surveys, because they can only rarely be directly observed and verified. Moreover, productive assets are the durable inputs used to generate income and offer the collateral base for expenditures based on credit rather than income. The stock of productive financial, physical, natural, social and human assets that households and individuals control largely determines their structural position in a society, and their ability to avoid poverty, or to escape from it if they find themselves falling backwards in the face of adverse shocks. As the Barrett et al. contribution demonstrates, the random noise inherent to flow-based measures can mask important features of the dynamics of household-level well-being. Understanding the dynamics of assets is thus fundamental to understanding persistent poverty and longer-term socio-economic dynamics.

The challenges posed by this asset-based approach to understanding poverty dynamics lead to a third distinguishing feature of the studies in this issue: they employ multiple methods and disciplinary approaches, mixing qualitative and quantitative information to better understand the problems of persistent poverty. The existing literature on African poverty has typically emphasised one or the other: the interpretive and historical (see Broch-Due and Anderson, 1999, Illife, 1987) or the quantitative, especially econometric dimensions (Grootaert and Kanbur, 1995; Baulch and Hoddinott, 2000). Recent work on poverty analysis has nonetheless underscored inherent methodological complementarities between qualitative and quantitative approaches in (cross-sectional) poverty analysis (Kanbur, 2003).

The papers in this issue try to take this integration to the next level, exploring the synergies between different ways of studying the dynamics of poverty and well-being across communities and countries. Measuring human well-being is inherently problematic, and becomes further complicated when trying to measure intertemporal changes in well-being. In this context, triangulation using multiple methods offers important advantages over single methodology approaches. That said, incorporating both qualitative and quantitative methods without strongly privileging one over the other is difficult to achieve. The Adato et al. article on poverty dynamics in South Africa gives one example of how to achieve this by comparing a poverty transition matrix based on econometric analysis with one constructed using qualitative methods.

A fourth and final distinguishing feature of the work in this issue is that it offers an in-depth look at a wide range of countries from across Africa, encompassing periods of political, climatic, and economic policy shocks that have had the potential to sharply impact poverty. These include successive and devastating droughts (Ethiopia, Kenya, Malawi and Zimbabwe), major political transitions (Ethiopia, Ghana, Madagascar, Malawi, South Africa and Uganda), and a range of different economic reform programmes (Ghana, Kenya, Madagascar and South Africa). Each of these macro-level processes have been previously linked with changes in poverty (Grootaert and Kanbur, 1995; Collier and Gunning, 1999; Carter and May, 2001; Elbers et al., 2002; Hulme and Shepherd, 2003; Dercon, 2004; Lybbert et al., 2004; Sachs et al., 2004). The explicit linkage of poverty dynamics to a wide range of different shocks (climatic, health, political, and other) represents an important step forward in linking the typically disparate literatures on risk and growth. In this sense we try to build directly on evolving conceptualisations of persistent poverty in Africa.

III. Evolving Conceptualisations of Poverty in Africa

The conceptualisation and measurement of poverty have been substantially rethought since most African states became independent in the early 1960s. Earlier anthropological assessments of poverty and rural differentiation highlighted labour and its organisation ('wealth in people') as the main measure of wealth, and control over people as the key to accumulating wealth (Guyer and Belinga, 1995; Meillassoux, 1981). The so-called 'wealth in people' argument remains important in relatively land abundant/low population savannah farming areas, as the Whitehead and Peters contributions emphasise. The converse problem, that the loss of labour power can precipitate a collapse into poverty, has become especially widespread in recent years with the rise of the HIV/AIDS pandemic and of increasingly drug-resistant malaria. As Krishna et al. document, health shocks are, in many places, the leading reason why previously non-poor households suffer a structural decline into persistent poverty. The 'wealth in people' perspective is therefore resurgent in much contemporary analysis of African poverty.

However, as population pressure has grown in important sections of Africa, and as rural economies have become more diversified, control over land, non-farm employment, and other key resources have become increasingly significant measures of wealth status. Ownership of livestock assets has been (and still is) a key wealth indicator in many parts of Africa, especially in the arid and semi-arid lands, as Barrett et al., Hoddinott and Little et al. document. Land and livestock have long been especially important in determining household food security and marketable surpluses.

One reason endowments of assets such as labour, land and livestock matter is that they condition households' ability and willingness to take advantage of emerging opportunities (see the Carter and Barrett paper). Technological change has played a central role in improvements in all measures of human well-being – income, life expectancy, health and nutritional indicators – throughout recorded human history (Fogel, 2004). Technological change in agriculture and natural resource management has played an especially important role in rural poverty reduction, not least of which in recent decades in Asia and Latin America (David and Otsuka, 1994; Datt and Ravallion, 1998; de Janvry and Sadoulet, 2002; Ravallion and Datt, 2002; Evenson and Gollin, 2003). Yet, the Green Revolution largely bypassed sub-Saharan Africa, with patterns of adoption of improved agronomic and natural resources management practices and higher yielding technologies closely associated with households' endowments of land, labour and livestock (Barrett et al., 2002). The opportunities afforded by liberalised domestic and international trade can likewise increase well-being through specialisation of production according to patterns of comparative advantage, helping reduce poverty where the micro-foundations of local factor and product markets permit poor households to seize the new opportunities (de Janvry and Sadoulet, 1993; Barrett and Carter, 1999). Where technologies remain rudimentary and terms of trade do not improve, households commonly remain poor.

The attention paid to markets and technologies as prospective handmaidens of rural poverty reduction has spawned increased attention to the geographic and socio-political determinants of poverty that condition market access and uptake of improved technologies. The relevant literature on Africa has focused especially on biophysical characteristics, such as how humidity and temperature affect agricultural productivity and health, and how population density, road infrastructure and distance to ocean ports affect commerce at the individual firm level (Sachs and Warner, 1997; Gallup and Sachs, 1998; Bloom and Sachs, 1998), but also on ethnic divisions, histories of political violence and patrimonial rule, and the complex, long-term effects of colonialism (Bates, 1981; Easterly and Levine, 1997; Collier and Gunning, 1999; Herbst, 2000; Acemoglu et al., 2001, 2002). The conclusion of much of this literature is that areas less favoured by nature and by states (both colonial and modern) have commonly become geographic poverty traps plagued by widespread destitution with limited opportunities for households to escape. Several papers in this volume offer evidence in support of this hypothesis of geographic poverty traps (Barrett et al., Little et al. and Whitehead).

The observation of geographically-based poverty pockets has motivated increased attention to the more general problem of persistent poverty in Africa. While much of the recent empirical work has been done by economists (Grootaert and Kanbur, 1995; Dercon, 1998; Baulch and Hoddinott, 2000; Carter and May, 2001; Elbers et al., 2002; Deininger and Okidi, 2003; Dercon, 2004; Lybbert et al., 2004), contributions have also come from anthropologists (Anderson and Broch-Due, 1999), political scientists (Chambers, 1997; Krishna et al., 2004), sociologists (Hulme and Shepherd, 2003), geographers (Watts, 1991) and historians (McCann, 1999).

Like many concepts in development studies, the term 'persistent poverty' – and synonymous terms such as 'chronic poverty' – is a convenient simplification of a very complex set of historical, social and political relations and is represented by a variety of empirical definitions in the literature. For the purposes of general policy analysis, one can isolate the distinguishing features and behavioural patterns associated with persistent poverty without naively assuming that history and political economy do not matter, nor getting caught up in complex webs of case-specific interpretations or sample-specific empirical operationalisations of the concept that so privilege context that comparison becomes implausible. This special issue attempts to balance site-specific social and cultural ('qualitative') and statistical ('quantitative') analyses with broader interpretations and generalisations about poverty dynamics in Africa.

To that end, the contributions to this volume explore a range of different measurements and indicators of poverty that reflect the considerable diversity in Africa's rural economies and societies. In South Africa, for example, (cash) pension transfers to the elderly play a key role (Adato et al.), while in the arid and semi-arid lands of Ethiopia, Kenya, and Zimbabwe livestock are central to well-being (Little et al.; Barrett et al.; and Hoddinott) and in Ghana, Madagascar and Malawi households' labour and land endowments heavily condition household well-being (Barrett et al., Peters, and Whitehead). Despite these and many other differences, the papers reveal a remarkable unity in showing how the mobility and immobility of certain households and individuals over time reflect their initial asset positions, the incomes and security that a greater initial asset stock generates, and the resulting cross-sectional variation in households' experience of shocks and their propensity to take up promising new technological and market opportunities.

IV. Key Findings on Persistent Poverty

Although these papers share a common perspective on the problem of persistent poverty in Africa and, at a methodological level, are bound together by a common reliance on longitudinal data and an effort to triangulate using mixed data and analytical methods, the specific cases studied are quite distinct. We can crudely lump these into three different sorts of cases, each yielding important findings that, together, help flesh out a coherent picture of the nature of persistent poverty in sub-Saharan Africa today.

In several cases, macro and sectoral level political and economic reforms or the introduction of improved technologies or new crops opened up new opportunities accessible and attractive only to some relatively better-off households. A key common denominator to this subset of the studies that encompass this special issue is their focus on identifying who has been able to take advantage of promising new opportunities, who has not, and what seem to be the keys to distinguishing between these two subgroups.

For example, Peters carefully documents how liberalisation in Malawi led to a boom in burley tobacco production, but that only a subset of the rural population was well-positioned to take advantage of these new opportunities. The benefits of policy change accrued mainly to those with requisite land, labour and access to cash or credit for seed and fertiliser, and who could join the growers' clubs that afford access to the auction floors and world market prices. Barrett et al. (2001) similarly found that only those farm households that were better-off ex ante were able to take advantage of the improved terms of trade generated by massive exchange rate devaluation in Côte d'Ivoire in 1994.

A very different sort of opportunity emerged in South Africa with the end of apartheid, which brought promise of new economic opportunities open to all South Africans. Yet Adato et al. demonstrate the existence of poverty traps caused by insufficient productive asset holdings and how social capital proves effective only for the relatively privileged in escaping that trap. Durable patterns of social exclusion and ineffective social capital impede upward mobility for the rest, leaving large numbers trapped in poverty or back-sliding into poverty even though they are temporarily non-poor.

The introduction of improved production technologies and higher-return livelihoods represent a third sort of opportunity – distinct from that created by market-oriented economic liberalisation or the removal of legal barriers that kept the majority of South Africans down – but one that likewise fails to stimulate a broad-based climb out of poverty among the poor. Barrett et al., building on Moser and Barrett (2003) and Barrett et al. (2004), discuss how poorer households in rural Madagascar have been effectively excluded by credit, insurance and labour constraints from uptake of a promising production technology that wealthier farmers have been able to use to raise rice yields by 60–80 per cent.

Whitehead similarly documents systematic patterns in who was able to take advantage of new higher-value crops and improved bullock plough technologies in rural Ghana. Those with relatively large initial holdings of land, livestock and, above all, adult male labour power were systematically better able to enjoy better yields and terms of trade and to accumulate wealth and remain secure in their livelihoods.

Other papers in the special issue study how major adverse shocks may differentially impact different subpopulations. Following northeastern Ethiopian households during and in the wake of the major 1999–2000 drought, Little et al. document a range of recovery patterns. Pre-drought livestock holdings provide a strong predictor of post-drought household wealth, a finding echoed in Barrett et al.'s empirical analysis of northern Kenyan households. And like Adato et al., Little et al. demonstrate the important role social networks play in assisting recovery from shocks while underscoring that this assistance nonetheless does not seem to offer a viable ladder out of long-term poverty. In Little et al.'s setting, social capital appears only to facilitate recovery to a low-level equilibrium. The drought had a devastating short-term impact on households, particularly among the poorest, but did not increase overall rates of poverty in the area in the medium term as households recovered reasonably quickly to their initial, albeit-impoverished state.

Hoddinott, utilising longitudinal data from rural Zimbabwean households, and Barrett et al., studying northern Kenyan households, both find strong evidence of wealth-differentiated risk management behaviours consistent with the existence of poverty traps. In particular, they posit that the churning evident in expenditure or income-based measures of well-being could partly reflect households' choice not to smooth consumption, as mainstream economic theory posits, but rather to smooth assets so as to defend one's structural position and future earning potential, as Zimmerman and Carter (2003) posited. Each paper presents strong evidence that while wealthier households indeed appear to smooth consumption as the standard theory hypothesises, as households approach what appears to be an asset poverty threshold, poorer households cease to use the few assets they possess to stabilise consumption, instead holding on to their limited assets, even if it entails destabilisation of consumption, often through reduced food intake.

Hoddinott's work also sheds light on intra-household variation in the experience of shocks. In the Zimbabwean households he studies, adult men suffered no observable change in nutritional status as a result of drought. Women, on the other hand, experienced a short-term decline in nutritional status, but recovered quickly. The greatest concern arises with respect to children younger than two, who lost, on average 15–20 per cent of growth velocity and are likely to have suffered permanent loss of stature – which is related to long-term educational attainment, health status and earnings – as a result of a short-term drought. Much as the experience of shocks varies across households, so too does it appear to differ within them according to relative initial power and wealth.

Covariate shocks such as drought are not the only adverse experiences that strike poor households. Individual and household-specific shocks such as injury and illness lead to loss of income, assets and, in extreme cases, life. Krishna et al., Barrett et al. and Whitehead all document how health shocks are managed differently by households in different economic positions and that such episodes are disproportionately responsible for knocking previously non-poor households into persistent poverty. Among the central and western Ugandan households Krishna et al. study, health shocks and associated costs and deaths of adult income earners account for nearly two-thirds of all household descents into poverty. Initial poverty is associated both with households' objective exposure to health risks, and with the ability and willingness to pay for preventive and curative care, sometimes sacrificing long-term prospects in the process.

Finally, while the above two kinds of cases look for bifurcated outcomes within a single region, a last class focuses more on the contrast between areas, emphasising the additional constraints that emerge in more remote areas. Barrett et al. exploit inter-site variation in Kenya and Madagascar to demonstrate higher rates of poverty and lower rates of escape from poverty in settings less favoured by nature and governments. Whitehead emphasises the extraordinary challenges faced by households in one of Ghana's most remote areas. Such places raise difficult policy questions as to whether and how to invest in less-favoured – not always 'lower potential' – lands.

V. Persistent Poverty Reduction Strategies

The challenge of poverty reduction is both most vexing and most urgent with respect to those who appear trapped indefinitely in a deplorable standard of living. The collection of papers that comprise this special issue offer important insights on the processes by which people become and remain persistently poor, and on interventions that might effectively help nudge them onto a sustainable growth trajectory. As donors, government policy makers and researchers struggle to understand and design appropriate policies to reduce persistent poverty in sub-Saharan Africa, it will become ever more important to clearly distinguish true structural mobility from simple, transitory churning around the poverty line, to identify the targetable characteristics of those who are structurally persistently poor, and to focus attention on the key productive assets and exclusionary processes that constrain the persistently poor's access to steady improvement in well-being.

The asset-based perspective brought by these papers suggests two broad classes of policy to address the problem of persistent poverty. The first is safety net policies that directly reduce the risks that may drive poverty-perpetuating survival strategies or that provide protection against loss of key assets to effectively insure vulnerable people, including the presently non-poor, against potentially catastrophic downside risk.

The second class might be termed 'cargo net' policies that help the persistently poor:

(i) build up their base of productive assets through education, land reform or other means, so that they can reach a minimum threshold of wealth necessary to self-finance or self-insure in ways that do not replicate their initial poverty;
(ii) improve the productivity of the assets held by the persistently poor through improved technologies or market access, thereby increasing their capacity to generate investible surpluses and to self-finance and self-insure; or,
(iii) access the finance (insurance and capital) necessary to protect and invest in assets and thereby to relax the constraints that often drive persistent poverty.

This conceptual view of poverty – with its implication that there may be minimum wealth thresholds that vary by location, group and types of capital – may imply a trade-off between helping more people versus helping a smaller number of people get over the threshold. For example, cargo net asset transfer programmes that are 'a mile wide and an inch deep' may be predictably ineffective in the presence of critical wealth thresholds that define structurally bifurcated accumulation trajectories. On the other hand, policies that try to relax risk directly, or to enhance access to finance, may not face such a trade-off. A safety net policy that successfully created a bankable index insurance mechanism would become cheaper – not more expensive – per beneficiary as it reached more people.

There is much yet to understand about persistent poverty and policies to combat it. With their focus on assets and the structural determinants of poverty, and their reliance on multiple methods of inquiry, the papers in this special issue offer some important first steps. We hope that these steps will help others advance further in order to allow communities, governments, NGOs and donors to take proactive, effective steps to reduce persistent poverty in Africa.

Acknowledgement

Authors' names are listed alphabetically, seniority is not assigned. The authors thank participants at the November 2004 BASIS CRSP policy conference on Combating Persistent Poverty in Africa for valuable comments and conversations, Harold Alderman, Paul Cichello, Cheryl Doss, Jane Guyer, Angelique Haugerud, Paul Heisey, Ravi Kanbur, Anirudh Krishna, Ken Leonard, John Pender, Agnes Quisumbing, Paul Siegel, Frances Stewart, Steve Younger and an anonymous reviewer for their expert assistance as manuscript reviewers and Eliza Waters for her assistance in assembling the special issue. This work has been made possible by support from the United States Agency for International Development (USAID), through grant LAG-A-00-96-90016-00 to the BASIS CRSP and the Strategies and Analyses for Growth and Access (SAGA) cooperative agreement, number HFM-A-00-01-00132-00. The views expressed here and any remaining errors are the authors' and do not represent any official agency.

Notes

1. The poverty gap index gives the mean percentage distance below the poverty line average over the entire population, counting the non-poor as having a zero poverty gap.
2. Data and computations available from authors by request.
3. See Baulch and Hoddinott (2000) or Hoddinott (2003) for excellent summaries of that literature.

References

Acemoglu, D., Johnson, S. and Robinson, J. A. (2001) The colonial origins of comparative development: an empirical investigation, *American Economic Review*, 91, pp. 1369–1401.

Acemoglu, D., Johnson, S. and Robinson, J. A. (2002) Reversal of fortunes: geography and institutions in the making of the modern world income distribution, *Quarterly Journal of Economics*, 117, pp. 1231–94.

Anderson, D. M. and Broch-Due, V. (Eds) (1999) *The Poor are Not Us: Poverty and Pastoralism in Eastern Africa* (Oxford, UK: James Currey Publishers).

Barrett, C. B., Bezuneh, M. and Aboud, A. (2001) Income diversification, poverty traps and policy shocks in Côte d'Ivoire and Kenya, *Food Policy*, 26, pp. 367–84.

Barrett, C. B. and Carter, M. R. (1999) Microeconomically coherent agricultural policy reform in Africa, in J. Paulson (Ed) *African Economies in Transition, Volume 2: The Reform Experiences* (London: Macmillan).

Barrett, C. B., Moser, C. M., McHugh, O. V. and Barison, J. (2004) Better technology, better plots or better farmers? Identifying changes in productivity and risk among Malagasy rice farmers, *American Journal of Agricultural Economics*, 86, pp. 869–88.

Barrett, C. B., Place, F. and Aboud, A. (Eds) (2002) *Natural Resources Management in African Agriculture: Understanding and Improving Current Practices* (Wallingford, UK: CAB International).

Bates, R. H. (1981) *Markets and States in Tropical Africa* (Berkeley: University of California Press).

Baulch, B. and Hoddinott, J. (2000) *Economic Mobility and Poverty Dynamics in Developing Countries* (London: Frank Cass).

Bloom, D. E. and Sachs, J. D. (1998) Geography, demography, and economic growth in Africa, *Brookings Papers on Economic Activity*, 1998, pp. 207–73.

Carter, M. R. and May, J. (2001) One kind of freedom: the dynamics of poverty in post-apartheid South Africa, *World Development*, 29, pp. 1987–2006.

Chambers, R. (1997) *Whose Reality Counts?: Putting the First Last* (London: Intermediate Technology Group Publishing).

Collier, P. and Gunning, J. W. (1999) Explaining African economic performance, *Journal of Economic Literature*, 37, pp. 64–111.

David, C. C. and Otsuka, K. (1994) *Modern Rice Technology and Income Distribution in Asia* (Boulder: Lynne Riener Publishers).

Datt, G. and Ravallion, M. (1998) Farm productivity and rural poverty in India, *Journal of Development Studies*, 34(4), pp. 62–85.

Deininger, K. and Okidi, J. (2003) Growth and poverty reduction in Uganda, 1999–2000: panel data evidence, *Development Policy Review*, 21, pp. 481–509.

de Janvry, A. and Sadoulet, E. (1993) Relinking agrarian growth with poverty reduction, in M. Lipton and J. van der Gaag (Eds) *Including the Poor* (Washington, DC, World Bank).

de Janvry, A. and Sadoulet, E. (2002) World poverty and the role of agricultural technology: direct and indirect effects, *Journal of Development Studies*, 38(4), pp. 1–26.

Dercon, S. (1998) Wealth, risk and activity choice: cattle in Western Tanzania, *Journal of Development Economics*, 55, pp. 1–42.

Dercon, S. (2004) Growth and shocks: evidence from rural Ethiopia, *Journal of Development Economics*, 74, pp. 309–29.

Easterly, W. and Levine, R. (1997) Africa's growth tragedy: policies and ethnic divisions, *Quarterly Journal of Economics*, 112, pp. 1203–50.

Elbers, C., Gunning, J. W. and Kinsey, B. H. (2002) Convergence, shocks and poverty, Tinbergen Institute Working Paper 2002–035/2.

Evenson, R. and Gollin, D. (2003) Assessing the impact of the Green Revolution: 1960 to 2000. *Science*, 300, pp. 758–62.

Fogel, R. W. (2004) *The escape from hunger and premature death, 1700–2100: Europe, America, and the Third World* (Cambridge: Cambridge University Press).

Gallup, J. L. and Sachs, J. D. (1998) Geography and economic growth, in B. Pleskovic and J. E. Stiglitz (Eds) *Proceedings of the annual World Bank conference on development economics* (Washington, DC: World Bank).

Grootaert, C. and Kanbur, R. (1995) The lucky few amidst economic decline: distributional change in Cote d'Ivoire as seen through panel datasets, 1985–1988, *Journal of Development Studies*, 31, pp. 603–19.

Guyer, J. I. and Belinga, S. L. E. (1995) Wealth in people as wealth in knowledge: accumulation and composition in Equatorial Africa, *Journal of African History*, 36, pp. 96–120.

Herbst, J. I. (2000) *States and Power in Africa: Comparative Lessons in Authority and Control* (Princeton: Princeton University Press).

Hoddinott, J. (2003) Pathways from poverty in sub-Saharan Africa, International Food Policy Research Institute working paper.

Hulme, D. and Shepherd, A. (2003) Conceptualizing chronic poverty, *World Development*, 31, pp. 403–24.

Illife, J. (1987) *The African Poor: A History* (Cambridge, UK: Cambridge University Press).

Kanbur, R. (Ed) (2003) *Q-Squared: Combining Qualitative and Quantitative Methods Of Poverty Appraisal* (Delhi: Permanent Black).

Krishna, A., Kristjanson, P., Radeny, M. and Nindo, W. (2004) Escaping poverty and becoming poor in twenty Kenyan Villages, *Journal of Human Development*, 5, pp. 211–26.

Lybbert, T. J., Barrett, C. B., Desta, S. and Coppock, D. L. (2004) Stochastic wealth dynamics and risk management among a poor population, *Economic Journal*, 114, pp. 750–77.

McCann, J. C. (1999) *Green Land, Brown Land, Black Land: an environmental history of Africa. 1800–1990* (Portsmouth, NH: Heinemann).

Meillassoux, C. (1981) *Maidens, Meals and Money: Capitalism and the Domestic Community* (Cambridge: Cambridge University Press).

Moser, C. M. and Barrett, C. B. (2003) The disappointing adoption dynamics of a yield-increasing, low external input technology: the case of SRI in Madagascar. *Agricultural Systems*, 76, pp. 1085–1100.

Ravallion, M. and Datt, G. (2002) Why has economic growth been more pro-poor in some states of India than others?, *Journal of Development Economics*, 68, pp. 381–400.

Sachs, J. D., McArthur, J. W., Schmidt-Traub, G., Kruk, M., Bahadur, C., Faye, M. and McCord, G. (2004) Ending Africa's poverty trap, *Brookings Papers on Economic Activity*, 1, pp. 117–240.

Sachs, J. D. and Warner, M. (1997) Sources of slow growth in African economies, *Journal of African Economies*, 6, pp. 335–76.

United Nations Millennium Project (2005) *Investing in Development: A Practical Plan for Achieving the Millennium Development Goals* (New York: United Nations).

Watts, M. (1991) Entitlements or empowerment? Famine and starvation in Africa, *Review of African Political Economy*, 51, pp. 9–26.

World Bank (2005) *World Development Indicators* (Washington, DC: World Bank).

Williamson, J. (2003) From reform agenda: a short history of the Washington Consensus and suggestions for what to do next, *Finance and Development*, Sept., 10–13.

World Bank (2000) *World Development Report 2000/2001 – Attacking Poverty* (New York: Oxford University Press).

Zimmerman, F. J. and Carter, M. R. (2003) Asset smoothing, consumption smoothing and the reproduction of inequality under risk and subsistence constraints, *Journal of Development Economics*, 71, pp. 233–60.

The Economics of Poverty Traps and Persistent Poverty: An Asset-Based Approach

MICHAEL R. CARTER & CHRISTOPHER B. BARRETT

I. Persistent Poverty and the Challenge of Forward-looking Poverty Measurement

Much empirical poverty analysis of poverty is dedicated to defining, measuring or locating who is recently poor. Such analysis is almost unavoidably backward looking in the sense that it creates a portrait of who was poor at the time survey data were collected. However, the observation of persistent or chronic poverty motivates a more forward-looking question: Who will likely remain poor into the future?[1]

The empirical papers that comprise this special issue contribute to answering this question by trying to understand the structural reasons that underlie poverty's persistence, asking when and why poverty reproduces itself over time, 'laying eggs' as one of the informants to the *Chronic Poverty Report* describes it (CPRC, 2004: 3). Some of the papers try to understand who among the poor is structurally positioned to take advantage of new economic opportunities when they appear (Adato et al., Barrett et al., Krishna et al., Peters and Whitehead).[2] Other papers ask who is positioned to ride out the negative shocks that destroy opportunities, while still maintaining a viable basis for future advance (Hoddinott and Little). In their search for viable and less viable structural positions, these studies implicitly define an asset-based approach to persistent poverty, where the term asset is understood to broadly include conventional, privately held productive and financial wealth, as well as social, geographic and market access positions that confer economic advantage. The goal of this paper is to frame this approach by developing the conceptual foundations for asset-based poverty measures that permit a forward-looking approach and help identify and ultimately understand the structure and persistence of poverty.

The remainder of this paper is organised as follows. Section II motivates an asset-based approach by noting the limited ability of conventional poverty measures to deal with time and poverty transitions. Section III then takes a first step towards a forward-looking, asset based approach to poverty by developing the concept of the (static) asset poverty line. A corresponding family of measures based on this line – modelled on the familiar Foster-Greer-Thorbecke (1984, hereafter FGT) logic – are then presented. These measures provide information on the depth of structural poverty given the current distribution of assets (and the returns to those assets).

Section IV then allows for the possibility of asset accumulation/decumulation dynamics. After a brief review of the economics of poverty traps, Section IV develops forward-looking measures of dynamic asset poverty based the concept of a dynamic asset poverty threshold (which we label the 'Micawber'[3] threshold) that potentially separates those able to move to a high (non-poor) asset position from those caught in a low-level equilibrium trap. Section V considers some of the econometric challenges that confront the identification of the Micawber threshold and forward-looking poverty measures, while Section VI concludes the paper with reflections on the policy implications and uses of these measures.

II. Why an Asset Based Approach to Poverty?

As a starting point for thinking about persistent poverty, it is useful to consider what standard expenditure-based poverty measures can and cannot tell us. Figure 1 schematically represents alternative approaches to measuring poverty. The most common (first generation) approach to poverty measurement relies on household expenditure (or income) data from a single point in time. Once a money metric poverty line is defined, the population can be divided into poor and non-poor categories, and the standard suite of headcount and other FGT measures can be calculated to gauge the extent and depth of poverty within an economy. Application of these first generation poverty analysis methods to repeated cross-sectional surveys allows insight into the evolution of poverty within a society.

However, as numerous authors have remarked, cross-sectional poverty measurement is unable to distinguish between two very different patterns of poverty, each with a very different meaning. Consecutive cross-sectional findings of, say, a 33 per cent poverty headcount ratio could reflect a society in which the same one-third of individuals are persistently poor, period after period. In such a society, poverty would be experienced by only a minority, but intensely and indefinitely for those unlucky few. Alternatively, repeated observations of the same headcount ratio could reflect a reality in which poverty is a purely transitory phenomenon in which individuals routinely swap places on the basis of random outcomes, or perhaps based on age or other demographic process. Over time, all households would be

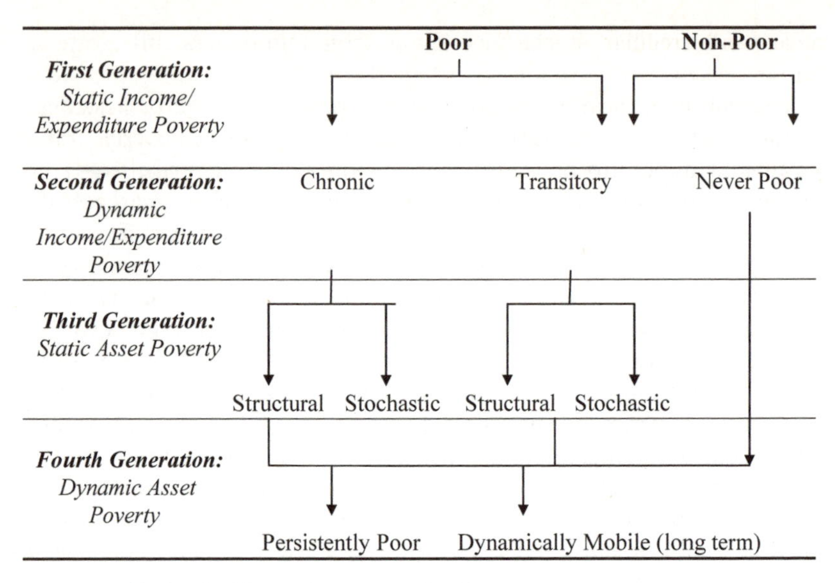

Figure 1. Alternative approaches to poverty measurement

poor one-third of the time, thus all would share the burden of poverty equally and only for a minority of the time.

Clearly a society typified by the first reality would be a much more polarised society, one vulnerable to hopelessness among a large subpopulation – and perhaps inter-class strife – and thus quite different from the one typified by the second poverty process. Unfortunately, first generation poverty measures are incapable of distinguishing between these starkly different poverty processes.

Interest in distinguishing between these two very distinctive situations has motivated a second generation of poverty analysis based on longitudinal or panel data that offer repeated observations over time on a single cohort of individuals or households. Grootaert and Kanbur (1995) offer an early and influential example of panel data-based expenditure or income poverty analysis. As illustrated in Figure 1, panel data permit a further decomposition of households into three categories: the always or chronically poor, the sometimes or transitorily poor, and the never poor.

In a summary of initial studies of panel data studies of poverty, Baulch and Hoddinott (2000) report on detailed studies of poverty dynamics based on panel data from ten countries. Updating that effort, Hoddinott (2003) found that the number of panel studies of African poverty had risen substantially. A common finding across all of these studies is that transitory poverty comprises a rather large share of overall poverty. The large share of transitory poverty based on income or expenditure underscores the inherent stochasticity of flow-based measures of welfare. People are better off one period than another without any significant or lasting change in their underlying circumstances, particularly the stock of productive assets under their control, due solely to random price and yield fluctuations and irregular, stochastic earnings from remittances, gifts, lotteries, and so forth.[4]

The Achilles heel of these informative, second generation poverty measures is that they cannot distinguish between very distinctive sorts of poverty transitions. Individuals may appear to be transitorily poor in a standard panel study, moving from the poor to the non-poor state over time due to either of two markedly different experiences. Some may have been initially poor because of bad luck. Their transition to the non-poor state simply reflects a return to an expected non-poor standard of living (a stochastic poverty transition). For others, the transition may have been structural, due to the accumulation of new assets, or enhanced returns to the assets that they already possessed.

Similarly, those transitorily poor individuals who move from being non-poor to poor, can represent a mix of experiences. For some, it could represent a return to an expected standard of living, after a brief non-poor hiatus afforded by a spell of good luck. For others, it could be a temporary transition caused by bad luck in a later survey period. Finally, for yet others, it could be a structural move caused by the loss of assets (due to illness, natural disaster or theft), or by a deterioration in returns to their assets brought on changes in the broader economy (for example, unemployment or declining terms of trade).[5]

In short, the inability of second generation poverty analysis to distinguish structural from stochastic transitions limits its ability to describe how well an economy works for its least well off members. Does an observed amount of upward mobility reflect an economy that functions for at least some of the poor, facilitating asset accumulation and increased returns to the assets held by the poor? Or, does it reflect a large amount of a large amount of structural stasis and hopelessness that is masked by the churning of households that already possess assets and enjoy expected returns that predict a non-poor standard of living on average?[6]

To overcome these limitations of second generation poverty measurement, this paper reformulates poverty measurement in asset space. Section III uses the work of Carter and May (1999, 2001) to identify an asset poverty line as a natural extension of the familiar flow-based concept of an expenditure or income poverty line. This asset poverty line can be used to distinguish stochastic from structural transitions, making it possible to decompose poverty transitions, as shown in Figure 1. The asset poverty line can also be used as the basis for a suite of structural poverty indicators that provide a snapshot of structural poverty, cropped of the influence of stochastic transitions.

While defining and measuring poverty based on the asset poverty line provides important information on the structural foundations of poverty, it does not speak to the long-term persistence of structural poverty. As illustrated in Figure 1, analysis based on the asset poverty line cannot by itself identify whether the currently structurally poor are likely to remain poor over the longer term, caught in a poverty trap, or indeed whether a subset of the structurally non-poor can sustain their positions over the longer term. To further decompose these groups according to their long-term, persistent poverty status requires a fourth generation approach to poverty based on an understanding of underlying patterns of asset dynamics. As discussed in Section IV, identification of the dynamic asset poverty threshold is the key to decomposing current structural poverty into its persistent and more transitory components.

III. The Asset Poverty Line and Measures of Structural Poverty

This section takes first steps toward developing forward-looking poverty measures that are informative about the nature of long-term, structural poverty. After defining the concept of an asset poverty line, this section shows how the asset poverty line can be used to identify those households who lack the assets that, on average, generate a non-poor level of expenditure or income. Such measures are informative about the likely prospects of a household possessing a given asset portfolio, given past asset productivity, much like increasingly-popular vulnerability measures (Christiaensen and Boisvert, 2000; Christiaensen and Subbarao forthcoming).

(a) Using the Asset Poverty Line to Decompose Poverty Transitions

Distinguishing between stochastic and structural transitions requires information on assets and expected levels of well-being. Conceptually, this is a relatively straightforward exercise, as indicted by Figure 2, adapted from Carter and May (2001). The vertical axis measures a standard flow indicator of achieved material well-being (or utility), typically measured as income or expenditure. The conventional money metric poverty line measured in this dimension is denoted $\underline{u}$. The horizontal axis measures the assets that generate a household's livelihood.

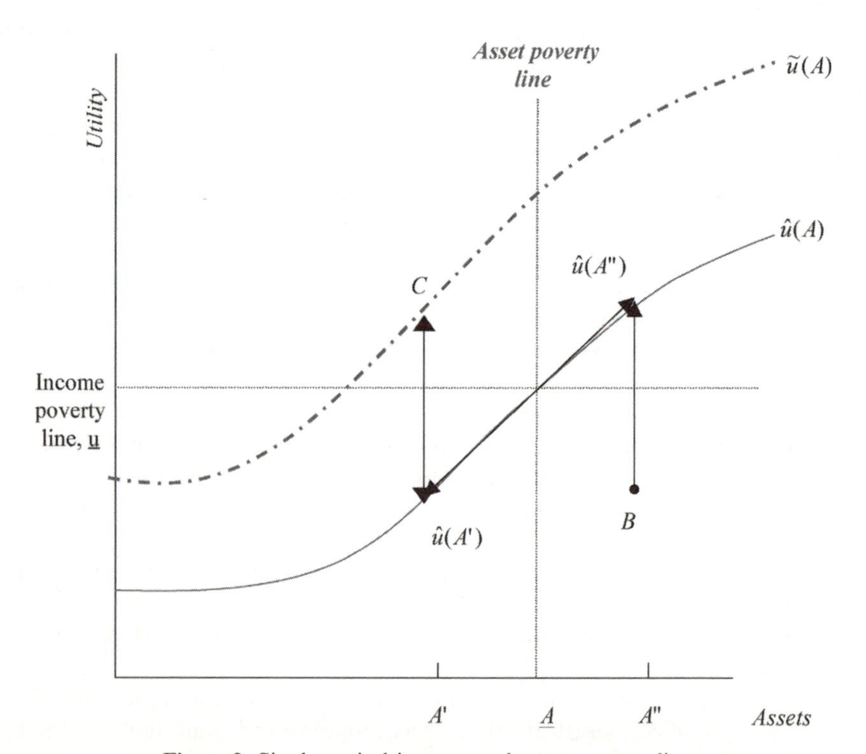

Figure 2. Single period income and asset poverty lines

While these assets are multi-dimensional, tangible and intangible, we assume here for illustrative purposes that assets are one-dimensional, or that we have non-problematically aggregated them into a one-dimensional index measure. We briefly discuss methods for building such an asset index in Section V.

One can map the relationship between assets and income, expenditures or some other flow measure of well-being, as illustrated by the (expected) livelihood function graphed in Figure 2.[7] The asset poverty line is then simply the level of assets (denoted $\underline{A}$ in Figure 2) that predicts a level of well-being equal to the poverty line, $\underline{u}$. Purely for expositional purposes, assume for the moment that the livelihood function does not change over time.[8] Then in any time period, a household is stochastically poor if it holds assets worth at least $\underline{A}$ yet its realised income or expenditure falls stochastically below $\underline{u}$. Conversely, the household is structurally poor if its stock of assets is less than $\underline{A}$ and its realised income or expenditure level falls, as expected, below $\underline{u}$.

Panel data permit estimation of the asset poverty line and enable the third generation decomposition of poverty transitions shown in the third row of Figure 1. A household that moved over time from above to below the standard expenditure-based poverty line could be said to have made a stochastic transition back to its expected status if the household's assets still mapped into an expected standard of living below the poverty line. In Figure 2, this transition is illustrated as the movement from point C back to the point $\hat{u}(A')$. Alternatively, a household that moves from $\hat{u}(A'')$ to $\hat{u}(A')$ would have made a structural transition below the poverty line due to a loss of assets from A'' to A'.

Similarly, a household that made the opposite observed expenditure transition (from below to above the poverty line) could be said to have made a structural transition if household assets predicted expenditure initially below the poverty line, at $\hat{u}(A')$, but in the subsequent period assets yield expected expenditures above the poverty line. Such a shift could occur either because of asset accumulation that moved the household to point $\hat{u}(A'')$, or because of improved returns on the household's stock of assets, which shifted the livelihood function from $\hat{u}(A)$ to $\tilde{u}(A)$, bumping expected and observed expenditures from $\hat{u}(A')$ to point C in Figure 2. Finally, in Figure 2, the stochastic transition out of poverty would be manifest as a movement from point B to $\hat{u}(A'')$, which merely reflects a return to a household's expected welfare level given its asset holdings and the livelihood function mapping assets into expenditures.

This asset-based approach thus moves us considerably closer to being able to address the key questions surrounding households' longer-term prospects of being non-poor. The challenge in implementing these ideas results from the need to estimate a livelihood mapping between assets and expenditures (or income) statistically. Carter and May (2001) illustrate an application of this method to South African households, cautiously denoting a household as stochastically poor only if one can reject the statistical hypothesis that their assets are expected to yield flow-based welfare measures below the standard expenditure or income poverty line.

While one could quibble with components of their methodology, the Carter and May analysis nicely illustrates both the strengths and limitations of the asset poverty line. They estimate that less than half of the observed transitions out of poverty in South Africa over the 1993–98 period are structural, as 60 per cent of the households who made the transitions had initial period assets that strongly predicted well-being in excess of the standard poverty line. In terms of downward mobility, Carter and May find that only a small fraction (15 per cent) clearly fell into poverty for stochastic reasons, while fully 51 per cent of those who fell behind suffered asset losses that left them structurally poor in the latter survey period.

In addition to helping unpack the nature of observed past transitions between poor and non-poor status, the asset poverty line can also distinguish households that have a current asset base that predicts a non-poor future standard living from those whose current circumstances predict a standard of living below the poverty line. This latter group is arguably of greater concern – and an appropriate target for intervention – as they would be expected to remain or become poor in the future, absent asset accumulation or further structural change in the economy.

(b) Structural Poverty Measures

The forward-looking, structural insights into poverty afforded by the asset poverty line can be used to create a class of structurally-based poverty measures based on the familiar FGT poverty measures. Recall that the FGT class of decomposable, single-period P_α poverty measures is defined as:

$$P_\alpha = \frac{1}{N}\sum_{i=1}^{N} I_i \left(\frac{\underline{u} - u_i}{\underline{u}}\right)^\alpha \tag{1}$$

where N is the sample size, $\underline{u}$ is the scalar-valued poverty line, u_i is the flow-based measure of welfare (income or expenditures), I is an indicator variable taking value one if $u_i < \underline{u}$ and zero otherwise, and α is a parameter reflecting the weight placed on the severity of poverty. Setting $\alpha = 0$ yields the headcount poverty ratio P_0 (the share of a population falling below the poverty line). The higher order measures, P_1 and P_2, yield the poverty gap measure (the money metric measure of the average financial transfer needed to bring all poor households up to the poverty line) and the squared poverty gap (an indicator of severity poverty that is sensitive to the distribution of well-being amongst the poor).

Consider now the FGT class of measures defined around the asset poverty line, $\underline{A}$:

$$P_\alpha^{\underline{A}} = \frac{1}{N}\sum_{i=1}^{N} I_i^{\underline{A}} \left(\frac{\underline{A} - A_i}{\underline{A}}\right)^\alpha \tag{2}$$

where A_i is asset stock of household i and the binary indicator variable $I_i^{\underline{A}} = 1$ if $A_i < \underline{A}$ reflects whether the household i's asset stock falls below the static asset poverty line. The order zero measure, $P_0^{\underline{A}}$ provides a head-count measure of the structurally poor, while $P_1^{\underline{A}}$ measures magnitude of the average asset transfer (or accumulation) needed to bring the structurally poor just up to the asset poverty line. Analogous to the flow-based FGT measures, higher order asset poverty measures ($\alpha > 2$) will be sensitive to the distribution of assets amongst the poor.

(c) The Temporal Dimension: Limitations of the Asset Poverty Line

As in the South African example discussed above, the asset poverty line gives a sharper picture of the nature of poverty dynamics. Analysis of P_α^A measures along with the standard flow-based FGT measures also promises a much more complete and forward-looking poverty portrait.

However, analysis based on the (static) asset poverty line suffers from two conceptual weaknesses. First, like the standard flow-based measures, its definition depends on an arbitrary living standard ($\underline{u}$ in the notation above). Second, analysis based on the asset poverty line does not account for any predictable future changes in the assets of the poor (nor predictable changes in the future returns to those assets). Analysis based on the static asset poverty line therefore cannot reliably indicate whether structurally poor households are likely to remain so into the foreseeable future, or whether they are headed in the right direction, nor whether structurally non-poor households can be expected to remain non-poor indefinitely, that is, are they free and clear of the poverty line for good? Put differently, how many of the structurally poor are likely to be structurally mobile over the long term? Alternatively, how many are caught in a long-term trap of persistent poverty? Similarly, how many of the structurally non-poor are actually in a sustainable situation?

Answering these questions requires an approach to poverty based on asset dynamics. Similar to the way in which the single period asset poverty line can distinguish between stochastic and structural poverty transitions in the short term, the remainder of this paper argues that a dynamic asset poverty line can help distinguish households caught in a long-term structural poverty trap from those expected to follow an upward trajectory, that is, those who enjoy structural economic mobility. The next section develops the theoretical foundations for the dynamic asset poverty line, the threshold at which accumulation dynamics bifurcate, leading to multiple dynamic welfare equilibria, including the possibility of a poverty trap.

IV. Poverty Traps and the Dynamic Asset Poverty Threshold

Households that can steadily accumulate assets or who enjoy steady technical change or favourable shifts in their terms of trade will grow their way out of poverty. Among very poor populations, this growth could take some time, but movement nonetheless proceeds steadily in the right direction. For these households, time would be a dependable ally in the fight against poverty and would oversee a domestic process of convergence as poor households climb out of poverty and catch-up to their better-off neighbours. But does time work in favour of poor households, or is the case that the many of the poor 'can't get ahead for falling behind' (Barrett and Carter, 2001–2)?

Analogous questions of convergence have figured prominently in the macro-economic debate over the growth of nations.[9] While there are some critical differences between economic growth at national and household levels, macro-economic growth theory and its attendant convergence controversy provide some useful insights and language for thinking about poverty and growth within nations. After a brief consideration of key ideas that have emerged from the macro growth and convergence literature, this section explores the microeconomics of household accumulation and poverty traps.

(a) Thresholds and Clubs: Insights from the Convergence Controversy over the Growth of Nations

The workhorse model of neoclassical economic growth relies on an assumption of diminishing returns to assets (that generate a stream of income) to hypothesise that poorer nations will tend to catch up over time, or converge, with the incomes of richer nations. However, there is overwhelming empirical evidence that income convergence does not accurately describe economic growth at the macro level of nation states. In the words of Lant Pritchett (1997), the observation of 'divergence, big time' has invited 20 years' debate and new theorising about alternative frameworks that might fit the data better.[10]

Within the macro-growth literature, two alternatives to the neoclassical growth model have emerged to account for the observed pattern of divergence. The first is the idea of conditional or club convergence, meaning that groups of countries that share similar intrinsic characteristics tend to converge to a living standard that is unique to their group or club. While there is convergence within clubs, there can be divergence between clubs.

The idea of conditional convergence dates back at least to Baumol (1986) and DeLong (1988) writing on 'club convergence', wherein distinct subpopulations (of nations, in their case) appear to converge on different steady-state growth rates. Quah (1993, 1996, 1997) extended this notion to more general distribution dynamics to explore the mobility of countries across income levels. Theories of conditional convergence turn fundamentally on the existence of an exclusionary mechanism, an immutable intrinsic characteristic that keeps members of one group or club facing a lower level equilibrium from moving to another group or club with a higher level equilibrium. The extant macro literature offers only rather vague suggestions as to why such exclusionary mechanisms might exist, hypothesising about distance from sea ports, agro-ecological conditions and their impacts on health and agricultural productivity, natural resource endowments and their effects on incentives to industrialise, or the institutional legacies of colonial history, including intra-national ethnic diversity (Acemoglu et al., 2001; Bloom and Sachs, 1998; Bloom et al., 2003; Easterly and Levine, 1997; Masters and Macmillan, 2001; Sachs and Warner, 1997).

The second alternative posits thresholds and multiple equilibria. From this perspective, there is no unique equilibrium for a country. Instead, controlling for a country's intrinsic characteristics, both high- and low-level equilibria are available. Whether the country reaches a high level equilibrium, or remains trapped at a low-level equilibrium, depends on whether the country begins above, or is able to boost itself over a critical minimum threshold level of capital or income.

In contrast to club convergence vision of intrinsic differences between nations, the multiple equilibria growth models posits the possibility of poverty traps related to thresholds at which returns are locally increasing (Azariadis and Drazen, 1990; Fiaschi and Lavezzi 2003; Murphy et al., 1989). These theories formalise earlier, informal models of economic 'take off' or 'big bang' (Young, 1928; Rosentstein-Rodan, 1943; Nurkse, 1953; Myrdal, 1957; Rostow, 1960), which likewise depended fundamentally on locally increasing returns. The key insight of these models is that without a coordinated push that dramatically increases the scale of production and, or market size past some threshold, so that firms can tap into (locally) increasing returns to scale, the economy will get stuck at a low income equilibrium.[11]

While both the club and threshold perspectives can account for patterns of divergence in the global economy, distinguishing between them empirically is clearly important from a policy perspective. While the econometric challenges are daunting, several recent papers have made significant progress on this front. Canova (2004) shows that countries can be divided into groups or clubs that gravitate toward distinct equilibrium income levels, while Hansen (2000) identifies critical threshold levels of (initial) per-capita GDP and literacy that divide low from high equilibrium countries. However, because Hansen's thresholds are cast in terms of time-invariant initial conditions (that is, initial conditions effectively define clubs), it is not yet clear whether the data support the notion that there are multiple equilibria available to any given country. Nonetheless, the notion that poverty traps can result from either unfavourable intrinsic characteristics, or from locally increasing returns processes that generate multiple equilibria is an important idea to carry forward to the analysis of household level poverty.

(b) Microeconomics of Poverty Traps and Asset Dynamics

As with nations, individuals may also have intrinsic characteristics (skills, savings propensities, discount rates, and geographic locations) that condition their desired level of accumulation and ultimate equilibrium level of well-being. However, there may also be analogues to the locally increasing returns to scale that generate multiple equilibria and thwart the ability of initially poor households to catch up and converge with their wealthier neighbours. This section focuses on forces that can create locally increasing returns at the individual level and draws out their implications for poverty traps and asset dynamics.

When returns are locally increasing, there will be a positive relation between wealth (level of assets) and the marginal returns to assets. At the microeconomic or household level, a positive relationship between wealth and marginal returns can exist for at least three reasons:

(1) the underlying income generating process may itself directly exhibit increasing returns to scale, either because the primal technology exhibits locally increasing returns or because input (output) prices, or transactions costs are negatively (positively) related to scale over some significant range;
(2) some high return production processes may require a minimum project size such that only wealthier households can afford to switch to and adopt the high return process; and
(3) risk and financial market considerations may cause some lower wealth households to allocate their assets so as to reduce risk exposure, trading off expected gains for lower risk, thereby making expected marginal returns to wealth lower for lower wealth households.

For expository purposes, we will examine the second of these three reasons in detail.

Consider the case where a household can allocate its productive wealth to two distinct productive activities, L_1 and L_2. Both activities exhibit diminishing returns to wealth, as under the canonical neoclassical growth model. However, activity L_2 has a minimum scale of operation due to sunk costs of operation or of switching into L_2 (that is, it generates no returns if the wealth dedicated to this activity is below this minimum level). Figure 3 graphs these two production technologies as well as the steady state asset values that a household would choose if it were exogenously restricted to one technology or the other. Note that the graph is drawn for a given set of intrinsic characteristics (individual time preferences, technical efficiency or skill, and so forth).

For an individual with these characteristics, the value A_1^* denotes the steady state value for a household restricted to livelihood activity L_1, yielding income or material well-being level U_L^*. The value A_2^* denotes the same thing for L_2, yielding the higher level steady state income, U_H^*.[12] For illustrative purposes, Figure 3 places the asset poverty line, $\underline{A}$, between A_1^* *and* A_2^*. Note that this implies that any individual who settles into equilibrium at A_1^* would be caught in a poverty trap even though in principle a higher, non-poor equilibrium exists.

So how would a household sort itself between activities and their implied equilibrium asset and well-being levels. Assuming that no risk or other constraints limit the adoption of the technologies, Figure 3 shows that the optimal livelihood choice for households is activity L_1 for households with asset stocks up to A_S, and L_2 for households with assets in excess of A_S. Although each of these livelihood functions exhibits diminishing returns, there are locally increasing returns in the neighbourhood of A_S, the threshold at which households optimally switch from L_1 to L_2. There are plentiful empirical examples of such patterns, for example, households possessing more assets who adopt higher return crop varieties or agronomic practices, wealthier households who get skilled salaried employment rather than unskilled casual wage labour, or households who graduate from poultry or small ruminants to indigenous cattle to improved dairy cattle and advanced

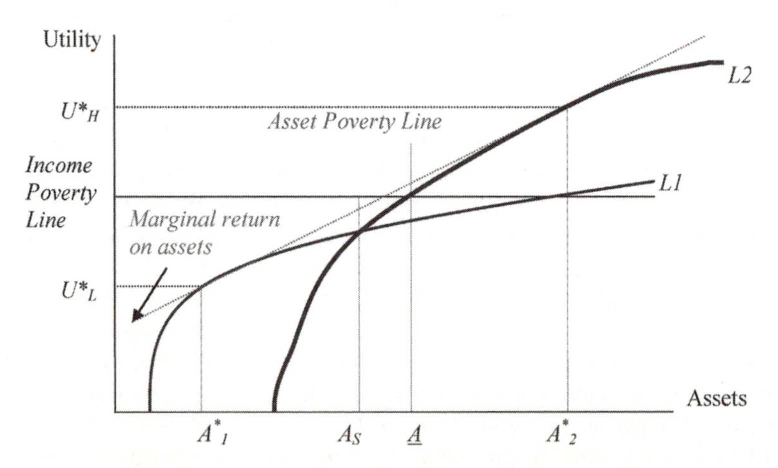

Figure 3. Asset poverty with multiple livelihood options

animal husbandry practices (for example, artificial insemination, supplemental feeding, and so forth) as wealth grows and these methods become affordable.

While it thus seems reasonable to postulate that poorer households might utilise technology L_l, the key dynamic question is whether or not the pattern of locally increasing returns would impede the ability of this household to accumulate, cross over asset level A_S, and catch up with wealthier households. Consider an individual with assets between A_1^* and A_S. Two features of this problem are relevant to the long-term accumulation choices of this individual. First, the individual will be earning relatively low rates of return on their modest asset holdings, a factor which further perpetuates their poverty because they earn less investible surplus, after meeting immediate consumption needs, than do richer households. Second, the marginal short-term, or myopic, incentives to save are depressed. If household accumulation decisions were driven by these depressed returns and liquidity constraints, then the household would indeed be expected to reach an equilibrium asset holding at the relatively low level, A_1^*.

The key question then becomes whether or not household savings and accumulation behaviour will be driven by these low marginal returns. A forward-looking household would know that while the marginal returns to further accumulation are low, increased accumulation has strategic value in moving the household closer to the asset level(s) where returns sharply increase. Clearly the household's first best option would be to borrow sufficient funds so that it could leap forward to a higher return asset level. Increasing returns would therefore not suffice by themselves to trap poor households at low asset levels.

If, however, poor households are rationed out of credit markets, as a now voluminous literature suggests, or if they lack socially mediated access to capital, as Mogues and Carter (forthcoming) suggest occurs in many polarised societies, then discrete jumps enabled by strategic borrowing may not be possible. In the face of exclusion from financial markets, a poor household's only option would be to move forward slowly with an autarchic savings strategy. This approach would require substantial short-term sacrifice (diminished consumption) with little return even in the medium term (as marginal returns to new assets are low until the household reaches A_S). If the poor household finds it desirable and feasible makes this sacrifice, then it will – with sufficient time – reach the asset level necessary to achieve the higher returns and will eventually converge toward the asset and income levels of initially wealthier households. But many very poor households cannot afford to reduce consumption further, or at least the opportunity cost of tightening their belts further – for example, in terms of foregone energy for work, withdrawing children from school, and so forth – make autarchic accumulation unattractive. If the poor household opts not to undertake extraordinary savings, it then settles into a poverty trap.

A somewhat complex theoretical literature explores the conditions under which each of these two outcomes is most likely to occur (for example, Loury, 1981; Banerjee and Newman, 1993; Galor and Zeira, 1993; Mookherjee and Ray, 2002). The basic intuition is, however, simple. It would seem likely that if a household was not 'too far', in some sense, from the asset level where increasing returns occur, then it would be likely to pursue the autarchic accumulation strategy. However, as the distance from that level increases, it seems less likely that households would find it feasible and desirable to pursue the autarchic accumulation strategy. Zimmerman and Carter (2003) identify a Micawber threshold, the critical asset threshold below which it is no longer rational or feasible to pursue the autarchic accumulation strategy. If it exists, the Micawber threshold thus constitutes a dynamic asset poverty threshold, analogous to the static asset poverty line discussed in the previous section. Households whose assets place them above that threshold would be expected to escape poverty over time, while those below would not. One needs to identify this dynamic asset poverty threshold in order to disaggregate the structurally poor into those expected to escape poverty on their own over time through predictable asset accumulation and those expected to be trapped in poverty indefinitely.

As with the existence of multi-equilibria in macro growth models, the existence of the Micawber threshold has important policy implications (some of which we discuss in the conclusion to this paper). While the theoretical literature offers insights as to when such a threshold will occur, the really important question is the empirical one of whether such a threshold exists and, if so, where. As a first step in this direction, we now consider testable implications of such a threshold if it exists.

For illustrative purposes, denote $A^* < A_S$ as the critical dynamic asset poverty threshold. As discussed before, households with assets in excess of A^* will choose to save and accumulate (despite low marginal returns to accumulation) until they reach the point A_S where it becomes optimal to switch to livelihood strategy L_2 and to grow to a steady state level of capital, A_2^* . Households below this threshold will by definition not find it optimal to make the sacrifices needed to reach A_S. Absent access to intermediate capital, such households will thus revert to a steady state level of capital, A_1^*. Figure 4 portrays this scenario and its implication for asset dynamics. The top panel depicts the two distinct livelihood strategies of Figure 3, L_1 and L_2. The bottom panel shows the asset dynamics that ultimately drive the system. Now we can better see how the critical threshold for poverty dynamics is neither $\underline{A}$, the static asset poverty line, nor A_S, the point at which households rationally switch from L_1 to L_2 in the static model, because while adoption of improved livelihood strategies is indisputably important, such choices are also reversible. Rather, the critical threshold is A^*, the unstable dynamic asset equilibrium, the threshold at which accumulation dynamics bifurcate. A household with initial wealth just above A^* will naturally accumulate assets, at some point pass A_S and switch from L_1 to L_2, and ultimately settle at a long-term equilibrium asset stock of A_2^*, yielding steady state utility U_H^* above the income poverty line. By contrast, a household with initial wealth just below A^* will naturally shed assets down to A_1^*, never switch to the more remunerative livelihood strategy, and settle ultimately at an equilibrium welfare level of U_L^*, well below the income poverty line. Note that in this particular case illustrated in Figure 4 ($A_1^* < A^* < \underline{A}$), the structurally poor at any point time (those with assets below $\underline{A}$) can be divided into those who will be persistently poor ($A < A^*$) and those who will eventually surpass $\underline{A}$ on their way to the high level equilibrium, A_2^* ($A^* \leqslant A < \underline{A}$)).

While Figure 4 was drawn with $A_1^* < A^* < \underline{A}$, other configurations are possible. Adato et al. (this volume) estimate that $A_1^* < \underline{A} < \underline{A}^*$ in South Africa. In this case, all the currently structurally poor, and a subset of the non-currently structurally poor would be expected to gravitate to the low-level equilibrium. These different cases

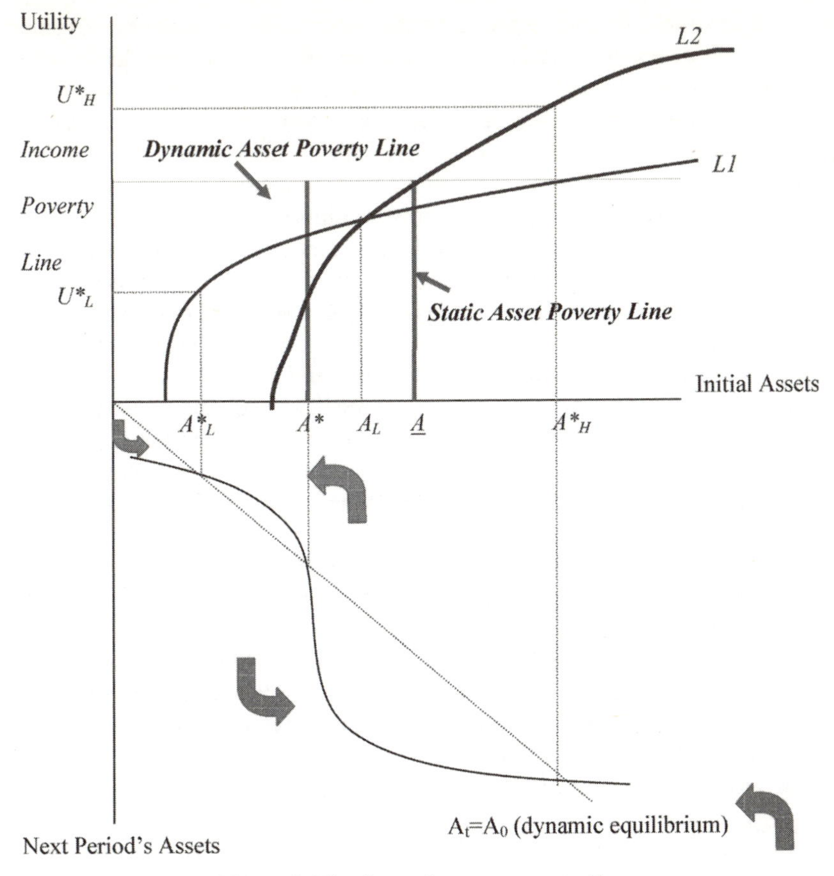

Figure 4. The dynamic asset poverty line

suggest the importance of poverty measures based on the Micawber threshold, something to which the next section now turns.

(c) Using the Dynamic Asset Poverty Threshold to Measure Chronic Poverty

The standard, money-metric poverty line is frequently criticised as an arbitrary construct which has no behavioural foundation.[13] In contrast, the Micawber or dynamic asset poverty threshold is an empirical construct whose foundation is observed behaviour. Conceptually, the Micawber threshold can separate households expected to be persistently poor from those for whom time is an ally that promises better standards of living in the future. Poverty measures based on the Micawber threshold thus promise not only to distinguish stochastic from structural changes, but also to identify the long-run health of an economy as judged by its ability to facilitate growth in living standards amongst its least well-off members.

Analogous to the discussion in Section III, consider the following restatement of the FGT family of poverty measures around the Micawber threshold:

$$P_{\alpha}^{A^*} = \frac{1}{N}\sum_{i=1}^{N} I_i^{A^*}\left(\frac{A^* - A_i}{A^*}\right)^{\alpha} \tag{3}$$

where A_i is asset stock of household i and the binary indicator variable $I_i^{A^*} = 1$ if $A_i < A^*$ and reflects whether the household i's asset stock falls below the dynamic asset poverty threshold. The dynamic asset poverty gap $(A^* - A_i)$ indicates the asset transfer that is necessary to place a household in a position from which they can grow and sustain a non-poor standard living in the future. This class of dynamic asset poverty measures allows for the very real possibility that some of those who are presently structurally non-poor would be expected to decumulate assets over time and fall into poverty. This is precisely the sort of forward-looking measure that policymakers need in order to gauge the health of an economy and to target poverty reduction interventions appropriately. Analogous to other FGT-based measures, $P_{\alpha}^{A^*}$ will give a persistent poverty headcount measure for $\alpha = 0$, a measure of the average transfers needed to eliminate persistent poverty for $\alpha = 1$, and a distributionally sensitive measure of the severity of persistent poverty for $\alpha \geqslant 1$. In conjunction with the standard poverty measures, and the measures based on the asset poverty line discussed earlier, which describe conditions in the recent past and the near future, respectively, $P_{\alpha}^{A^*}$ measures offer a longer-term perspective on the likely evolution of well-being, and thereby flesh out the dynamics of well-being at the lower tail of the wealth distribution.

V. Empirical Strategies to Identify Poverty Dynamics and Critical Asset Thresholds

A very recent empirical literature has begun to test statistically for the existence of poverty traps.[14] Unfortunately, much of this literature has taken its cue from the macroeconomic growth literature on convergence and often uses parametric methods that assume globally decreasing returns to scale to explore the dynamics of household income or expenditure. However, as the discussion here has made clear, poverty traps are defined by a threshold in *asset* space around which accumulation dynamics bifurcate and are defined by the existence of some range over which increasing returns might prevail. A household that suffered a temporary income shock that pushed it below the poverty line, but which did not degrade its asset base, would be expected to recover to its pre-shock level of well-being.[15] That is, in the language of this paper, households that suffer stochastic income poverty transitions should not be expected to fall into poverty traps.

In contrast, a household that suffered a loss of productive assets (for example, a loss of assets that pushed it below the dynamic asset poverty threshold A^* in Figure 4) might indeed fall into a poverty trap. In short, without a firm grounding in an asset-based approach to poverty – which permits us to distinguish the dynamics of households that experience stochastic from structural transitions – we cannot test empirically for the existence of poverty traps.[16] Furthermore, imposing assumptions of strict concavity (that is, globally decreasing returns), assumes away one of the key features for which one ostensibly wishes to test.

To date there has been no systematic development of empirical strategies to identify poverty dynamics and critical asset thresholds. This section briefly maps out key elements of the extant tool kit for exploring this exciting topic.

(a) Flexible Methods for Estimating Dynamic Asset Poverty Thresholds

Estimation of the sort of asset dynamics displayed in Figure 4 in order to test for the existence of a dynamic asset poverty threshold confronts two basic problems. First, not only is the relationship potentially highly non-linear, but also the dynamic asset poverty threshold is an unstable equilibrium, away from which households move over time. This means that we would expect few observations in the neighbourhood of the threshold itself in any data set and an unstable equilibrium can easily be mistaken for heteroskedastic errors (Barrett, 2005). The second problem is that most households possess a portfolio comprised of multiple assets. Estimation of asset dynamics must somehow deal with this dimensionality problem.

Lybbert et al. (2004) examine a pastoral population whose major productive asset is livestock. This feature of the economy they study makes the second basic issue, asset aggregation, relatively easy to solve.[17] To solve the first problem, Lybbert et al. estimate livestock dynamics using a non-parametric kernel estimator. This estimator is sufficiently flexible to capture high-order non-linearities. In addition, because it is non-parametric, local curvature is estimated using nearby points, meaning that a local twist in the asset dynamics relationship is not overwhelmed by the weight of distant points, as might happen using parametric regression methods. Lybbert et al. find strong evidence of a dynamic asset poverty threshold as well as evidence that, as predicted, recovery from shocks depends fundamentally on whether or not the shock casts the household below that threshold. These results corroborate qualitative ethnographic research among the same subject population.

The asset aggregation issue is less easily solved in the case of more complex economies. Barrett et al. (this volume) and Adato, Carter and May (this volume) flexibly estimate asset aggregation weights using factor analysis or by regressing expenditure or other well-being measures on households' productive assets. As detailed in those papers, these approaches permit the creation of asset indices in which the weights can both vary over time and depend themselves on the presence or absence of complementary assets in the household's wealth portfolio. While the properties of these asset indices have yet to be fully worked out, they permit the authors to test for the presence of dynamic asset poverty thresholds in more complex economies, again using relatively simple non-parametric kernel or nearest neighbour estimators.[18] Both papers find evidence of such thresholds.

(b) Directions for Future Analysis of Asset Dynamics

The bivariate non-parametric methods employed by Lybbert et al. (2004), Barrett et al. (this volume) and Adato, Carter and May (this volume) depend on two non-trivial econometric assumptions. First, these studies presume that all households in the same structural position all lie within the same accumulation regime. However, as the theory of poverty traps makes clear, households facing otherwise identical initial conditions may follow different accumulation trajectories if one enjoys better capital or insurance access than the other. And households with equal access to finance may face quite different accumulation trajectories when they have different livelihood functions due to spatio-temporal variation in agro-ecological or policy conditions. The challenge is to find ways of separating households into distinct capital access and accumulation regimes conditional on underlying livelihood mappings, either via ex ante measurement or through the development of sufficiently flexible econometric methods. In addition, a secondary problem is to control for other factors may influence accumulation (for example, life cycle household savings patterns) that could be spuriously correlated with initial asset holdings.

In addition to these regime identification and prospective omitted relevant variables problems, these existing studies implicitly assume that that unobserved household characteristics are uncorrelated with initial asset condition. If this assumption is incorrect, then these analyses are likely to confound the true structural state dependence of multiple equilibria models with what might be termed a spurious state dependence. The later would result if households with initially low levels of assets remain in a structurally poor state, not because of barriers to accumulation, but because they share intrinsic characteristics (for example, low work ethic or a high discount rate) that place them in a low-level equilibrium 'club.'

To resolve this identification problem, one would conceptually like to observe an experiment in which higher and lower asset households experienced fundamental changes in their asset positions (for example, through weather or other exogenous shocks that fundamentally altered asset holdings). True structural dependence would suggest that households with these exogenously altered asset positions would shift between low and high equilibrium positions. Under spurious dependence, households would be expected to return to their original equilibrium attractor point. In practical econometric terms, resolution of this problem is likely to require at least three periods of observations with significant random perturbations in the asset positions of households. As with the macro-growth literature reviewed above, significant additional work needs to be done before we can fully distinguish between club convergence and multiple equilibrium theories.

Short of resolving these econometric challenges, the study of poverty dynamics and the identification of critical asset thresholds are among the tasks best suited to mixing qualitative and quantitative methods (Hulme and Shepherd, 2003). Panel data can be used to stratify households for qualitative study via oral histories (for example, Barrett et al. this volume, Adato, Carter and May, this volume), participatory methods can be used to define poverty transitions then studied quantitatively using survey methods (Krishna, 2003; Krishna et al., 2004; Kristjanson et al., 2004; Krishna et al., this volume), or other means of sequential or simultaneous mixing of qualitative and quantitative methods can be effectively employed. Qualitative analysis can be especially valuable in identifying historical causes of structural transitions that predate initial surveys.

VI. Toward Persistent Poverty Reduction Strategies

Reformulating poverty analysis explicitly on an asset basis offers important advantages. Identification of the asset poverty line makes it possible to distinguish structural from stochastic poverty transitions. Identification of the dynamic asset poverty threshold permits a further refinement of poverty measurement, making it possible to distinguish households likely to escape poverty over the longer term from those apparently mired in a poverty trap. Application of these structural or asset-based approaches to poverty should ultimately underwrite a more satisfying analysis of the contentious question of the impact of market-oriented liberalisation policies on long-term poverty dynamics.

While these measurement issues are important, perhaps the deeper value of an asset-based approach is that it offers three important policy insights. First, it permits us to determine whether there exists a minimum configuration of assets or economic conditions required for households to ultimately engineer their own escape from poverty. From this perspective, the asset-based approach we advance adds specificity to John Williamson's (2003) call for minimum asset bundle.

Second, the asset based approach promises insights into the enabling conditions necessary to assure that time is an ally of poor households. As discussed above, the existence of the threshold depends on the degree to which the household is excluded from intertemporal exchange through credit, insurance or savings, whether formally or through social networks. A household with perfect access to capital over time and across states of nature would not face a critical threshold. Such a household would always be able to access the funds needed to build assets so as to move onto a natural growth trajectory. Similarly, such a household could use (formal or informal) insurance relationships to protect its assets from shocks that might otherwise threaten its ability to generate a high rate of return and reach or recover to a non-poor equilibrium.

Third and finally, this asset approach has implications for the design and positioning of safety net policies. The arguments put forward here indicate that the long-term implications of shocks depend not on the absolute magnitude of the shock, but where a shock leaves the household ex post. Households that do not fall below the Micawber threshold would be expected to use time and markets to engineer an eventual recovery to a higher, non-poor equilibrium living standard. Households that fall below that threshold would not be expected to recover but, instead, to suffer a permanent deterioration in their position (Carter et al., 2005). Thus households' need for a safety net depends less on the magnitude of the shock they experienced – as it is usually conceptualised based on the standard economics of insurance – and more on their asset position ex post of a shock.

As policymakers and development practitioners increasingly turn their attention to the problem of persistent poverty and its correlates of hopelessness and polarisation, we researchers must adapt our analytical toolkits. In this paper, we have made a case for availing ourselves of emerging longitudinal data on households and individuals and framing poverty analysis using an asset-based approach that pays particular attention to the underlying, systemic dynamics of critical assets. This is the only way to distinguish deep-rooted, persistent structural poverty from poverty that passes naturally with time due to economywide growth processes. While empirical research that takes asset dynamics and the possibility of poverty traps seriously remains in its infancy, the promise of such research is considerable in its capacity to inform targeting of interventions, the identification of key enabling conditions to open up pathways out of poverty for the structurally poor, and the design of safety net programming.

Acknowledgement

The authors thank Harold Alderman, Felix Naschold, participants in the November 2004 USAID BASIS CRSP policy conference on Combating Persistent Poverty in Africa and an anonymous referee for helpful comments on an earlier draft. This work has been made possible by support from the United States Agency for International Development (USAID), through grant LAG-A-00-96-90016-00 to the BASIS CRSP, and the Strategies and Analyses for Growth and Access (SAGA) cooperative agreement, number HFM-A-00-01-00132-00. The views expressed here and any remaining errors are the authors' and do not represent any official agency.

Notes

1. Vulnerability-based approaches to poverty, which ask who is at risk of being poor in the future, share this forward-looking approach to poverty (for example, Dercon, 2004).
2. The sense that the development liberalism of the 1980s and 1990s came up short on reducing poverty has led to a similar search to understand the minimum asset positioning needed for households to constructively participate in the opportunities afforded by a market economy. John Williamson, who coined the term Washington Consensus that is often used to label the suite of liberalisation policies popular in the 1980s and 1990s, argued that governments must ensure that citizens have the minimum asset base and market access required to save, accumulate and succeed in a market economy (Williamson, 2003). Williamson suggests that without such assurance, some households will be trapped in poverty, unable to use time and markets to fundamentally improve their well-being or that of their children.
3. We owe this label to Michael Lipton (1993), who wrote of a 'Micawber threshold', below which it is difficult for agents ever to accumulate assets. The image echoes the Dickensian travails of Wilkins Micawber, the perpetually insolvent debtor with whom David Copperfield took up residence, who moves in and out of different jobs and debtor's prison, unable to advance until he encounters and ultimately exposes the evil Uriah Heep.
4. The magnitude of measured transitory expenditure or income poverty may also reflect the measurement error to which flow-based welfare measures are especially prone. Transitory poverty would be purely a statistical artefact of imprecise measurement when, for example, non-poor households are mis-measured as poor in one period, but correctly measured as non-poor in another period when nothing fundamentally changed between survey periods. Barrett et al. (this volume) show that measurement error and stochastic components to income data generating processes can completely mask structural patterns of income change over time.
5. Slightly more formally, the second generation approaches to poverty measurement cannot differentiate between stationary and non-stationary shocks to individuals' welfare.
6. None of these observations are meant to imply that the stochastically poor are somehow not 'really' poor. Instead, the message is that the transition of a stochastically poor person to a non-poor status conveys fundamentally different information about the economy than does the identical transition made by a structurally poor person.
7. The curvature of the livelihood mapping is itself interesting, as Carter and May (1999) and Finan, Sadoulet and de Janvry (forthcoming) discuss in detail.
8. In general, we would expect the livelihood function, and therefore the asset poverty line, to move as rates of return change due, for example, to price changes or to technological change that affects productivity. We address this possibility shortly, as illustrated by the dashed livelihood function, $\tilde{u}(A)$ in Figure 2.
9. See the account given in Romer (1994).
10. Empirical work has been cast almost exclusively in terms of income, not in terms of assets (capital stocks of various sorts). The primary exception has been the literature on 'green national accounts', which worries about depreciation of the stock of natural capital (that is, environmental resources) and the resulting sustainability of income levels as measured in the standard national accounts. Given that

asset transactions overwhelmingly occur within rather than between countries, a large part of the asset changes that matter considerably at more micro (for example, household) levels of analysis do not matter at the macro level of nation states.

11. Note that private firms will also be in this low-level equilibrium trap. A big push based on public coordination is thus typically seen as necessary to cross the threshold and move toward a higher equilibrium.
12. Note that the household restricted to *L1* would choose a lower steady state level because the marginal returns to further accumulation (given by the slope of the production function) do not warrant additional savings. As illustrated in Figure 3, households restricted to either technology accumulate assets only up to the point where marginal returns are equalised.
13. Similar criticisms would also apply to the static asset poverty line, introduced earlier in this paper.
14. See for example, Adato, Carter and May (this volume), Barrett et al. (this volume), Dercon (2004), Elbers et al. (2002), Jalan and Ravallion (2002, 2004), Lokshin and Ravallion (2002), Lybbert et al. (2004), Ravallion and Jalan (1996).
15. The experience of graduate students who leave professional employment to go back to school offers an intuitive example from a very different context. The student's income typically falls sharply, often dropping the student and her family below the income poverty line, but her asset stock is preserved, even built up, enabling predictable, subsequent recovery to a non-poor equilibrium income level.
16. In principle, the same comment could be made about the macroeconomic literature. Note that growth models ultimately concern the steady state levels of productive assets (capital), with steady state growth equal to the rate of technological change. However, in the case of nations, national output or income is a relatively stable index of the underlying level of productive assets as national income deviates relatively little from its expected value. At the micro-economic level, household income can depart far more significantly from its expected income and thus offers a far less reliable index of underlying assets.
17. Following common practice in the study of livestock, Lybbert et al. (2004) aggregate heterogeneous livestock into 'tropical livestock units' using a generally accepted weighting system that permits sheep and goats to be aggregated with larger animals such as cattle and camels.
18. Barrett et al. (this volume) also use parametric methods that yield qualitatively identical estimates of the critical asset threshold, but which fit the data far less well in the tails of the wealth distribution.

References

Acemoglu, D., Johnson, S. and Robinson, J. A. (2001) The colonial origins of comparative development: an empirical investigation, *American Economic Review*, 91, pp. 1369–1401.

Adato, M., Carter, M. and May, J. (this issue), Exploring poverty traps and social exclusion in South Africa using qualitative and quantitative data, *Journal of Development Studies*.

Azariadis, C. and Drazen, A. (1990) Threshold externalities and economic development, *Quarterly Journal of Economics*, 105, pp. 501–26.

Banerjee, A. V. and Newman, A. F. (1993) Occupational choice and the process of development, *Journal of Political Economy*, 101, pp. 274–98.

Barrett, C. B. (2005) Rural poverty dynamics: development policy implications, in D. Colman and N. Vink (Eds) *Reshaping Agriculture's Contributions to Society* (Oxford: Blackwell).

Barrett, C. B. and Carter, M. R. (2001–2) Can't get ahead for falling behind: new directions for development policy to escape poverty and relief traps, *Choices*, 16, pp. 35–8.

Barrett, C. B., Marenya, P. P., McPeak, J. G., Minten, B., Murithi, F. M., Oluoch-Kosura, W., Place, F., Randrianarisoa, J. C., Rasambainarivo, J. and Wangila, J. (this issue), Welfare Dynamics in Rural Kenya and Madagascar, *Journal of Development Studies*.

Baulch, B. and Hoddinott, J. (2000) *Economic Mobility and Poverty Dynamics in Developing Countries* (London: Frank Cass).

Baumol, W. J. (1986) Productivity growth, convergence, and welfare: what the long-run data show, *American Economic Review*, 76, pp. 1072–85.

Binswanger, H. and Rosenzweig, M. R. (1993) Wealth, weather risk and the composition and profitability of agricultural investments, *Economic Journal*, 103, pp. 56–78.

Bloom, D. E., Canning, D. and Sevilla, J. (2003) Geography and Poverty Traps, *Journal of Economic Growth*, 8, pp. 355–78.

Bloom, D. E. and Sachs, J. D. (1998) Geography, demography and growth in Africa, *Brookings Papers on Economic Activity*, 2, pp. 207–295.

Canova, Fabio (2004) Testing for convergence clubs in income per-capita: a predictive density approach, *International Economic Review*, 45, pp. 49–77.

Carter, M. R. (1997) Environment, technology and the social articulation of risk in West African agriculture, *Economic Development and Cultural Change*, 45, pp. 557–90.

Carter, M. R., Little, P. D., Mogues, T. and Negatu, W. (2005) Poverty traps and environmental shocks: tracking the impacts of natural disasters on assets in Ethiopia and Honduras, working paper, University of Wisconsin.

Carter, M. R. and May, J. (1999) Poverty, livelihood and class in rural South Africa, *World Development*, 27, pp. 1–20.

Carter, M. R. and May, J. (2001) One kind of freedom: the dynamics of poverty in post-apartheid South Africa, *World Development*, 29, pp. 1987–2006.

DeLong, J. B. (1988) Productivity growth, convergence, and welfare: comment, *American Economic Review*, 78(5).

Dercon, S. (1998) Wealth, risk and activity choice: cattle in Western Tanzania, *Journal of Development Economics*, 55, pp. 1–42.

Dercon, S. (2004) Growth and shocks: evidence from rural Ethiopia, *Journal of Development Economics*, 74, pp. 309–29.

Dercon, S. and Krishnan, P. (1996) Income portfolios in rural Ethiopia and Tanzania: choices and constraints, *Journal of Development Studies*, 32, pp. 850–75.

Easterly, W. and Levine, R. (1997) Africa's growth tragedy: policies and ethnic divisions, *Quarterly Journal of Economics*, 112, pp. 1203–50.

Elbers, C., Gunning, J. W. and Kinsey, B. H. (2002) Convergence, shocks and poverty, Tinbergen Institute Working Paper 2002–035/2.

Esteban, J. and Ray, D. (1994) On the measurement of polarization, *Econometrica*, 62, pp. 819–52.

Feder, G. and Nishio, A. (1998). The benefits of land titling and registration: economic and social perspectives, *Land Policy Studies*, 15, pp. 25–43.

Fiaschi, D. and Lavezzi, A. M. (2003) Distribution dynamics and nonlinear growth, *Journal of Economic Growth*, 8, pp. 379–401.

Field, E. (2003) Entitled to Work: Urban Property Rights and Labor Supply in Peru Harvard University working paper.

Finan, F., Sadoulet, E. and de Janvry, A. (forthcoming). Measuring the poverty reduction potential of land in Mexico, *Journal of Development Economics*.

Foster, J., Greer, J. and Thorbecke, E. (1984) A class of decomposable poverty measures, *Econometrica*, 52(3), pp. 761–66.

Galor, O. and Zeira, J. (1993) Income distribution and macroeconomics, *Review of Economic Studies*, 60(1), pp. 35–52.

Gonzalez-Vega, Claudio (1977) Interest rate restrictions and income distribution, *American Journal of Agricultural Economics*, 59(5), pp. 973–6.

Grootaert, C. and Kanbur, R. (1995) The lucky few amidst economic decline: distributional change in Cote d'Ivoire as seen through panel datasets, 1985–1988. *Journal of Development Studies*, 31, pp. 603–19.

Hansen, Bruce (2000) Sample splitting and threshold estimation, *Econometrica*, 68, pp. 575–603.

Hoddinott, J. (2003) Pathways from poverty in sub-Saharan Africa, International Food Policy Research Institute working paper.

Hulme, D. and Shepherd, A. (2003) Conceptualizing Chronic Poverty, *World Development*, 31(3), pp. 403–23.

Jalan, J. and Ravallion, M. (2002) Geographic poverty traps? A micro model of consumption growth in rural China, *Journal of Applied Econometrics*, 17, pp. 329–46.

Jalan, J. and Ravallion, M. (2004) Household income dynamics in rural China, in S. Dercon (Ed.) *Insurance Against Poverty* (Oxford: Oxford University Press).

de Janvry, A. and Sadoulet, E. (1993) Relinking agrarian growth with poverty reduction, in M. Lipton and J. van der Gaag (Eds) *Including the Poor* (Washington, DC, World Bank).

Krishna, A. (2003) Escaping poverty and becoming poor: Who gains, who loses, and why? Accounting for stability and change in 35 North Indian villages, *World Development*, 32, pp. 121–36.

Krishna, A., Kristjanson, P., Radeny, M. and Nindo, W., 2004, Escaping poverty and becoming poor in twenty Kenyan villages, *Journal of Human Development*, 5, pp. 211–26.

Krishna, A., Lumonya, D., Markiewicz, M., Mugumya, F., Kafuko, A. and Wegoye, J. (this issue), Escaping poverty and becoming poor in 36 villages of Central and Western Uganda, *Journal of Development Studies*.

Kristjanson, P., Krishna, A., Radeny, M. and Nindo, W. (2004) Pathways out of poverty in Western Kenya and the role of livestock, Working paper for the FAO/Pro-Poor Livestock Policy Initiative.

Lipton, M. (1993) Growing points in poverty research: labour issues, ILO Symposium: Poverty: New Approaches to Analysis and Policy. Geneva: International Labour Organisation.

Lokshin, M. and Ravallion, M. (2002) Household income dynamics in two transition economies, World Bank working paper.

Loury, G. C. (1981) Intergenerational transfers and the distribution of earnings, *Econometrica*, 49, pp. 843–67.

Lybbert, T. J., Barrett, C. B., Desta, S. and Coppock, D. L. (2004) Stochastic wealth dynamics and risk management among a poor population, *Economic Journal*, 114, pp. 750–77.

Masters, W. A. and Macmillan, M. S. (2001) Climate and scale in economic growth, *Journal of Economic Growth*, 6, pp. 167–86.

Mookherjee, D. and Ray, D. (2002) Contractual structure and wealth accumulation, *American Economic Review*, 92(4), pp. 818–49.

Mogues, T. and Carter, M. R. (forthcoming), Social capital and the reproduction of inequality in socially polarized economies, *Journal of Economic Inequality*.

Murphy, K. M., Schleifer, A. and Vishny, R. W. (1989) Industrialization and the Big Push, *Journal of Political Economy*, 97, pp. 1003–20.

Myrdal, G. (1957) *Economic Theory and Under-developed Regions* (London: Duckworth).

Nurkse, R. (1953) *Problems of Capital Formation in Underdeveloped Regions* (Oxford: Oxford University Press).

Pritchett, L. (1997) Divergence, big time, *Journal of Economic Perspectives*, 11(3), pp. 3–17.

Quah, D. (1993) Empirical cross-section dynamics for economic growth, *European Economic Review*, 37, pp. 426–34.

Quah, D. (1996) Twin peaks: growth and convergence in models of distribution dynamics, *Economic Journal*, 106, pp. 1045–55.

Quah, D. (1997) Empirics for growth and distribution: stratification, polarization and convergence clubs, *Journal of Economic Growth*, 2, pp. 27–59.

Ravallion, M. (2001). Growth, inequality and poverty: looking beyond averages, *World Development*, 29(11), pp. 1803–15.

Ravallion, M. and Jalan, J. (1996) Growth divergence due to spatial externalities, *Economics Letters*, 53, pp. 227–32.

Ray, D., Duclos, J. Y. and Esteban, J. (2004) Polarization: concepts, measurement, estimation, *Econometrica*, 72(6), pp. 1737–72.

Romer, P. M. (1994) The origins of endogenous growth, *Journal of Economic Perspectives*, 8(1), pp. 3–22.

Rosenstein-Rodan, P. (1943) Problems of industrialization of Eastern and South-Eastern Europe, *Economic Journal*, 53, pp. 202–11.

Rostow, W. W. (1960) *The Stages of Economic Growth* (Oxford: Oxford University Press).

Sachs, J. D. and Warner, A. (1997) Fundamental sources of economic growth, *American Economic Review Papers and Proceedings*, 87, pp. 184–88.

De Soto, H. (2000) *The Mystery of Capital: Why Capitalism Triumphs in the West and Fails Everywhere Else* (New York: Basic Books).

Williamson, J. (2003) From reform agenda: a short history of the Washington Consensus and suggestions for what to do next, *Finance & Development*, (Sept.), pp. 10–3.

Young, A. A. (1928) Increasing returns and economic progress, *Economic Journal*, 38, pp. 527–42.

Zimmerman, F. J. and Carter, M. R. (2003) Asset smoothing, consumption smoothing and the reproduction of inequality under risk and subsistence constraints, *Journal of Development Economics*, 71, pp. 233–60.

'Moving in Place': Drought and Poverty Dynamics in South Wollo, Ethiopia

PETER D. LITTLE, M. PRISCILLA STONE, TEWODAJ MOGUES, A. PETER CASTRO, & WORKNEH NEGATU

> Every year is drought time for me (woman farmer, South Wollo, based on P. Stone's field notes, 2003).

I. Introduction

In conversations with farmers of South Wollo, Ethiopia, it is common to hear horrific stories of poverty and heart-wrenching tales of death and massive asset losses during droughts. People's ability to make a living in this impoverished and risky part of the world is clearly challenging, even when compared to other low-income areas of rural Africa. Ethiopia is a nation that ranks among the poorest in the world (171 of 174) with an annual per capita income of only $104 or US$ 0.28/day (see United Nations Development Programme, 2001; World Bank, 2002). Most studies indicate incidences of rural poverty above 50 per cent and as high as 78 per cent when food aid transfers are discounted (see Bevan and Joioreman, 1997; Dercon and Krishnan, 1998; and Dercon, 2002). In one recent study the prevalence of destitution (extreme poverty) in North and South Wollo was noted to be 14.6 per cent, a situation that is said to have worsened over time through frequent droughts (see Sharp et al., 2003: xiii).

Notwithstanding the prevalence of poverty in Ethiopia, the extent to which it has declined or increased in recent years is widely debated, as is the role that frequent droughts figure in these dynamics (see Dercon, 2002; Dercon and Krishnan, 2000; Devereux and Sharp, 2003). Drawing on a recent study by the authors in the South Wollo and Oromiya Zones of northeastern Ethiopia, this paper addresses: (1) the extent to which poverty and vulnerability to poverty has changed in rural Ethiopia in recent times; and (2) the degree to which the 1999–2000 drought affected poverty and wealth dynamics. The paper uses drought, a common occurrence in Ethiopia, as an entry point for discussing the more challenging issue, poverty. Our discussion will show that drought does not have a uniformly impoverishing impact on agricultural households. Some very poor households actually came out of the recent drought better than when the event began, while some of the wealthier households benefited both from a favourable livestock market and increased opportunities to share herd out animals in the post-drought period. During droughts poor households also generally held on to their limited assets more effectively than others and also recovered quicker from disasters.[1] It will be shown that while the incidence of poverty changed very little during 1997 to 2003, the fortunes of the poorest improved, but not enough to keep them from poverty. For the majority it is a kind of 'moving in place' without sustained material improvement, but enough resilience that households and families survive and stay together despite significant hardships. Finally, the paper underscores how households rely on local social relations for access to material resources, especially for post-drought recovery.

The article utilises several different concepts that require explanation. First, vulnerability, a common term in the poverty and food security literature (Davies, 1996; Moser, 1998; Watts, 1983), refers to households on the economic margins that have a relatively high likelihood of moving into poverty during some pre-determined length of time. In the words of Hoddinott and Quisumbing, 'vulnerability is the likelihood that at a given time in the future, an individual will have a level of welfare below some norm or benchmark (2003:9).' In this paper, we consider 'vulnerability to poverty' to mean that a household has at least a 50 per cent chance of being poor within a six-year period. Resilience, on the other hand, is the ability of a household (poor or other) to withstand and recover from hardships (for example, drought or illness), and to return to its pre-existing asset and welfare levels within a three- to five-year period. In short, they are able to resist further deterioration in wealth and welfare even in drought-prone environments. As used in the article, poor households in South Wollo can be relatively resilient if they are able to survive and recover to pre-existing asset and welfare levels, even though their benchmarks are low.

In this study a household is considered to be persistently or chronically poor if they have been continuously poor for at least six years. This time span is consistent with other measures for distinguishing persistent cases from other types of poverty (see Chronic Poverty Research Centre 2004). The time duration (six years) is adequate to capture most of the normal effects of life course/developmental factors on household welfare. As individuals and households progress through life, they often temporarily move in/out of asset-poverty. While developmental factors play some role in explaining poverty dynamics in South Wollo, we find poverty among all ages of household heads and at different stages in the developmental cycle. Finally, a threshold refers to an asset or wealth level – in this case defined by livestock ownership – that marks a qualitative difference for households in terms of income strategies, consumption, and vulnerability to poverty. By their very nature, thresholds are arbitrary divisions, but necessary for analytical purposes.

The article itself is organised into six parts, including the introduction. The next section provides a general background to the area's ecology and history and an overview of social and economic conditions, while Section III discusses the drought of 1999–2000 and its general impacts in the region. Sections IV and V use both quantitative data and ethnographic case studies to explore the different household and individual trajectories that have been pursued during 1997–2003, with an emphasis on the post-drought period (2000–2003). They assess which households were able to hold on to assets and recover from the drought and which were not. These two parts of the article rely on an asset indicator (ownership of livestock) to establish poverty and vulnerability thresholds, in part because: (1) virtually all local measures of wealth and poverty emphasise livestock ('the poor have no animals') (also see Devereux and Sharp, 2003: 18); and (2) more than 90 per cent of total asset values are held in the form of livestock in rural Ethiopia (see Dercon 2004: 316). Furthermore, the quantitative household survey includes seven years of data on herd ownership and, thus, we are able to trace welfare changes using livestock as an asset indicator over a reasonable span. As the paper will show, ownership of livestock also is correlated with other key indicators of welfare, such as income, expenditures and food availability, and serves as a universal store of value and source of traction for agriculture.

Along these lines, we suggest that asset ownership is a better predictor of long-term welfare and household viability, than is consumption, income, or other 'flow' variables that are subject to massive measurement problems and dramatic, short-term changes.[2] Asset endowments (social and economic) largely determine a household's or individual's future capacity to earn income and withstand shocks. By utilising asset-based wealth groups, households are shown to move in/out of different categories of poverty and vulnerability over time, often with only negligible improvements in welfare. The final part of the article addresses policy implications and asks how current policies affect patterns of poverty and inequality and what might be done to improve welfare in South Wollo.

The study relies on an unusually rich mix of quantitative and qualitative data from a multiple round (seven) study of 416 randomly-selected households during 2000 to 2003, case studies of 62 of these households, and a series of detailed interviews with separate groups of males and females and mixed groups. The original sample was 448 households, but attrition over three years reduced it to 416. The smaller sample of 62 households was selected to represent poor, middle, and better off households and male versus female-headed households. However, it is generally representative of the large sample in most respects. In addition to household heads, key economic agents (particularly spouses and adult children) within households were interviewed in five of the seven rounds. We used the criterion that a household member had to have a separate income-earning activity or activities – farming, trading, waged employment, or other – for the person to qualify as a 'key economic agent.' Less than 25 per cent of spouses and older children (18 years or older) indicated that they had 'separate' income earning streams, and many of those who did were concentrated in Bati *wereda* (district) where there are good opportunities for trading activities. Petty trading, beer brewing, and other non-farm activities were the main 'separate' income streams that were identified.

Recall data on household assets and drought-induced losses also were collected for the period 1997–99. Analyses in the article will move between the larger sample, the group interviews, and the smaller, more familiar group of case study households. In doing so, the article hopefully will demonstrate that analyses of individual 'stories' are as necessary and convincing for understanding the causes of poverty as large statistical datasets (also see Hulme, 2003).

II. The Study Region

The research area is located in South Wollo and neighbouring Oromiya Zones,[3] the heart (or buckle) of what often is called the Ethiopian 'famine belt' (see Mariam, 1984; Rahmato, 1986). This region was the most severely affected part of Ethiopia in the well-known famines of 1971–74 and 1983–84, both of which were greatly aggravated by political factors. To this day, some households in the area have not fully recovered from the debilitating effects of the 1983–84 crisis. The research location covers four *wereda* – Legambo, Desie Zurie, and Jamma of South Wollo and Bati of Oromiya Zone – and in each *wereda* data were collected in two *kebele* (an administrative unit made up of approximately four to five villages) for a total of eight different research *kebele* (see Figure 1). Compared to most other parts of highland Ethiopia, the area has slightly smaller average land holdings (about 15 per cent smaller), lower incomes, and is less food secure because it depends more on the short (*belg*) rains than other areas (see Abegaz, 2004). South Wollo is relatively unique in the Ethiopian highlands because of the region's reliance on the *Belg* rains. The area also lies in a rainfall 'shadow' that makes the *meher* (long rains) season undependable in certain locations (personal communication, James McCann).

Culture and History

Ethnically the area is a mix of Oromo and Amhara populations with a large mixture of Oromo migrating into the area during the sixteenth and seventeenth centuries. The two lowland *kebele*, Kamme and Chachato, are inhabited by the Oromo, while the other *kebele* are predominantly Amharic speakers. The population of the study area is predominantly Muslim (>85 per cent) and Orthodox (Coptic) Christian. There are important differences in local social structure. The Oromo trace descent through male kinship lines (patrilineal) while the Amhara are generally bilateral (trace relations through male and female relations), which has important implications for settlement and inheritance patterns – especially for women. While polygyny was once noted to be widespread in the Oromo areas, we found no cases in our sample. Respondents indicate that poverty and land shortages are the main reasons for the institution's decline.

The notion of persistent poverty in South Wollo has an important historical dimension. Politics and history both have played key roles in shaping patterns of wealth accumulation and poverty in South Wollo, specifically, and rural Ethiopia, generally. Prior to the overthrow of the late Emperor Halle Selassie in 1974, only

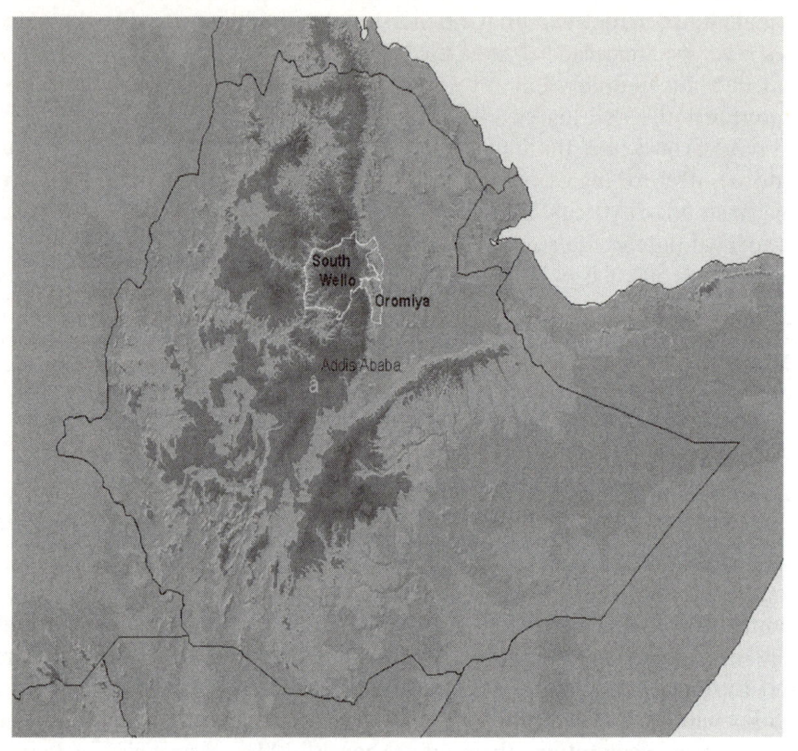

Figure 1. Location of study region in Ethiopia. *Note*: Map was composed and drawn by Michael Shin

slightly over 50 per cent of households in the study region possessed their own farms. Instead, many were rent-paying tenants or sharecroppers on lands owned by the previous imperial government and its representatives (Kiros and Assefa, 1977:5). Under the imperial system peasants also were heavily indebted because of the need to borrow cash to buy food and pay taxes (Mariam, 1984: 88–92). As recently as 1992 and 1997, additional land redistributions were held in the study region under the new Ethiopia People's Revolutionary Democratic Front (EPRDF) government that was formed in 1991 after the violent downfall of the previous regime. Approximately 49 per cent of current households received the bulk of their land from recent land reform acts.

The Marxist-leaning Derg[4] government headed by Major Mengistu Haile Mariam prohibited private markets and inter-regional labour movements and land could not be sold or bought. After the 1991 coup that replaced the Derg state with the current EPRDF party, agricultural and labour markets were relaxed, but restrictions on land use and transactions were kept in place (for details of the recent political history, see Zewde and Pausewang (2002)). The latter constraint weighs heavily on an individual's decision to migrate for employment outside his/her home area. As in the Derg period, farmers have an upper limit on land ownership (2.5 hectares in South Wollo) and can have their farm(s) reallocated by the local administration if they are absent for more than two seasons. In fact, more than one-third of household heads (male and female) fear that further land redistributions will take place and, consequently, are concerned that unless they remain on the farm, their land will be reallocated. Many people recall at least one case where a household head pursued an outside opportunity and lost access to his/her land.[5]

Land policies also contribute to a peculiar national demographic picture that has a trickle down effect for regions like South Wollo. For a country of 70+ million people Ethiopia has one of Africa's largest percentages of population still residing in rural areas (approximately 85 per cent) and only one city (Addis Ababa) with a population over 500,000 people. Thus, while political ideologies and regimes have drastically changed since the 1960s, the underlying policy principle of 'tying the peasant to the land' persists and it results in a relatively undiversified and undifferentiated rural sector.

Geography and Agro-Ecology

The study region is anchored by two key market towns, Dessie and Kolmobolcha, and comprises four major agro-ecological zones: *wurch* (highlands above 2,800 metres above sea level [a.s.l.]), *dega* (highlands approximately 2000–2800 metres a.s.l.), *woina dega* (midlands approximately 1500–2000 metres a.s.l.), and *kolla* (lowlands below 1,500 metres a.s.l.). It is approximately 120 kilometres from north-to-south and at its widest point is about 160 kilometres east-to-west (approximately 19,200 square km). There is little infrastructure and only one tarmac road that connects the cities of Dessie and Kombolcha with the capital of Addis Ababa. Although South Wollo has few important towns, proximity to them affects rural livelihood strategies as farmers can pursue petty trading and informal employment in these locations.

Despite the fact that the area is generally famine prone, it is difficult to generalise across the different *wereda* and *kebele* in the study area. One of the study *wereda*, Jamma, is a surplus farming area that was only moderately affected by the 1999–2000 drought. Another study *wereda* (Legambo), in turn, experienced devastating loses from the 1999–2000 drought and has only partially recovered from this event. Unlike other areas of East Africa where highlands generally are the most food secure parts of a country (see Little, 1992), the opposite often is the case in Ethiopia. In fact, the crowded, steep-sloped highlands above 2,000 metres a.s.l., including large parts of South Wollo, are among the country's most famine-prone.

South Wollo is a particularly rugged terrain and has very steep slopes, with drops of 1,000 metres over a few kilometres not uncommon. Most of the area has thick vertisol soils that require animal or mechanised traction to effectively utilise. No farmers in our sample used mechanised traction. However, all who farmed used oxen traction, with the exception of a few farmers who utilised horses. In terms of soil classification, farmers in the area classified 40 per cent of their farms as fertile (*lem*), 42 per cent as semi-fertile (*lem-tef*), and 18 per cent as unfertile (*tef*).

An Overview of Poverty

As indicated earlier, by almost any statistical indicator of poverty, large numbers of rural households of South Wollo are very poor. Per capita incomes in the area are less than $50 per year for more than 80 per cent of households and even the 'wealthiest' 10 per cent of households have average livestock assets of less than 10 TLUs,[6] or the equivalent of seven cattle, two donkeys and 20 small stock (goats and sheep). Non-income measures of welfare – for example, housing, consumer durables, and savings – also are shockingly low. For example, less than 1 per cent of households have a bank account and the average value of housing is only 1,100 birr (or US $127). Moreover, fewer than 5 per cent of household heads (male and female) own a radio. These measures are considerably below even the poorest areas of neighbouring Kenya (see Little et al., 2001).

A quick 'snapshot' of local livestock and land ownership further confirms the relative poverty and lack of differentiation in the area. Using ownership of at least one oxen, a level at which at least some sharecropping arrangements can be avoided through social mechanisms, such as *maganjo*,[7] 38 per cent of households in South Wollo owned no oxen in August 2003 more than three years after the end of the 1999–2000 drought. With at least one ox, a family is said to be making some progress and can pursue *maganjo* rather than 'beg oxen from others' (Tebasit farmer, June 2003; Stone and Kassahun, 2003: 32). Moreover, average land holdings (excluding rented and sharecropped in) is only 0.82 hectare in South Wollo, and even the largest land owning quartile has an average farm size only of 6.86 *timad* (1.72 hectare), or about four times larger than the average of the poorest land-owning quartile. More than 25 per cent of households had average farms of less than 0.5 ha, a miniscule farm size that Rahmato (1986) refers to as a 'starvation plot'. Interestingly, open-ended interviews of male and female respondents provided very similar breakdowns in land distribution and average farm sizes as the household survey.

Female-headed households, which make up about 24 per cent of households in the area, reveal a much greater tendency toward poverty than male-headed households.[8] In other studies in the area female-headed units are noted to be 'four times more likely to be destitute than male-headed households (Sharp et al., 2003: xv).' In our study, female-headed households in South Wollo control on average less than 50 and 70 per cent of the total livestock and land, respectively, that males do. They also have fewer adult labourers in the household and only about 60 per cent of the annual food stocks that male-headed households control.[9] However, there are important exceptions since a small number of female-headed households are in the wealthiest livestock and landholding quartiles (see the case of Amina discussed later).

Importantly, the poorest households do control land, often having received it from government redistribution programmes. In the words of one respondent, 'Land ownership is not a good indicator of wealth because everybody was given land at redistribution – even the poor' (P. Little, unpublished notes, January 2004). Consequently, the poorest families with land are able to lease or sharecrop it out (normally on a 50/50 basis) and receive some income. During the drought recovery period, 2000–2003, sharecropping arrangements began to favour the landowner as agricultural conditions improved and the demand for land increased. Cash payments and in-kind compensation of fertiliser and seeds to poorer households became more common and many of the 'better off' farmers complained bitterly about the increased costs of sharecropping.

Poverty and Wealth Thresholds

The depth of material poverty, in terms of assets and incomes, is such that different categories of the poor and non-poor need to be distinguished. Based on asset/herd ownership, we establish thresholds to distinguish the poor from the non-poor, the poor from the very poor, and the 'vulnerable to poverty' group from other non-poor households. As Table 1 shows, annual incomes, food and labour availability, returns from assets, and income from farm/non-farm activities correlate with these different livestock asset categories. Most importantly, at the point where a household controls about 4.5 TLUs (or about 1.0 TLU per capita), or the equivalent of two oxen, one cow and 15 small stock, it has sufficient oxen and labour to avoid sharecropping and oxen rental arrangements; generate sufficient non-agricultural income to reduce dependence on risky rainfed agriculture to about 40 per cent or less; have sufficient food stocks to sustain the family for several months during the year; and have at least a 50 per cent chance of staying above this threshold for at least six years, even with the occurrence of drought. These households, which we crudely label the 'non-poor,' also are likely to have strong social networks and relationships that they can draw on in times of need. Below this level households, which can be considered materially 'poor', tend to rely more on rainfed agriculture; earn relatively small amounts from their livestock assets; face critical labour shortages; have less extensive social networks, and sometimes sharecrop out their land. While only about 35 per cent of households were at or above the 4.5 TLU level in 2001–2002, for the above reasons we have chosen it as the approximate divide between non-poor and poor.

As noted earlier, the depth of poverty is such that within the asset poor category there are those who can be treated as very or extremely poor (TLUs of 1.0 or less). Many of them were poor or very poor for at least six years and own the equivalent of six sheep, four goats, and one chicken, or less than this. Another group, those who are highly 'vulnerable to poverty,' are distinguished from other non-poor households. Above an asset threshold of 6.0 TLU, which defines the 'better off' households, there is a considerably smaller probability of moving into poverty for any duration of time (2+ years) and the chances greatly decrease as herd assets rise.

During 1997–2003 there was some stability (what economists like to call 'equilibrium') in the number of households at a low-level of poverty, although there was a lot of 'churning' within this broad category and considerable inter-annual changes. Beyond a relatively high asset level (in this case, 10+ TLU), households were on a trajectory of accumulation and production that kept them virtually free from poverty during the six-year study period, despite the occurrence of drought (see discussion later in the article). Unfortunately, this asset group, where the risk of poverty is virtually nil, is very small (less than 10 per cent of the study population in 2001–2002).

Table 1 shows the extent to which our herd asset categories correlate with other poverty/welfare indicators, and generally confirms the importance of livestock as a wealth/poverty indicator. For example, among 'better off' households in the table income from livestock-based assets account for more than 40 per cent of total household income, while among the 'very poor' it is only 8 per cent. In addition, household food availability (stocks) exceeds seven months on average for the 'better off' asset group, while it is only 2.28 and 4.05 months for the very poor and poor, respectively. Additionally, per capita income among the 'better off' is twice that of

Table 1. Annual incomes (cash/in-kind): March 2001–March 2002 (birr)[1]

		Poor (66%)		Non-poor (34%)	
	All (100%)	V. Poor (20%)	Poor (46%)	Vulnerable (13%)	Better off (21%)
Income source	All HH (n = 416)	HH ≤ 1.0 TLU	HH 1–4.45 TLU	HH 4.5–5.9 TLU	HH ≥ 6.0 TLU
Subsist crop[2]	734 (42%)	439 (62%)	680 (43%)	799 (41%)	1119 (40%)
Waged	21 (1%)	24 (3%)	17 (1%)	11 (1%)	32 (1%)
Remittance	89 (5%)	39 (6%)	44 (3%)	164 (8%)	192 (7%)
Business	118 (7%)	53 (7%)	51 (3%)	45 (2%)	88 (3%)
Crop sales	225 (13%)	92 (13%)	271 (17%)	278 (14%)	218 (8%)
Animal product	85 (5%)	9 (1%)	45 (3%)	113 (6%)	230 (8%)
Livestock sales	489 (28%)	51 (7%)	480 (30%)	555 (28%)	906 (33%)
All: Eth Birr (US $)	1,761 ($193)	707 ($83)	1588 ($187)	1965 ($231)	2785 ($328)
Annual per capita Inc. ($)	$36	$23	$35	$41	$48
Other indicators					
HH size	5.38	3.68	5.38	5.70	6.84
Adult units (AU)	3.52	2.54	3.50	3.71	4.4
Farm size (ha)	0.82 (0–2.5)	0.60 (0–1.75)	0.79 (0–2.0)	0.93 (0–2.5)	1.03 (.25–2.13)
AVG TLU (March 2002)	3.95 (0–28)	0.2 (0–1.0)	2.70 (1.05–4.45)	5.18 (4.50–5.95)	9.7 (6–28)
Annual household expenditure (birr)	660	532	606	793	914
Food stocks (March 2002) (kg)	305	103	254	325	606
Food stocks per AU (kg)[3]	87	41	73	88	138
Estimated no. months of food[4]	4.83	2.28	4.05	4.89	7.67

Notes: [1]Data collection covered a nine-month period, 1 July, 2001–1 March, 2002. The figures were annualised by multiplying sums by 1.33 per cent, except for subsistence crop income which represented the full agricultural year. The exchange rate at the time was approximately 8.5 birr = $1.

[2]This is the estimated value of crop produced.

[3]More than 90 per cent of this was in grain (mainly wheat).

[4]This was in March 2002 and right after the main harvest season (*meher*). It is assumed that 0.6 kg of grain is required per day along with some vegetables and other foods, to meet minimum energy requirements (2,100 Kcal) of an adult. One adult unit is equivalent to male/female 15–59 years; 0.5 AU is used for a person (<15 years or >59 years).

the very poor, while differences in farm size between the three groups is less, due in part to the country's equity-oriented land polices and reforms.

Non-farm/livestock income sources show an interesting pattern in Table 1. Because waged employment in the region is limited mainly to non-lucrative casual and unskilled work, which is compensated at 0.45 to $0.55 per day, it is pursued by the poor as a survival strategy. In a similar fashion, business opportunities in the region are predominantly limited to petty trading and other low-revenue enterprises (Gebre-Egziabher and Demeke, 2004) and are also mainly important for the poor. Among the very poor business (especially petty trading) activities account for about 7 per cent of their annual income, while it accounts for only 1 per cent of total income among the non-poor. In terms of other non-farm/livestock activities, some of the 'better off' households have family members who work outside the region – mainly in neighbouring Djibouti – and remit income. This pattern accounts for the relatively high percentage of remittance income among the non-poor, especially when compared to their waged income, and it is a very important factor in explaining their improved welfare.

Because land sales are illegal and there is a cap on land holdings, it is not surprising that dependence on cultivation declines at higher asset levels. Among the very poor dependence on rainfed farming is very high (75 per cent of total income), while dependence on livestock-based income is low. By contrast, among the 'better off' livestock-based income (excluding returns from natural herd reproduction) is almost as important as crop-based income. At higher levels of assets the reliance on cultivation declines even more and the dependence on livestock-based income is even greater.

III. The 1999–2000 Drought and its Effects

In the past 20 years there were major food security disasters in 1983–84, 1991–92, 1999–2000, and, again, in 2002, and minor ones in almost one out of three years. In the 1999–2000 drought, about 75 per cent of the population in our study area received food aid. A much smaller proportion received food assistance during the 2002 disaster, an event that received considerable international attention although our data show its impact was minimal in most of the area (Little, 2005).

The drought of the late 1990s was a prolonged event with uneven consequences, but its onset was gradual. Indeed, the first signs of disaster can be traced to the poor short rains (January–April) (called the *Belg* season) of 1998 (DPPC, 1998; Hammond and Maxwell, 2002). In our study region approximately one-half of our households reside mainly in *Belg* growing areas and the others in predominantly *Meher* zones where there is a June-to-September growing season. Because the *Meher* rains of 1998 were uneventful for some locations, drought and relief agencies in Ethiopia failed to see the looming disaster until the *Belg* season of 1999 emerged as a massive failure (approximately 90 per cent loss of crops) and that year's *Meher* season was poor (see Castro et al., 1999). Thus, the drought of the late 1990s was keyed by the failure or near failure of three successive agricultural seasons that resulted in a massive humanitarian crisis (DPPC, 2000; Hammond and Maxwell, 2002). While food aid distribution started in the region in June 1999, it was not widespread until 2000.

In looking at what happened to livestock herds in the area, a similar pattern of gradual decline is revealed (see Figure 2). Aggregate numbers of animals began to decline as early as late 1997 and interviews conducted during the drought indicate that some of these died, but a larger number were sold at 'throwaway' prices of 30 per cent or less of normal rates. Not surprisingly, our group interviews at the time (1999) showed 'livestock sales' as the main drought coping mechanism for 90 per cent of male and 71 per cent of female herd owners (see Amare et al., 2000). Aggregate declines in oxen and total herds were almost 40 per cent from 1998 to mid-2000.

If one looks at Figure 2, it is apparent that the local impact of the drought was unevenly distributed. The poorest quartile of households (based on 1997 asset categories) did their best to hold on to their very meagre assets, although they started at very low levels. Their miniscule herd assets actually grew during the pre-drought period until right before the last part of the drought when they experienced a decline. In many cases, these households reduced consumption to two meals per day, ate smaller portions and wild foods, and sold their labour, and/or engaged in petty trade (especially firewood and charcoal sales), in order to avoid selling their few animals. The wealthiest quartile, in turn, experienced the steepest decline during the drought as they sold off their rapidly-devaluing herds. The cost of purchasing fodder to keep animals alive and the need to purchase food also motivated drought-induced sales among the top quartile of herd owners. The better off group (quartile I) lost much at this time, but most stayed above the poverty threshold or experienced only transitory poverty (one to two years).

Post-drought rates of herd growth were relatively high for the poorest two quartiles.[10] During 2000 to 2003, the average livestock assets of the poorest quartile of households grew from 0.17 to 1.85 TLUs, although most in the poorest quartile were starting from near zero. This equates to starting off with holdings of one sheep and one chicken, and increasing these to one oxen, seven sheep, and three chickens after three years – a small but impressive gain. A slightly different, but equally encouraging picture emerges when the near asset-less or destitute in this group (that is, those with 0.1 TLU or less) are considered. These households represent the poorest of the 'very poor' category in Table 1. While the drought clearly created a large number of destitute households (27 per cent of total households), the number had declined to 10 per cent in 2003, which is an 80 per cent improvement over the

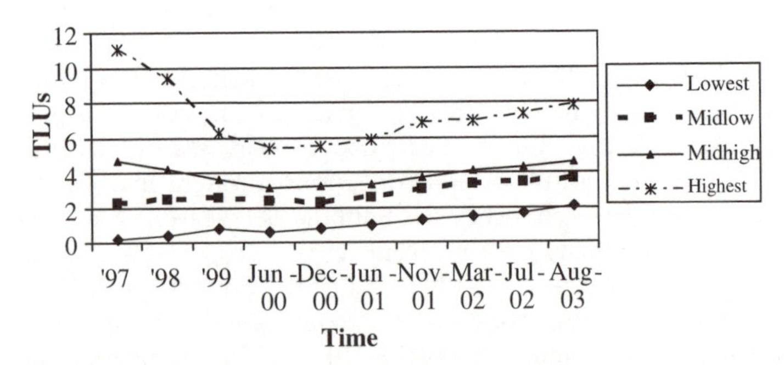

Figure 2. Herd asset changes, 1997–2003. *Source*: BASIS/IDR Household study co-directed by Peter D. Little and Workneh Negatu

1997 figure (see Figure 3). The reduction is a positive sign, but the study region still remains with a large number of virtually asset-less households. In the words of one respondent, 'because the poor [without oxen] sharecrop out their land, they depend on credit to purchase food and this becomes a problem because they must borrow to buy food' (P. Little, unpublished notes, January 2004). With only land and sometimes labour as their main assets, the poorest households share-crop out their farms and borrow to buy food.

The occurrence of periodic droughts tends to wipe out asset gains that poor households attain. At a very optimistic post-drought annual growth rate of about 0.3 TLU/year, very poor households would still take about eight to ten years to reach an asset threshold of around 1.0 TLU per capita (an average of 4.5 TLU per household). In this scenario it is very likely that a drought or other shock (for example, family illness) would occur in the intervening years and obliterate asset gains. The main difference between the poor and non-poor is not that the former have higher post-drought recovery rates, but that they rarely reach a level where they can sustain themselves out of poverty before the next drought strikes. Figure 4 shows that the drought increased the percentage of asset poor from 60 to 78 per cent of total households. With the recovery period, the rate of poverty dropped to 59 per cent in 2003, which was about the same as in 1997.

IV. Poverty Dynamics and Social Mobility

So which households were able to improve or even move out of asset poverty during 1997 to 2003 despite the setback of a drought? Table 2 shows the percentage of households that were able to transition out of poverty during 1997–2003 based on their initial asset holdings. As the data show, 46.5 per cent of the very poor stayed very poor, while about 30.9 per cent improved, but were still below the poverty level in 2003. Another 8 per cent had moved above the poverty threshold but were still considered to be vulnerable, while 6 per cent had moved into the highest wealth category ('better off'). Those in the poor asset category had slightly better outcomes, with 16 per cent moving into the 'better off' group by 2003. Overall, of the 251 households (out of 416) that were in poverty in 1997, 76 per cent were still in this state six years later while 24 per cent had moved out of poverty.

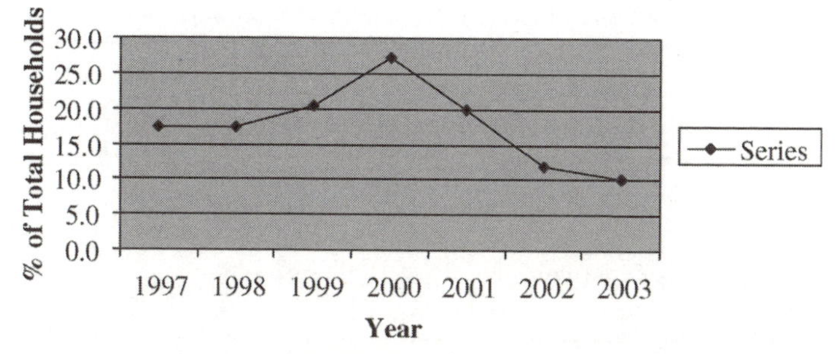

Figure 3. Percentage of asset destitute (0.1 TLU or less), 1997–2003. *Source*: BASIS/IDR Household study co-directed by Peter D. Little and Workneh Negatu

Households in the 'vulnerable' category (Table 2) experienced considerable instability during the period. Of the households who could be classified as 'vulnerable to poverty' in 1997, 50 per cent of them had become poor or very poor by 2003. Only 21 per cent had improved their status while the remaining 29 per cent stayed the same. In short, over a six year period, households who started with asset holdings between 4.5 and 5.95 TLU were 2.5 times more likely to become poor than to improve their status. Clearly, the drought was an important external factor that pushed asset vulnerable households into poverty, which many had not recovered from by 2003.

By contrast, among 'better off' households only 20 and 1 per cent, respectively, became either poor or very poor during 1997 to 2003. However, while most of the 'better off' stayed out of poverty, their average asset/TLU holdings declined about 30 per cent during the period from 10.92 to 7.69 TLU. It should be noted that unlike the poor, better off households are able to time sales more efficiently, selling off large

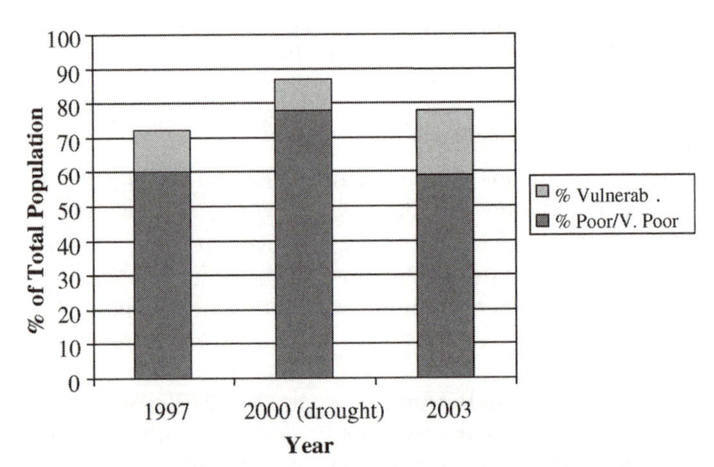

Figure 4. Impact of drought on poverty, 1997–2003. *Source*: BASIS/IDR Household study co-directed by Peter D. Little and Workneh Negatu

Table 2. Asset transitions among different categories of households, South Wollo, 1997–2003

		2003 (% of households)			
		Very poor	Poor	Vulnerable	Better off
1997 asset categories[1]	Very poor (n = 101)	(47) 46.5%	(40) 39.5%	(8) 8%	(6) 6%
	Poor (n = 150)	(17) 11%	(87) 58%	(24) 16%	(22) 15%
	Vulnerable (n = 58)	(6) 10%	(23) 40%	(17) 29%	(12) 21%
	Better off (n = 107)	(1) 1%	(23) 21.5%	(28) 26%	(55) 51.5%
	All (n = 416)	(71) 17%	(173) 42%	(76) 18%	(95) 23%

Note: [1]Very Poor < = 1.0 TLU; Poor: 1.05 to 4.45 TLU; Vulnerable: 4.5 to 5.95 TLU; Better off: 6.0+ TLU.

numbers of animals during drought when prices drop and continue selling in the post-drought era when prices rise (see the discussion later in the article).

Figure 5 shows the relationship between initial asset holdings and wealth status during the six-year period. As the data depict, 95 per cent of those households with one or fewer TLU remained poor or vulnerable after six years. With initial asset holdings beyond eight TLUs, on the other hand, most households were able to stay out of poverty even with an intervening drought. As was argued earlier, these households depend less on risky rainfed agriculture than poor and vulnerable households. In the next section, it will be shown that the larger the herd, the greater the reliance on natural reproduction – rather than purchases – to recover after a drought.

V. Case Studies

Individual cases show the kinds of strategies used to recover assets following a drought. They also highlight the difficult circumstances that impoverished households confront and why some of them are unable to improve their status. When we look at how the poor managed their meagre livestock assets during 2000–2003, wide differences are revealed. When questioned about which households were most vulnerable to drought and unable to recover from it, local respondents provided their own categories of poor and vulnerable households:

- households headed by the elderly;
- landless and land-poor households ('many do casual labour');
- female-headed households, especially those with many children but no older children;
- households without oxen or other livestock and without labour;
- households who must share-crop out their farms and 'can produce only enough food for three months of household needs.'

Some of the poorest households manifest several of the above characteristics and may cope with drought by 'lending' out members to better off relatives or neighbours. The most desperate of these may send out an adolescent child to another

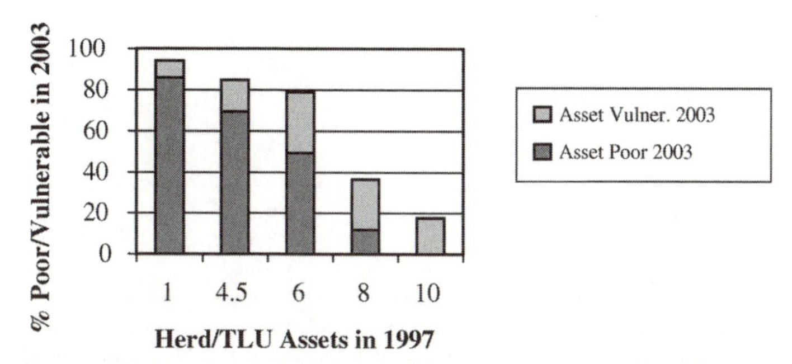

Figure 5. Relationship between initial herd assets and poverty/vulnerability, 1997–2003. *Source*: BASIS/IDR Household Study co-directed by Peter D. Little and Workneh Negatu

household where the child becomes a type of 'indentured' servant, earning less than $10 and food rations per month for herding and farm work. During the 1999–2000 drought, some children were away from their families for more than two years. As a result of this and the practice of sending out migrant labourers when times are tough, household sizes of the poor can be 20 to 25 per cent smaller during a drought than at other times (Little, 2005).

The cases discussed below highlight some of the difficulties that the poor confront, but also their incredible resourcefulness against daunting odds. In some cases, they are contrasted with examples of 'better off' households to show different trajectories and opportunities. The cases are organised according to certain coping/recovery activities and their impacts on poverty dynamics and welfare.

Engaging Livestock Markets

Those families with few livestock assets confront special problems recovering from droughts because their breeding herds are so limited. In contrast to better off households, they are forced to borrow or purchase animals during the post-drought period when livestock prices are especially high, and also are constrained in pursuing cultivation just as conditions are improving (see Table 3). For example, the 'very poor' category relied heavily on purchases and borrowing (often on a share-herd basis) to re-stock their herds during 2000–2003. They accumulated a much smaller percentage (42 per cent) through natural reproduction than wealthier households (68 per cent) and, surprisingly, in relative terms they actually engaged more in the

Table 3. Sources of herd accumulation and de-accumulation among the poorest and best off households, 2000 to 2002[1]

	Poorest (bottom 20 per cent)	Best off (top 10 per cent)
Source of annual accumulation		
Births (TLU/%)	0.30 (42%)	2.38 (68%)
Purchases (TLU/%)	0.30 (42%)	0.94 (27%)
Borrowed[2] (TLU/%)	0.12 (16%)	0.18 (5%)
Source of annual de-accumulation		
Deaths (TLU/%)	0.13 (37%)	1.04 (31%)
Sales (TLU/%)	0.19 (56%)	1.67 (50%)
Lend	0.015 (5%)	0.37 (11%)
Eat/slaughter	0.005 (2%)	0.26 (8%)
Total annual gain per HH (TLU) (%)	0.72 (100%)	3.5 (100%)
Total annual loss per HH (TLU) (%)	0.34 (100%)	3.34 (100%)
Net TLU gain per year	0.38	0.16
Ratio of births/purchases	1	2.53
Ratio of sales/purchases	0.63	1.78
Ratio of births/deaths	2.31	2.28
Ratio of total gains/losses	2.12	1.05

Notes: [1]Data on herd changes were based on three- and six-month recall periods, and the data were collected at five different times: November/December 2000, June 2001, November/December 2001, March 2002, and June 2002. The data were analysed on a 12-month basis. [2]Includes animals borrowed on a share herd basis.

market as buyers during this time than did better-off households. As Table 3 shows, the ratio of animal births-to-purchases was 2.5 times higher among the best off (top decile) of herders than among the very poor. Because the poorest households do not have good access to larger traders, they also receive lower prices (as much as 25 per cent below the average) for their animals and pay more per animal for purchases than better-off households.[11]

By contrast, the best off households in Table 3 were selling off their excess stock – much of it gained through natural reproduction – during 2000–2002 when prices increased about 50 and 40 per cent, respectively, for cattle and small stock. This pattern partially explains why they accumulated fewer TLUs after the drought than poorer households. In Table 3 the ratio of sales-to-purchases is more than three times higher for the best off households than the very poor, a strong indication that the former were able to benefit disproportionately from the post-drought boom in livestock prices. At a time when the very poor were desperate to recover their few animal assets they also took on animals from wealthier households on a share-herd basis (that is, a contract where in exchange for herding the poor share in herd offspring usually on a 50/50 basis), permitting the best off households to avoid labour and feed costs while reaping gains in herd growth. In this case, the drought has opened up an opportunity for the wealthiest households to benefit both from a favourable livestock market and from share-herd contracts to desperately poor households. While some poor households may benefit from share herd arrangements, others paint a different portrait: 'If you are given a sheep by a rich man, you are like a "servant" to the person. He can call on you anytime, make you prepare *injera* [a type of Ethiopian bread] and work on his farm – he can take the sheep back if you do not help him. He can organise what they call *debo* [a work party] in which people come or they can lose share herd animals. The rich prepare food and sit while others/poor are working' (Little, unpublished notes, January 2004).

The case of Mengistu is illustrative of the problem of insufficient herd capital among the poor and very poor.

> *Case of persistent poverty*: Mengistu[12] occasionally works as a casual labourer in Dessie town or on neighbours' farms. He is 27 years old and resides in Tebasit *kebele* with his wife. His family is in the 'very poor' category of households. He relies heavily on his father, who resides nearby, to help plough his 0.75 hectare farm. His father's household also is poor and the father's ability to help Mengistu's family is limited. In June 2000, Mengistu had no animal assets, but bought one heifer in 2003. He and his wife hope eventually to use it as a milk cow. The price he paid for the animal was equivalent to more than three months of wages, but he had no other option to increase the family's herd.

The following example of what we term 'sustained well-being' provides an informative contrast to Mengistu's case:

> *Case of sustained well-being*: Belay is 45 years old, married with six children, and resides in Yedo *kebele*. He does no wage or non-farms activities but, instead, concentrates solely on his 1.5 hectare farm and herd of five cattle and 18 sheep (June 2002). During 2000 to 2002 his herd increased by 12 sheep and three

calves through breeding. He also managed to sell two oxen during this time at very good prices and purchased one small bull. By August 2003, Belay had recovered 65 and 95 per cent, respectively, of the cattle and sheep he owned prior to the drought. He was in the wealthiest quartile of herd owners in 1997 and was still in this group in 2003.

The contrasting cases of Belay and Mengistu show the advantages of having sufficient herd capital for breeding rather than relying on purchases. Belay's assets allow him to maintain his current favourable status, while the poor like Mengistu are disadvantaged because they either must borrow, share-herd, and/or purchase livestock to recover drought-induced losses.

Relying on Social Relations

Social relations based on kinship and other principles are extremely important for many households, especially the poor and very poor. They can sustain them even at very low levels of welfare, or provide just enough to move them near or above the poverty threshold. In our study sample loans between kinsmen (both through husbands' and wives' families) account for almost 50 per cent of informal money borrowing and much of the sharecropping also takes place among relatives (40+ per cent). Table 4 shows the social basis of assistance and the fact that about 63 per cent of all assistance is between kin or marriage relations. Most of the assistance had to do with provision of money, labour, oxen/livestock, and food.

Contrary to what might be expected, levels of material assistance between households actually decline during droughts. Like the poor, 'better off' households are also hit during these times and often cannot help relatives as much as during recovery years. This difference may partially explain why poor households are hit so hard during a drought, but are able to recover relatively quickly after the event when assistance from relatives re-emerges.

Table 4. Social basis of assistance, 2002–2003[1]

Relationship	Number	% of total	Cumulative %
Brother	17	5.8	5.8
Sister	15	5.1	10.9
Son	23	7.8	18.8
Daughter	29	9.9	28.7
Father	12	4.1	32.8
Mother	7	2.4	35.2
Other relative (including in-laws)	81	27.6	62.8
Friend	8	2.7	65.5
Neighbour (non-relative)	93	31.7	97.3
Iddir (funeral club) members	1	.3	97.6
Other non-relative	7	2.4	100.0
Total	293	100.0	

Note: [1]Data were collected from 416 households under the BASIS/IDR Household Study co-directed by Peter Little and Workneh Negatu.

Examples from our in-depth interviews show the importance that kin-based relations can assume in the lives of the persistently poor.

> *Case of persistent poverty*: Abazen is a widow who lives in Yedo *kebele* with her two sons (ages 17 and 14). Her assets place her in the very poor category of households. After her husband died in 1997, she has relied heavily on her relatives. She was born in this *got* (village) and married a person from there. There are six houses in the village from her side of the family and she can drop in on them at anytime and 'they give me food and other things'. Her husband had brothers in the village but they all died – she gets no support from the deceased husband's family. She share-herds two sheep from her aunt's son. She owns one of her own sheep and the older boy herds the animals. Abazen is glad that he has now reached an age (17 years) where he can manage the farm's activities. She share crops out part of her farm to her cousin who provides fertiliser, seed, and gifts of grain prior to harvest. Abazen does other economic activities, like making and selling local liquor (*tella*) once a week on market day. Last year she also did cash-for-work on a government road project in the area.

A poor household like Abazen's heavily relies on loans and gifts from better off households, especially from relatives. Her economic condition is not good, but she and her children are kept alive and away from severe hunger through assistance by relatives.

Relying on Remittances

As noted earlier, opportunities for decent waged employment are very scarce in South Wollo. Individuals who pursue non-farm waged employment usually leave the area, either migrating to Addis Ababa, the Awash Valley where some large-scale irrigation schemes exist, or neighbouring Djibouti. The latter has been the most lucrative option in the past ten years and has allowed certain households and individuals to avoid poverty, as the following example attests:

> *Case of sustained well-being*: Amina is 60 years of age and owns two oxen, nine other cattle, and 15 shoats (case based on Stone, 2002). She heads a relatively wealthy household and resides in Chachato *kebele*, Bati *wereda*. She and her husband (who died around 1996) lost most of their cattle in the 1983–84 drought but were able to rebuild by the late 1980s. During the 1983–84 drought she sent two children (sons) to neighbouring Djibouti to work and one of them still sends cash remittances. Amina depends heavily on this source of cash, to buy food and livestock. She also relies on the son (20 years of age) who lives at home to plough her 1.0 hectare farm. In the post-drought period of 2000 to 2003 she was able to increase herds from 13 to 15 cattle and three to 23 sheep, and actually was better off in 2003 than in 1997.

Amina's case of sustained welfare contrasts sharply with the realities of many female-headed households like Abazen's, which do not receive remittances and remain very poor in 2003. Amina and her late husband were fortunate to have three adult children and were wise enough to send two of them to Djibouti rather than, in her words, 'letting them all die here' (Stone, 2002: 23). This strategy has paid off well.

Utilising Food Aid Transfers

There is little doubt that the massive amount of food aid available in the area assisted in asset recovery for some of the poor, although for the general population it does not show up as a statistically significant variable in recovery (Carter et al., 2004). The latter may stem from the fact that food aid was broadly distributed among most households and not well targeted at the poor. However, what is clear is that food assistance in the recent drought did little to save assets since more than 95 per cent of animal assets were depleted before it showed up in the region (Little, 2005). This finding suggests that the timing of food aid deliveries is more important than the duration of its distribution and other related factors.

The case of Mohamed highlights the complex role that food aid plays in household recovery strategies:

> *Case of persistent poverty*: Mohamed is a 60 year old household head who lives with his wife and six children in Chachato. His family had only one head of cattle and one camel in 2000. During June 2000 to December 2000 he received about 200 kg of food aid (wheat), which made up 35 per cent of his household's consumption needs. The remainder of his food needs came from purchases (first), farm production, and gifts from local relatives. Mohamed acknowledges that food aid helped him to hold on to his few animals after the drought, but that he could not depend on it. He notes that 'food aid is useless because they do not give it to all of us – just sprinkle it among some.'

As the case of Mohamed suggests, food aid is an important resource in the area, but other sources of food (for example, market purchases) often are more important (see Little, 2005).

Disposing of Assets

As indicated above, the asset profile of some better off households worsened during 1997 to 2003, but very few of them fell into the poorest asset group (see Table 2). However, several vulnerable households did become poor or very poor.

> *Case of entry into poverty*: Menonen and Zinesh have been married since the 1980s and reside with their eight children in Temu *kebele*, Legambo *wereda*. They are 50 and 45 years of age, respectively. Their assets declined considerably as a result of the recent drought and they have not been able to recover them. During 1997 to 2000 they lost five cattle (including two oxen) and eight sheep through sale and death and by August 2003 they had only recovered one ox and two sheep. During the drought, Menonen left the area to work outside and he was away for a considerable period of time. Animals had to be sold to finance food purchases and without Menonen there was nobody to assist with herding.

What has been particularly devastating for the family is that Menonen hurt his leg in 2001 and this has hampered his farming work since he returned. The household now takes in animals on a share-herd basis and with Menonen's injury Zinesh does waged casual farm work to help meet income needs. They are barely making it and are unlikely to reach their pre-drought wealth status before the next drought strikes.

The above example shows a dramatic, perhaps permanent impact on poverty as a result of the recent drought and health problems. For most other households, however, the drought may have worsened their status, but it did not have as dramatic an effect on their welfare as the above case.

Surviving through Casual Labour

As noted earlier, there are households (about 8 per cent of the total) that were virtually stockless (0 to 0.1 TLUs) during the entire seven-year period (1997–2003) (see Figure 3). The drought had virtually no impact on their wealth holdings since they had little or nothing to lose. The persistence of these asset-less households raises several interesting questions about how they are able to persist; why they have been unable to accumulate assets; and what kinds of informal/community safety nets are in place to protect them.

Case of Persistent Poverty: Zeila of Gerado, South Wollo is a divorced woman, 37 years of age, who heads a household with three children. She has a farm of about 2.0 *timad* (0.5 ha), but sharecrops out part of it because she does not have oxen or adequate labour. During the recent drought her 15-year old son worked outside the area as a hired herder and received a wage of about 50 birr ($6.00) plus food every two months (this is an example of the kinds of unfair labour contracts that individuals pursue as a result of poverty). In 2001 he returned home and now works in the area as a daily casual labourer at the rate of about 4 birr (US$ 0.45)/day and when the opportunity arises he works on food-for-work schemes. Stone and Kebede describe how Zeila's recent illness has made it especially difficult: 'Since her illness three to four years ago, she has been unable to do strenuous agricultural and trading work – she says the sun bothers her skin – so her sources of off-farm income are limited. She used to trade, but now that her health has not been good she needs to limit herself to activities that do not require a lot of energy' (2003:1).

Zeila's household is chronically poor. Like the households of Menonen and Zinnesh, her poor health has been a critical constraint on the welfare of her family. Yet, as bad as her situation is, she is actually better off than others who head asset-less households, because she has children (labour) who can help.

Access to waged and self-employed income activities are important drought-coping strategies for people like Zeila, but with extraordinarily low education levels (79 per cent of household heads are illiterate) the work tends to be for very low wages. In South Wollo self-employed petty trading can be an important short-term response to drought as it was for Zeila before she became sick, but rarely is it a source of long-term wealth accumulation.

VI. Conclusions and Policy Implications

The preceding discussion has demonstrated the importance of examining both drought coping and recovery periods to understand poverty dynamics in areas like South Wollo. It also shows the significance of initial asset holdings (in this case, livestock) as a predictor of whether a household will be poor six or more years later. What may seem to be a downward trend in poverty from a two- to three-year optic can look very different from a medium- to long-term perspective with an intervening drought. The 1999–2000 drought had a devastating short-term impact on households, particularly among the poorest, but did not increase overall rates of poverty in the area in the medium term. Generally, the rate of poverty (and destitution) actually declined slightly during a six-year period despite a disastrous drought. As the article argues, a large percentage of poor households actively pursue a range of different economic activities that allowed most to attain their pre-drought wealth status, but not to escape poverty. The findings show that the greater the dependence on rainfed agriculture-based incomes and the less diversification there is, the greater the risk of poverty.

As our study has shown, the 'poor' are not static, mired in despair and paralysed into inaction. Indeed, to the contrary, the poor are extraordinarily resourceful and show a great capacity to re-build assets and livelihoods. The ability of the poor and very poor, however, to move beyond a certain threshold of asset viability before the next drought strikes is limited, and this has been the case for many households since at least the 1984 famine. Indeed, many poor households have reached a low-level poverty equilibrium, where they move between very meagre quantities of asset ownership and despite intermittent shocks (droughts) return to their pre-existing asset levels or even slightly improve them. Because droughts occur frequently, the poor face a situation where once they begin to re-build their assets, the next drought wipes out the gains and recovery ensues again.

The article has shown that local social mechanisms assume considerably more importance for the poor in the recovery period than during droughts. Wealthier community members are loaning considerable numbers of livestock, cash, and food to the poor during recoveries, but this drops off steeply when conditions begin to deteriorate. Consequently, there should be a concern that the wealth of the 'better off' actually is declining faster than that of others, and wealth differences between households are narrowing in some locations. As one male household head of Kamme noted, 'There used to be rich people in the village, helping those who faced problems. But now they are impoverished. The people must look to government for help' (Castro and Kebede, 2003:26). In short, current social mechanisms are not sufficient to halt massive asset depletion and suffering among the poor during a drought and this makes the timing of disaster assistance (especially food aid) so vitally important.

That the 'better off' households seem to be moving toward reduced welfare levels speaks loudly of the structural constraints to rural economic diversification and growth under current policy conditions in Ethiopia. Limits on land ownership and property transactions, a lack of physical and social infrastructure (schools and health clinics) and investment opportunities, and serious natural constraints (pasture shortages) on herd accumulation retard long-term wealth accumulation. In contrast to other African countries, there is little investment in non-farm businesses, rental properties, and human capital among the top strata of South Wollo households (cf. Bryceson, 2000). Like the poorest households, the 'better off' in South Wollo amazingly earn more than 90 per cent of their income from farm/livestock activities. Unfortunately, the 'better off' households are caught in a situation where they hold most of their wealth in an asset (livestock) that clearly experiences diminishing returns after a certain level and that is also very susceptible to drought. In a land-constrained economy like South Wollo's, there are real costs (in terms of management, availability of fodder, and animal deaths) to maintaining herds – especially oxen – beyond a certain number.

With such a large number of households coping below or just above the asset-poverty line, what possible policy prescriptions are there? Some researchers are calling for nothing short of a complete transformation of the South Wollo economy: 'At this point in time, anything less than a structural transformation of the Wollo economy seems inadequate to the task of reversing the poverty ratchets in which the people of Wollo seem trapped, but the source of such a transformation is by no means clear' (Sharp et al., 2003: 174). We do not feel the situation is desperate enough to justify radical, costly measures, which the government has pursued with its current programme to resettle thousands of families from famine-prone zones to better watered, lowland areas (see Mulugeta, 2004). In our opinion, there are incremental and less radical actions for alleviating poverty, but most require a long-term commitment on the part of government and funding agencies.

If the immediate effects of a drought could be ameliorated through guaranteed transfers (income or food) or safety nets, the poor might not have to deplete their limited assets 'to eat'. They might also be able to build up sufficient assets to withstand the next drought. Because of the erratic timing and nature of food aid distribution, these programmes do not achieve this at present. Nor do effective primary health programmes exist to help people, like Zeila and Menonen. Under current conditions, drought – and misfortunes like illness – are recurrent shocks that keep the poor from ever getting ahead enough to sustain themselves out of persistent poverty.

Current Ethiopian government and donor efforts to insure a safety net in chronically poor/food insecure areas, such as South Wollo, is a step in the right direction (see Raisin, 2003). As our data show, once the food crisis of a drought ends, poor households – including many headed by females – show considerable resourcefulness in rebuilding assets and livelihoods, and there is no reason to assume that they would not do the same if food risks were diminished through safety nets.

As we argued earlier, access to non-farm income can be an important aspect of asset protection and accumulation among both the poor and 'better off', but to date it is: (1) limited to a few areas with relatively good market access; and (2) restricted to low-wage 'survival' jobs. Two options are possible to improve the non-farm employment situation in the region, so that some diversification out of high-risk rainfed agriculture and livestock activities can take place. The first is the development of viable market towns, with reliable infrastructure and tax and credit incentives to bring in small-scale industries. The desperate demographic and land holding situation means that the future of South Wollo requires vibrant non-farm and urban sectors, to generate jobs and reduce over dependence on risky agriculture and external assistance.

A second aspect to improving non-farm incomes relates to land tenure insecurity in the area. This problem, however, does not call for an expensive land titling programme as a means of insuring tenure, but rather a halt to the mini-land redistributions that have occurred since the government changed in 1991. As we have argued, current land tenure polices keep people 'tied to the land' even when it is limiting their future prospects.

Despite its problems, rainfed agriculture remains the livelihood that drives most economic activities in the region, and is pursued by households from all socio-economic strata. Local demand and markets are strongly determined by how agriculture is doing, and this in turn affects the employment generated by trading and other small business activities. In the area there are possibilities for improved fodder management, water harvesting techniques in dryland areas, and the extension of drought adaptive packages that could decrease the risk of agricultural losses. In the post-drought period local grant and loan programmes for the poor to assist them to recover at least one ox for agriculture also will diminish loses from sharecropping and rentals by the poor.

Finally, the above suggestions are not dramatic development experiments like resettlement, but they would go a long ways toward improving asset levels and resiliency without the massive human suffering usually associated with resettlement (see Rahmato, 2003). South Wollo will continue to be challenged to feed itself even in good rainfall years, but with increased investments to generate meaningful employment, urban markets, and agricultural diversification, the incidence of persistent poverty in the region could decline in this decade.

Acknowledgements

This paper stems from an interdisciplinary research project, entitled 'Assets, Livelihoods, and Cycles: Addressing Poverty and Food Insecurity in the Horn of Africa and Central America', funded by the Broadening Access and Strengthening Input Market Systems-Collaborative Research Support Program (BASIS-CRSP) (USAID Grant No. LAG-A-00-96-90016-00). The project and this paper are products of strong collaboration among several US and Ethiopian researchers associated with the BASIS-CRSP. In particular, the authors would like to acknowledge the assistance of Yigremew Adal, Mesfin, Degefa Tolossa, Mengistu Dessalegn Debela, Kassahun Kebede, Yared Amare, Michael Carter, Michael Roth, and Ragan Petrie. The authors and not the above agency or individuals are solely responsible for the contents of this paper.

Notes

1. Drought is the main agricultural risk that farmers face, but pests, crop diseases and frost also can be major problems in certain areas of South Wollo.
2. We accept the fact that asset/livestock ownership is not the only way to measure something as complex as poverty in Ethiopia, but given the lack of economic and asset diversity in our study area, it remains the best wealth indicator. In the different studies of rural poverty in Ethiopia various

measurements of poverty have been used, including food consumption, income, livestock ownership, labour units, and so on (Webb and von Braun 1992; Dercon and Krishnan 1998, 2000).

3. When plans for the study began in 1998, part of Oromiya zone was actually included in South Wollo zone, but a subsequent re-demarcation of boundaries changed this. Both zones, however, remain part of the Amhara Regional State. In the paper when we talk of the South Wollo area or region, we are including the Oromiya zone in it.
4. The Derg, which approximately translates as 'committee' in Amharic, was the term that was used to refer to the Mengistu regime (1977–91).
5. Another factor that keeps 'the poor on the land' in South Wollo has to do with the distribution of malaria in the country. Despite the hardships and risks in the area, locations above 2,100 metres a.s.l. are virtually malaria free, whereas many other areas where land and employment can be found are malaria-ridden.
6. As used here, a TLU (Tropical Livestock Unit) is: TLU = 1 head of cattle (oxen, bull, cow, calf, heifer); 0.5 TLU = 1 Horse/Donkey/Mule; 1.4 TLU = 1 camel; TLU = 10 sheep/goat; 0.05 TLU = 1 chicken. The TLU ratios approximate weight, subsistence (food), and market value of different animals.
7. *Maganjo* is when the owners of one ox combine their animals so they can plough their fields with the required number (2). It is a widespread institution in South Wollo and Oromiya zones.
8. The paper mainly addresses gender differences based on the sex of the household head, and does not explore intra-household relations. While we believe the latter issue could provide important perspectives on poverty dynamics, we have yet to explore our data on this topic.
9. Strong cultural norms constrain women from ploughing fields. Thus, for a female-headed household without an adolescent or adult son(s) the head frequently must share-crop out her farm to have it plowed.
10. A common post-drought recovery strategy by farmers is to focus initially on fast-breeding sheep and goats, and then invest later on in oxen and cattle.
11. We have not explored in detail the reasons for the price discrepancies. Part of it might be explained by the fact that the poor may be selling lower-quality animals than 'better off' households, but this would not account for why they also are paying higher animal prices than others. We feel that there are other factors involved, including the poor people's lack of access to more lucrative markets, good market information, and large traders.
12. Pseudonyms are used throughout the paper to protect the identity of individuals.

References

Abegaz, B. (2004) Escaping Ethiopia's poverty trap: the case for a second agrarian reform, *Journal of Modern African Studies*, 42, pp. 313–42.

Amare, Y., Adal, Y., Tolossa, D., Castro, A. P. and Little, P. D. (2000) Food security and resource access: a final report on the community assessments in South Wello and Oromiya zones of Amhara Region, Ethiopia, BASIS CRSP, Department of Applied and Agricultural Economics, University of Wisconsin.

Bevan, P. and Joireman, S. (1997) The perils of measuring poverty: identifying the 'poor' in rural Ethiopia, *Oxford Development Studies*, 25, pp. 315–43.

Bryceson, Deborah (2000) 'African peasantries' centrality and marginality: rural labour transformation, in C. Kay and J. Mooji (Eds) *Disappearing Peasantries? Rural Labour in Africa, Asia and Latin America*, (London: Intermediate Technology Publications) pp. 37–63.

Carter, Michael, Little, P. D., Mogues, T and Negatu, W. (2004) Tracking the long run economic impacts of disasters: environmental shocks and recovery in Ethiopia and Honduras, BASIS CRSP, Department of Applied and Agricultural Economics, University of Wisconsin.

Castro, A. P., Amare, Y., Adal, Y. and Tolossa, D. (1999) BASIS/IDR Community Assessments: Kebele Profiles, Parts I, II, III and IV. BASIS CRSP, Department of Applied and Agricultural Economics, University of Wisconsin.

Castro, A. P. and Kebede, K. (2003) Detailed field notes from interviews in Oromiya and South Wello Zones, Amhara Region, Ethiopia, 17–23 July, 2003 (unpublished).

Chronic Poverty Research Centre (2004) *The Chronic Poverty Report, 2004–05*, Manchester: Institute for Development Policy and Management, University of Manchester.

Davies, S. (1996) *Adaptable livelihoods: Coping with Food Insecurity in the Malian Sahel* (New York: St. Martin's Press).

Dercon, S. and Krishnan, P. (1998) Changes in rural poverty in rural Ethiopia 1989–1995: measurement, robustness tests and decomposition, CSAE Working Paper Series WPS 98.7, Centre for the Study of African Economies, Oxford University.

Dercon, S. and Krishnan, P. (2000) Vulnerability, seasonality, and poverty in Ethiopia, *Journal of Development Studies*, 36, pp. 25–53.

Dercon, S. (2002) Growth and shocks: evidence from rural Ethiopia, Paper prepared for the IMF Conference on Macroeconomic Policies and the Poor, Washington, DC.

Dercon, S. (2004) Growth and shocks: evidence from rural Ethiopia, *Journal of Development Economics*, 74, pp. 309–29.

Devereux, S. and Sharp, K. (2003) Is poverty really falling in rural Ethiopia? Paper presented at the conference on 'Staying Poor: Chronic Poverty and Development Policy,' University of Manchester, Manchester, England. 7–9 April, 2004.

DPPC (Disaster Prevention and Preparedness Commission) (1998) Food Supply Prospect in 1998, DPPC, Addis Ababa, Ethiopia.

DPPC (Disaster Prevention and Preparedness Commission) (2000) Assistance Requirements in 2000 for Victims of Natural Disasters, DPPC, Addis Ababa, Ethiopia.

Gebre-Egziabher, T. and Demeke, M. (2004) Small businesses in small towns of the eastern Amhara Region: nature and economic performance, BASIS CRSP Research Report, Department of Agricultural and Applied Economics, University of Wisconsin.

Hammond, L. and Maxwell, D. (2002) The Ethiopian crisis of 1999–2000: lessons learned, questions unanswered, *Disasters*, 26, pp. 262–79.

Hoddinott, J. and Quisumbing, A. R. (2003) Methods for microeconometric risk and vulnerability assessments: a review with empirical examples, Social Protection Discussion Paper No.0324, The World Bank, Washington, DC.

Hulme, D. (2003) Thinking 'small' and the understanding of poverty: Maymana and Mofizul's Story. Working paper No. 22, Chronic Poverty Research Centre, University of Manchester.

Kiros, F. G. and Mehretu, A. (1977) Survey of socio-economic characteristics of rural Ethiopia. Research Bulletin 15: Comparative review and analysis, Institute for Development Research, Addis Ababa University.

Little, P. D., Smith, K., Cellarius, B., Coppock, D. L. and Barrett, C. B. (2001) Avoiding disaster: diversification and risk management among East African herders, *Development and Change*, 32, pp. 401–33.

Little, P. D. (1992) *The Elusive Granary: Herder, Farmer, and State in Northern Kenya* (Cambridge: Cambridge University Press).

Little, P. D. (2005) Food aid dependency in rural Ethiopia: myth or reality? Paper presented at the workshop on 'What Have We Learned About Poverty and Food Insecurity in Eastern Amhara Region, 1998–2004: Research and Policy Implications of the BASIS CRSP/IDR Project,' Addis Ababa, Ethiopia, 7–8 March, 2005.

Mariam, M. W. (1984) *Rural Vulnerability to Famine in Ethiopia, 1958–1977* (New Delhi: Vikas Publishing House).

Moser, C. (1998) The asset vulnerability framework: Reassessing urban poverty reduction, *World Development*, 26, pp. 1–19.

Mulugeta, S. (2004) Ethiopia's plan to rapidly move millions to avoid starvation could harm more than it will help, *Newsday*, 15 Dec., p. A22.

Raisin, J. (2003) Transitional asset protection systems (TAPS): Integrating a transitional asset protection system (TAPS) into the federal food security strategy and regional programs, United States Agency for International Development, Addis Ababa, Ethiopia.

Rahmato, D. (1986) Hunger and destitution in rural Ethiopia, IDR Discussion Paper, Institute for Development Research, Addis Ababa University.

Rahmato, D. (2003) *Resettlement in Ethiopia: The Tragedy of Population Relocation in the 1980s* (Addis Ababa: Forum for Social Studies).

Sharp, K., Devereux, S. and Amare, Y. (2003) Destitution in Ethiopia's northeastern highlands (Amhara Regional State), Institute for Development Studies, University of Sussex.

Stone, M. P. (2002) Retrospective accounts of responses to drought by female and male headed households of Bati and Dessie Zuria Woredas, South Wello and Oromiya Zones: General observations from qualitative interviews. BASIS CRSP, Department of Applied and Agricultural Economics, University of Wisconsin.

Stone, M. P. and Kebede, K. (2003) Interview notes, South Wollo and Oromiya zones, June 2003 (unpublished).

Stone, M. P. (2003) 'Every year is a drought year for me': are female-headed households in Ethiopia a case of sustained unsustainability? Paper presented at the panel on Poverty and Food Security in Amhara Region, Ethiopia, Annual Meetings of the African Studies Association, Boston, MA, 30 Oct.–2 Nov.

United Nations Development Programme (UNDP) (2001) *Human development report: Ethiopia.* (New York: UNDP).

Watts, Michael (1983) *Silent violence: food, famine, and peasantry in northern Nigeria* (Berkeley: University of California Press).

Webb, P. and Von Braun, J. (1992) *Famine and food security in Ethiopia* (Chichester: John Wiley).

World Bank (2002) *World development indicators* (Washington: The World Bank).

Zewde, B. and Pausewang, S. (Eds) (2002) Ethiopia: the challenge of democracy from below (Uppsala: Nordiska Afrikainstitutet; Addis Ababa: Forum for Social Studies).

Exploring Poverty Traps and Social Exclusion in South Africa Using Qualitative and Quantitative Data

MICHELLE ADATO, MICHAEL R. CARTER, & JULIAN MAY

I. Rethinking the Washington Consensus in Polarised Societies

To no one's surprise, South Africa in the immediate post-apartheid period was characterised by high economic inequality and levels of poverty not usually found in an upper middle income country. In the Poverty and Inequality Report (PIR) prepared for then Deputy-President Thabo Mbeki, May et al. (2000) capture this distributional reality most succinctly when they calculated that South Africa was economically two worlds: one, populated by black South Africans where the Human Development Index (HDI) was the equivalent to the HDI of Zimbabwe or Swaziland. The other, was the world of white South Africa in which the HDI rested comfortably between that of Israel and Italy.

More surprising, however, has been the further deepening of inequality, and poverty, in the post-apartheid period.[1] While it is always possible to argue that these trends are the temporary aberrations of structural adjustment, this paper explores the idea that they represent a deeper and more systemic component of the South African social and economic reality, arising from poverty traps such as those identified by Woolard and Klasen (2004). In particular, this paper explores the idea that the apartheid pattern of socio-economic polarisation – in which class and colour were almost perfectly correlated – created a world of inequality in which conventional avenues of upward mobility were cut short, and that highly segmented, and ultimately ineffective patterns of social capital accumulation play a role in the persistence of this constrained mobility.[2] While social capital has been identified in the literature as an important avenue of upward mobility for poorer people (see the comprehensive, though often critical review in Durlauf and Fafchamps, forthcoming), this paper explores whether a legacy of apartheid is an economy in which social exclusion and poverty continue to interact in a mutually self-sustaining fashion, an attribute that could be a general feature of unequal societies such as South Africa.

This question, or legacy hypothesis, has particular salience given the general tenor of economic policy making in South Africa over the last decade. National economic policy in the first post-apartheid government adopted the liberal stance of the so-called Washington Consensus with the adoption of the GEAR (Growth, Employment and Redistribution) programme in 1996. Its name not withstanding, GEAR displaced the emphasis that the ANC and its allies in the trade unions and NGO sector had initially given to direct government responsibility for meeting basic human needs. With its emphasis on fiscal discipline and incentives for private investment, South Africa under GEAR was clearly betting that time would prove to be an ally of the poor on the playing field of an expanding free market economy.

In retrospect, this confidence in time as an ally appears to have been misplaced. As May, et al. (2004) document, despite the fact that macroeconomic policy met its targets and conformed closely to the discipline of the Washington Consensus, time and the South African economy have proven to be rather feeble allies in the fight against poverty, generating neither sufficient growth, nor improvements in income distribution and poverty measures. The recent South African Human Development Report (UNDP, 2003) goes further and argues that the employment elasticity of growth actually declined during the implementation of GEAR, while inappropriately targeted fiscal discipline and a preoccupation with cost recovery undermined advances in the delivery of social services.

It seems that the current South African government is recognizing the need for alternatives. In the September 2003 issue of its popular periodical *Finance & Development*, the International Monetary Fund published a set of papers that revisit the wisdom of the Washington Consensus. Included among them is a piece by South African finance minister, Trevor Manuel, the architect of GEAR (Manuel, 2003). Manuel argues that government needs to take a more pro-active stance than foreseen in the Washington Consensus, and must now take affirmative steps to ensure that citizens are positioned to be able to respond to the new opportunities provided by the liberalised, post-apartheid economy. In the same issue of *Finance & Development*, John Williamson (who coined the term Washington Consensus in 1990) more pointedly says that governments must assure that citizens have the minimum asset base and market access required to save, accumulate and succeed in a market economy (Williamson, 2003).

The failure of time and the Washington Consensus suggests the existence of a persistent, time-resistant poverty that is not easily eliminated. Section II begins this paper's analysis with a brief review of polarisation and exclusion, providing a foundation for the legacy hypothesis. Section III develops some of the analytical tools needed to investigate the structural poverty dynamics suggested by this hypothesis. Section III then implements an analysis of structural dynamics using the 1993–98 KIDS panel data set and finds that South Africa over that time period was indeed characterised by the sort of low level structural poverty trap suggested by the legacy hypothesis. Section IV then deepens the analysis, drawing on qualitative data gathered from a subset of 50 KIDS households that was undertaken in 2001. This later data confirms the general patterns of immobility found in the quantitative data, and explores the factors that constrain or enable mobility. It also provides some insight into what social capital does (help less well-off households stabilise their level of well-being), versus what it does not do (help less well-off households move ahead over time). Section V concludes the paper with some reflections on economic policy and income distribution dynamics in polarised societies.

II. Apartheid's Legacy of Polarisation and Exclusion

Carter and Barrett (this volume) emphasise that poverty traps can emerge when: (1) Increasing returns to scale, fixed costs or risk create a reality in which marginal returns to investment increase as wealth increases over some range; and, (2) Poor households have inadequate access to financial services (loans and insurance). In this circumstance, poor households may become mired in situations of low assets and failed attempts to accumulate and move ahead. Income distribution would, in this case, be a divergent process, with the initially poor trapped at low levels of well-being, while the initially better-off move ahead to higher levels of well-being. On the other hand, when poor households can borrow against future earnings to capitalise investment projects, and enjoy insurance that permits them to ride out economic downturns without sacrificing past gains, then income distribution will tend to be characterised by a convergent process in which the initially poor tend to catch up economically with the rest of their society.

If the economic theory of poverty traps is correct, then the ability of the poor to access capital and insurance becomes a key determinant of longer term poverty dynamics. Unfortunately, the ability of markets themselves to deliver financial services to poor people is suspect. As now well-developed theoretical and empirical literatures make clear, such markets may simply not exist, may carry disproportionate costs for poor people, or indeed, they may tend systematically to exclude low wealth people.

The arm's length anonymous transactions of markets are, of course, not the only mechanisms of access to capital and insurance. A variety of informal, relational or socially mediated mechanisms can, and in many places do, provide access to financial services. Indeed, much of the growing interest within economics about social capital stems precisely from an interest in understanding the ability of social mechanisms to substitute for incomplete markets.

What then determines socially mediated access to capital and insurance? Figueroa et al. (1996) point out that social capital has resonance with the concept of social exclusion that has been the subject of debate concerning poverty in Europe. In this debate, social exclusion is seen to focus 'primarily on relational issues (such as) the lack of social ties to the family, friends, local community, state services and institutions or more generally to the society to which an individual belongs' (Bhalla and Lapeyre, 1997: 417). In a similar spirit, Townsend (1985: 665) talks of social needs such as being able/unable to fulfil the roles of parent, kin, citizen, neighbour and so forth. Being ashamed to appear in public and not being able to participate in the activities of the community are also noted by Sen as being aspects of deprivation (Sen, 1985:169, 161). In this way, exclusion may be posed as the opposite of social integration.

Exclusion has both economic and social dimensions. The economic dimension refers to exclusion from the opportunities to earn income, the labour market and access to assets. The social dimension refers to exclusion from decision making, social services and community and family support. At one level then, social exclusion can refer to the exclusion to the rights of citizenship; while at another, the concept refers to relationships within families and communities. The usefulness of the concept is the support that it lends to the importance of social relationships in resource allocation and usage. Social exclusion may thus be linked to the existence of discriminatory forces, such as racism, and the outcome of market failures and unenforced rights. Alternatively, it could be argued that exclusion is a consequence of hierarchical power relations, in which group distinctions and inequality overlap (de Haan, 1998:13) and it is conceivable that inclusion may occur, but under unfavourable or exploitative conditions, sometimes referred to as 'adverse incorporation' (Bracking, 2003). In South Africa, Moser (1997) has gone further, linking the exclusionary policies of apartheid and the social dynamics set in motion by the apartheid struggle to the erosion of social capital.

In a recent theoretical paper, Mogues and Carter (forthcoming) further explore these themes by asking how an individual's investment in social capital is shaped by social identity. In particular they show that as what Stewart (2001) calls horizontal inequality increases (that is, as ethnicity or other markers of social identity becomes increasingly correlated with economic status), social capital becomes more narrowly constructed and increasingly ineffective as a mechanism of economic advance for poor people.

Taken together, these theoretical considerations and empirical observations suggest that social mechanisms of access to capital and insurance are likely to be ineffectual in highly unequal societies such as South Africa. The remainder of this paper will now use both quantitative and qualitative data to see if social exclusion and ineffectual social capital help explain emerging South African patterns of economic mobility and poverty dynamics.

III. Quantitative Evidence of Asset Thresholds and Poverty Traps

Both the quantitative and qualitative portions of this study draw on data collected from households in the KwaZulu-Natal Income Dynamics Study (KIDS). KIDS households were originally selected at random in 1993 from the universe of KwaZulu-Natal households (as part of a broader national survey), and were again interviewed in 1998. The province of KwaZulu-Natal is home to approximately 20 per cent of South Africa's population of 44 million. Although not the poorest province in South Africa, it arguably has the highest incident of deprivation in terms of access to services and perceived well-being (Klasen, 1997; Leibbrandt and Woolard, 1999).

Table 1 presents a suite of poverty indicators drawn from prior analysis of the household expenditure data from the KIDS study.[3] The rows of the table present information on 1993, while the columns present information on 1998. When measured against a standard poverty line, 27 per cent of KIDS households were poor in 1993 with an average poverty gap that was 27 per cent of the poverty line. The number of poor had risen to almost 43 per cent by 1998, while the average poverty gap rose to 33 per cent. While these figures are striking, they do not reveal the extent of mobility (for example, how many of the initially poor households were also poor in 1998), nor do they identify the causes of mobility.

Table 1 allows a first look at these mobility issues by including a standard mobility decomposition. The rows of the table give the 1993 well-being class, while the columns give the 1998 classification. Looking at the top bold row in each cell of the table first, the results of this two-way classification scheme are provided. As can be seen, 18 per cent of the households were poor in both periods, or were chronically poor in the language of standard dynamic poverty analysis. Another 35 per cent of households were poor in one period only and hence can be classified as transitorily poor. The chronically or twice poor thus constitute between 42 per cent and 64 per cent of overall poverty.[4]

While these standard mobility indicators are informative, they do not address a key challenge facing the empirical analysis of poverty, that of distinguishing between households that can expect to escape poverty over time from those that cannot. Carter and May (2001) take a first step towards answering this challenge by defining the asset poverty line, defined as the level of assets needed to generate an expected living standard equal to the poverty line.[5] Households with assets below the asset poverty line would be expected to be poor (at least in the short to medium term), while those with assets above that line would be expected to be non-poor. Stochastic shocks can of course move people away from these expected positions.

Using the asset poverty line, Carter and May are able to further decompose the mobility patterns shown in Table 1. The 25 per cent of the KIDS sample that fell

Table 1. Decomposing poverty transitions in South Africa (per cent surveyed households)

		1998	
		Poor 43%	Non-poor 57%
1993	Poor 27%	***18%*** *Chronically poor, of which:* • 8% dual entitlement failures*** • Structurally poor/ ≤92%	***10%*** *Got ahead, of which:* • 58% Stochastically mobile* • Structurally mobile ≤42%
	Non-poor 73%	***25%*** *Fell behind, of which:* • 15% Stochastically mobile** • Structurally poor/ ≤85%, of which 51% had entitlement losses	***48%*** *Never poor*

Source: Based on Carter and May (2001).

behind between 1993 and 1998 can be split into those whose movement was structural, based on the accumulation of assets (or increased returns to assets), and those whose movement was stochastic, based on bad luck and the failure to earn expected returns to assets. As can be seen in Table 1, perhaps 15 per cent of the households that fell behind did so for stochastic reasons, meaning that their asset base in 1998 was firmly above the 1998 asset poverty line. The fact that they were observed to be poor in 1998 despite being above the asset poverty line thus indicates bad luck in the form of failure of to achieve expected returns to their assets. In the short- to medium-term (with no further changes in assets or in the structure of the economy), these households would be expected to return to a non-poor status.

The other 85 per cent of the households that moved downwards between 1993 and 1998 are likely structurally poor, with assets below the asset poverty line. Either they were non-poor in 1993 for reasons of good fortune (returns to their assets in excess of the expected returns), or they suffered asset losses between 1993 and 1998 which moved them beneath the asset poverty line. Indeed, over 50 per cent of the households that moved downward between 1993 and 1998 report losses of productive assets (for example, death of a wage earner, or loss of enterprise assets to fire or other disaster). In contrast to the households whose downward mobility was stochastic, these households have a structural basis to their poverty and would be expected to remain poor over the short- to medium-term.

Carter and May similarly decompose the 10 per cent of KIDS households that moved ahead between 1993 and 1998 into those whose upward mobility was structural versus those whose mobility reflected the operation of random factors. Stochastic upward mobility – which Carter and May estimate was the case for 58 per cent of the upwardly mobile households – could occur when a household that was above the 1993 asset poverty line was observed to be poor in 1993, presumably because of bad luck that depressed returns to assets (for example, a lost job, poor business performance). The move by such a household to a non-poor standard of living would reflect a return to the standard of living that would be expected given the household's asset base. Upward structural mobility, on the other hand, would occur when a household that was below the 1993 asset poverty successfully engineered an escape from poverty by accumulating additional assets, moving above the 1998 asset poverty line, and gaining the returns expected for those assets. Carter and May estimate that no more than 42 per cent of upward mobility (roughly 4 per cent of the overall sample) reflected this structural process of poverty relief. Thus modest pattern of upward structural mobility, coupled with the relatively large amounts of structural poverty, are at least consistent with the hypothesis that social exclusion and ineffective social capital are an important legacy of apartheid.

While the Carter and May decomposition gives important information about how the economy is working, and also gives a sense of how much poverty is likely to persist in the short- to medium-term (holding assets and the structure of the economy constant), it does not tell us how many of the structurally poor are likely to remain poor over the longer term. Are some structurally poor households on an upward trajectory of steady asset accumulation such that they would be expected to some day exit poverty? Is another subset caught in a poverty trap from which upward mobility is not possible?

Similarly, the Carter-May decomposition does not tell us whether all of the structurally non-poor are in a defensible position. Is there a subset of households above the asset poverty line in 1998 that are on a downward trajectory of de-accumulation such that they would be expected to become poor over the longer term? In other words, are they below a critical threshold of assets necessary to successfully sustain a non-poor standard of living or move ahead over time? Alternatively are all structurally non-poor households in positions from which they can maintain or improve upon their non-poor status? In an effort to answer these questions, we turn now to further quantitative and qualitative analysis.

(a) Poverty Traps and Asset Dynamics

As discussed by Carter and Barrett (this volume), if poverty traps exist, they should be visible in the pattern of asset dynamics. Figure 1 illustrates hypothetical alternative asset dynamics. For the moment, assume that we have devised an appropriate index that compresses the multiple economic assets of a household at time t, given by the vector $\boldsymbol{A}_t$, into a one-dimensional index, $\Lambda(\boldsymbol{A}_t)$. In the next section we will discuss the creation of an appropriate multi-asset index. The horizontal axis in Figure 1 measures initial or early period stocks of the assets used to generate incomes and livelihoods, $\Lambda(\boldsymbol{A}_0)$. The vertical axis measures asset stocks for a later period, $\Lambda(\boldsymbol{A}_t)$. The different curves express $\Lambda(\boldsymbol{A}_t)$ as a function of $\Lambda(\boldsymbol{A}_0)$. Note that the 45-degree line gives equilibrium points where $\Lambda(\boldsymbol{A}_t) = \Lambda(\boldsymbol{A}_0)$.

The convergent trajectory in Figure 1 illustrates the case in which poorer households tend to build up assets and livelihood potential over time, converging to

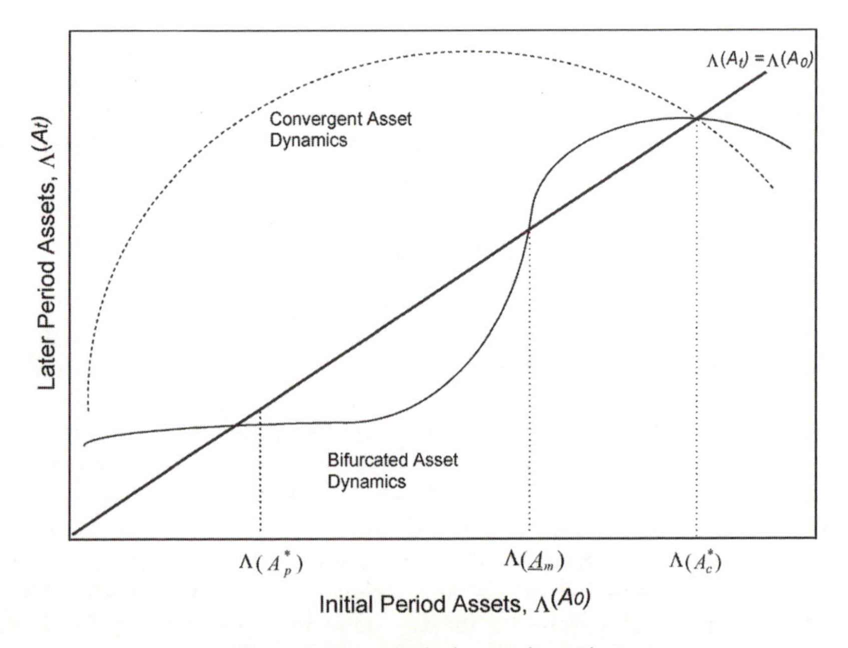

Figure 1. Hypothetical asset dynamics

the equilibrium level, $\Lambda(A_c^*)$.[6] Households with stocks initially in excess of $\Lambda(A_c^*)$ would tend over time to retreat back towards that level.

In contrast, the stylised bifurcated asset trajectory in Figure 1 illustrates the case of a poverty trap. Asset level $\Lambda(\underline{A}_m)$ is the critical asset threshold (which Zimmerman and Carter, 2003 label the 'Micawber threshold'[7]) around which accumulation trajectories split. Households that begin below this level tend to fall behind (as $\Lambda(A_t) < \Lambda(A_0)$) and approach the low-level poverty trap of $\Lambda(A_p^*)$. Households above that critical threshold will tend to get ahead and approach the high asset and income equilibrium, denoted $\Lambda(A_c^*)$.[8] While either convergent or bifurcated dynamics can in principal exist, the empirical challenge is to identify whether the South African economy exhibits convergent dynamics or the sort of poverty trap equilibrium hypothesised by the social exclusion perspective.

(b) A Livelihood-Weighted Asset Index

Prior to estimating the relation between $\Lambda(A_t)$ and $\Lambda(A_0)$, assets themselves must be measured and aggregated. Fortunately, the asset poverty line, discussed above suggests a simple and analytically convenient measure. Note that identification of the asset poverty line requires estimation of the following regression function that relates livelihood of household i at time t (ℓ_{it}) to the bundle of assets held by the household at that time (A_{it})

$$\ell_{it} = \sum_j \beta_j(A_{it})A_{ijt} + \varepsilon_{it}, \qquad (1)$$

We measure household livelihood or material well-being as household consumption expenditures divided by the money value of the household's subsistence needs. The dependent variable thus equals one if expenditures exactly equal the poverty line. Note that the coefficients of the regression relationship (the $\beta_j(A_{it})$) give the marginal contribution to livelihood of the j different assets.[9]

Given estimates of the β_j, we can then calculate the fitted value of the regression function, Λ_{it}, defined as:

$$\Lambda_{it} = \sum_j \hat{\beta}_j(A_{it})A_{ijt}. \qquad (2)$$

Note that Λ_{it} is an asset index, where assets are weighted by their marginal contribution to livelihood as given by the estimated regression coefficients, $\hat{\beta}_j$. The advantages of this livelihood-weighted asset index Λ_i are several. First its weights can be estimated quite flexibly such that returns to assets depend on levels of other assets. In addition, the coefficients can be permitted to vary over different years as macro policy and other changes influence the returns to assets and endowments. Second, the index is expressed in a convenient livelihood metric. In the particular application used here, the asset index is expressed in poverty line units (PLUs), such that a value of one means that the particular bundle predicts a poverty level of material well-being, a value of 0.5 would mean that the assets predict a livelihood at half the poverty line, and so forth.

Four key assets were used as the base for the index: human capital (educated labour and uneducated labour), natural and productive capital (land, livestock, small business machinery and equipment, and so forth), and unearned or transfer income which includes South Africa's much discussed Old Age Pension grant. The latter was included as a measure of resources available for self-finance of income earning and investment activities. Not included among the core assets was social capital or other less tangible economic assets.

Returns to these core assets were estimated using a polynomial expansion of the basic assets. This specification permits marginal returns to assets to both diminish (or increase) with the level of the assets, as well as to be influenced by holdings of other assets (for example, marginal returns to capital assets may be boosted by the presence of educated labour or exogenous income). The interest with these regressions is less in identifying the precise marginal returns to any individual assets, and more with deriving a set of weights that reliably predict the impact of an asset bundle on expected livelihood. Many of the estimated coefficients are significant, and the overall regression fit yields an R^2 of 0.56 for the 1993 and 0.37 for the 1998 data. Using these estimated coefficients, a fitted value, or estimated livelihood index, was calculated for each observation in the dataset. Full results of the regression analysis are available from the authors.

(c) Bifurcated Asset Dynamics in South Africa

Using these estimated asset indices for 1993 and 1998, we are now in a position to explore patterns of asset dynamics in South Africa. As discussed in Carter and Barrett (this volume), flexible, non-parametric methods offer significant advantages in estimating the sort of non-linear relationships that are hypothesised to characterise asset dynamics. For purposes of the analysis here, local regression methods (see Cleveland et al., 1988) were employed to estimate the bivariate relationship between the a household's estimated 1998 asset index, Λ_{i98}, and its 1993 index, Λ_{i93}.[10] The solid curve in Figure 2 graphs the resulting estimate of expected 1998 asset index given Λ_{i93}, while the two surrounding dashed lines represent the 95 per cent confidence band estimate of Λ_{i98}. The range of the graph has been truncated at 4 PLUs. As can be seen, the curve first cuts the 45-degree line at about 90 per cent of the poverty line, and cuts it a second time at an asset index value of two PLUs. The curve crosses the 45-degree line for a third and final time at about 5 PLUs.

The dynamics implied by this figure are precisely those of the hypothetical case of bifurcated dynamics. The Micawber Threshold is estimated to be at an asset level that predicts a level of well-being that is about twice the poverty line. Households with assets below that level would be expected to experience deterioration in their position, heading back toward the poverty trap level of assets that predicts a level well-being of about 90 per cent of the poverty line. Households with asset indices above the Micawber threshold would be expected to move toward an upper equilibrium asset level that predicts a living standard of about 5 PLUs. Households that begin in abject poverty with asset indices less than 90 per cent of the poverty line would be expected to improve their situations, moving toward the poverty trap equilibrium.

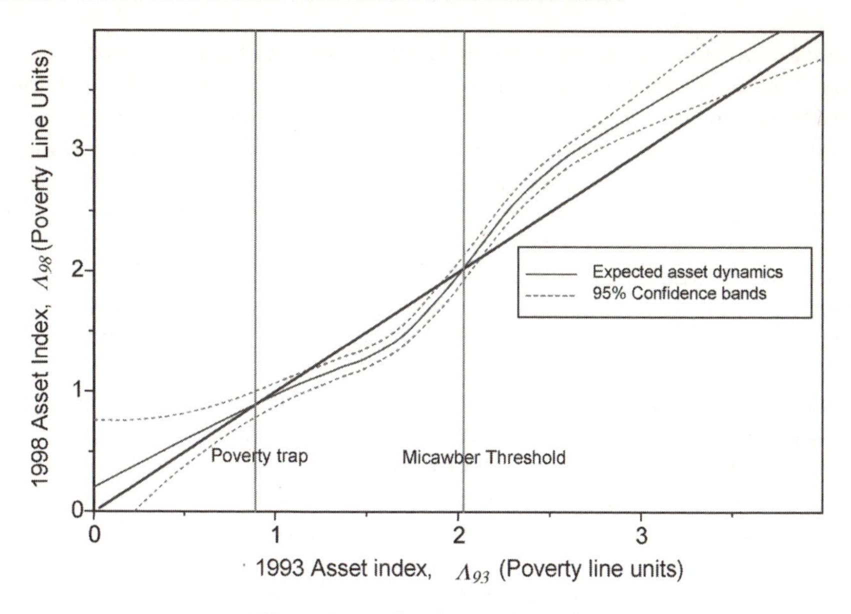

Figure 2. Predicted asset dynamics

Using Figure 2, households can be assigned to one of three long-term mobility classes:

(1) Caught in the poverty trap equilibrium $\leftrightarrow \Lambda_{98} < 0.9$ *PLUs*
(2) Downwardly mobile toward the poverty trap $\leftrightarrow 0.9$ *PLUs* $< \Lambda_{98} < 2.1$ *PLUs*
(3) Converging to the non-poor equilibrium $\leftrightarrow 2.1$ *PLUs* $< \Lambda_{98}$

Using these class assignments as predictors of the long-term position of households of course assumes that the underlying mobility process captured by the 1998 data persists over time. The next section will use later period qualitative information in part to test the accuracy of this assumption.

The estimates that underlie Figure 2 can be used to calculate the implied velocity of asset changes for households with different initial asset levels. A household that began just above the Micawber threshold (with an asset index of 2.5 PLUs) would have a predicted annual growth in assets of about 2.5 per cent, or over five years would experience a 15 per cent increase in expected well-being – meaning that its level of well-being would be expected to rise from 2.5 to almost 2.9 PLUs. A household that began below the Micawber threshold (at an asset level of say only 1.5 PLUs) would be expected to have assets that predict a living standard of only 1.25 times the poverty line after five years.

Figure 2 is as striking for what it does not show as for what it does show. Given the low standard of living and the high levels of unemployment suffered by households in our sample, it is surprising that these figures do not exhibit significant asset accumulation by less well-off households. Such households would appear to have every incentive to accumulate and surplus resources that could be profitably brought into use. Their failure to do so would seem to reflect the lack of access to capital and risk management services as discussed earlier. While there may, of course, be other constraints at work, this pattern is at least consistent with an unequal and polarised society in which neither market nor social mechanisms broker opportunities for upward mobility for the least well-off households.

In addition to these structural patterns, the estimated asset dynamics also imply that temporary shocks or setbacks can have permanents effects. For example, imagine a household that initially enjoyed an asset index above the Micawber threshold. If this household experienced an asset shock that pushed its assets below the Micawber threshold, then the estimated pattern of bifurcated asset dynamics predicts that this household will experience long-term effects as its expected long-term asset position drops from 4 PLUs to the lower equilibrium of 0.9 PLUs. This observation of the potentially permanent effects of one time shocks is of much more than academic interest. Fully 60 per cent of the KIDS households that exhibited downward mobility between 1993 and 1998 had experienced shocks that reduced their assets, as discussed above. In addition, households that experience income (not asset) losses may still find themselves in a position where they are forced to liquidate assets to meet immediate consumption needs. If drawing down such assets pushes the household below the Micawber threshold, the pattern of bifurcated asset dynamics again predicts that the temporary shock will have permanent, long-run effects.

Before turning to a deeper consideration of these results, one statistical comment is in order. As the confidence bands show, the estimated asset dynamics are quite imprecise at lower asset levels. Projecting the asset index data onto Figure 2 shows that this imprecision is not only the result of somewhat thinly distributed data, but also of a highly variable experience. We thus need to be extremely cautious with inferring that households below the poverty trap level of 0.9 PLUs will grow towards that level. Put differently, the interval estimate includes values that are both above and below the 45-degree line, meaning that we can have little confidence as to whether households below that level will improve or fall further behind over time. The contrast with asset positions above the Micawber threshold is both striking and somewhat discouraging if the convergent trajectory of pro-poor growth was anticipated. Not only can we be more certain of the data for this group, but we are also more certain that this group will carry on improving, as shown by their steeply rising rate of growth.

In summary, we thus find evidence that the very low ceiling of a poverty trap truncated upward mobility derived from the conventional set of assets in South Africa over the 1990s. While this pattern is consistent with the hypothesis that ineffectual social capital truncates upward mobility in polarised societies, it would be nice to have more direct confirmation of the roles played by social capital. In an effort to explore this issue further we turn to qualitative methods to see what role social capital played – or failed to play – in facilitating and constraining mobility.

IV. Qualitative Analysis of Poverty Traps, Mobility and Social Capital

In 2001, in-depth interviews from a sub-set of nearly 50 KIDS households were carried out.[11] The data from these interviews offer insights on three key issues relevant to this paper. First, they provide detailed accounts of the role of different types of events and assets in explaining mobility. Second, they allow observations on a second time span (1998–2001) that can be used to confirm, or reject, the predictions of the quantitative analysis of poverty traps. Third, they permit a close look at the role social capital plays, or does not play, in patterns of mobility and stasis.

The qualitative study combined 'household events mapping' (Adato et al., A, forthcoming) with semi-structured interviewing to trace and elicit stories about events from 1993 through 2001.[12] 'Households' were defined more broadly than in the quantitative study. All immediate or extended family members who gave or took resources from the household on a regular basis or in a significant manner, and thus affected the household's poverty or well-being status, were included.[13] The construction of 'household trees' probed for additional relationships not initially mentioned by household members; the household events map also discovered additional members of significance over the course of the interview (Adato et al., A, forthcoming). Using the assets framework adopted by this paper, we examined all events that had an impact on a household's well-being status for each year, and then categorised each event by its impact on the four types of assets already analysed: human, productive, natural and financial. To this list, we were able to examine a fifth category: social assets.[14] Events affecting each of the asset categories were first considered separately, and then in relation to each other. Outcomes were evaluated separately for each of the two periods: 1993–98 and 1998–2001.[15] Detailed accounts of household events throughout two periods, the processes that followed events (that is, whether a household gained, coped, or did not cope), and the impacts over time were all used to assess whether a household became better or worse off, the stability of that movement, and the characteristics of the households that explain mobility.

(a) Findings of the Qualitative Analysis

Using this information, and following the discussion in Section III, households can be divided into six mobility classes that closely mimic those used by Carter and May (2001):

(1) Chronic structural poverty
(2) Structurally downwardly mobile
(3) Stochastically downwardly mobile
(4) Stochastically upwardly mobile
(5) Structurally upwardly mobile
(6) Stable non-poor.

While these mobility patterns are not defined around a rigid asset poverty line, they do permit analysis of the ongoing mobility processes, an analysis that allows insight into the existence of poverty traps and longer-term poverty dynamics.

Using these mobility classes, Table 2 shows where the qualitative analysis places households for each of the two periods, 1993–98 and 1998–2001. As in the quantitative analysis, Table 2 shows that over an eight-year time horizon, most households are locked into one of two unequal positions: either poor and unable to change this situation or non-poor and relatively stable. The 36 cells in Table 2 are clustered into four groups. Group 1 (gray shading) includes households that appear to be trapped in poverty. This the largest cluster of households at 44 per cent of the

Table 2. Qualitative analysis of mobility over two periods (per cent of total households in qualitative sample)

1993–98 mobility (*Qualitative Observation*)	1998 to 2001 mobility						
		Chronic poor	Structurally downward	Stochastically downward	Stochastically upward	Structurally upward	Never poor
	Chronic poor	14%	2%		4%	2%	
	Structurally downward	10%	10%		4%	2%	
	Stochastically downward		2%	2%			6%
	Stochastically upward						
	Structurally upward			2%			
	Never poor		10%	2%			26%

total. Group 2 (horizontal stripe shading) represents those households that manage to move structurally upward – at 2 per cent of the total – displaying a striking absence of upward mobility. Group 3 (vertical stripe shading) represents households that fell structurally downward, with 12 per cent of the total. Group 4 (no shading) represents the cluster of households who were stably non-poor, with 38 per cent of the cases.

We now analyse the characteristics of the households that fall into each of these mobility classes. An important finding to note at the outset is the particular significance of stable income sources, such as formal employment or state grants. In the South African context of high and rising unemployment throughout the 1990s, formal employment is more than a matter of possessing a stock of human or financial capital; it also involves opportunities to obtain such employment. Such opportunities depend largely on the extent to which the economy provides them. Social networks can help in enabling access, though these are more effective for better-off households. Similarly, the Old Age Pension (OAP) grant is more than an immediate and exogenous source of financial capital; by providing access to a stable and secure income stream, the OAP also serves as surety with which to leverage further financial and – potentially – social resources. In both cases, the *stability* of the availability/accessibility of the income source is what enables the initial economic asset to make a structural difference.[16] An assets framework narrowly interpreted may be inadequate to explain poverty dynamics. The qualitative methodology that we adopt allows the interpretation to be broadened to include notions of availability, access and stability when assessing economic assets and their implications for household well-being and mobility. Below is a more detailed analysis of the characteristics of the four mobility groups, including the role of social assets.

Group 1 – Households trapped in structural poverty: In Group 1, households that were poor in both periods (1993–98 and 1998–2001), there is often no formal work, or only one formal job that is insufficient given the household size or other factors. Instead, the household relies on members that move in and out of informal or casual jobs. Some households depend on one OAP as the major, or only, reliable income source. Households that were structurally poor in 1998 and fell structurally further downward start out with similar conditions, but then lose their one stable income stream. Formal work is replaced by informal or casual work. There may be a substantial increase in the number of dependents as a former guardian dies or moves away. Ubiquitous in both periods are shocks, such as fire, illness, accident, death of a wage earner or pensioner, funeral and attendant expenses, or the payment of a dowry (*lobola*). Households in both the above categories tend to belong to burial societies when they can afford the membership dues, but have few other important social assets. Furthermore, they lose *potential* social assets when a formal worker with connections to employment opportunities dies, or when an employer who used to provide loans no longer does so.

Households that were moving structurally downward over the 1993–98 period and either remained poor or became worse off after 1998 look similar to those described above, though the situations are reversed across the two periods. In these cases, the significant event occurs *before* 1998: the death of a wage earner or pensioner, major job loss, or failure of a small business. Organisational memberships that could keep the household from falling deeper into crisis (burial societies, food stokvels[17]) are out of reach because of small but unaffordable membership fees. In the case of households that fall structurally downward again between 1998 and 2001, the household usually loses more than one major financial asset. This may be compounded by other events, such as family conflict that leads to the disintegration of the family or loss of social capital. For the structurally poor households that stochastically improve their situation, a one-time influx of or cash from a retrenchment package or savings are used to improve their home or buy furniture. They thus feel that they are improving their lives, but there are no structural changes in terms of livelihood earning potential in the long run, and they are likely to be found back in poverty in the next period.

Group 2 – Upwardly mobile households: Group 2 households look like the structurally poor households in the 1993–98 period, but after 1998 their situation changes. In one household, two small businesses were started and grew after 1998, appearing stable and relatively lucrative. The businesses involved investment in productive assets made with funds provided after a formal employer closed down and from income from the businesses. In another case, investment in human capital paid off, with two teaching jobs acquired between 1998 and 2001 and another household member studying at the technikon. Social assets do not appear to be substantially changed with this upward movement; however, the households in this cell do not report the type of family conflict that plagued a number of downwardly mobile households.

Group 3 – Downwardly mobile households: Group 3 households experienced stable conditions over the 1993–98 period, but things fell apart thereafter. Stable income (some mix of formal, domestic and informal work, and a pension over) was lost after 1998. Investments do not provide stability in the long run. Businesses started during 1998–2001 fail. There is also a large shock in the second period, such as death of a major wage earner or pensioner, or loss of retirement savings due to severe illness in the family, or a bureaucratic error. In some of these cases, social exclusion means a lack of status, power and resources to use the legal system to exercise rights to financial assets. Burial societies and community gardens are helpful, but do not provide any structural change. Family members can be relied on to prevent destitution, but they are not in a position to help the household out of poverty because they too lack resources.

Group 4 – Stable non-poor households: Group 4 households are structurally non-poor in both periods. Conditions are the reverse of those in Group 1 households. There is more than one formal job and/or pension. There are also casual, domestic and informal jobs *in addition to*, rather than instead of, formal work. Multiple small businesses operate simultaneously, so that if one fails there are still others, or else a new business quickly replaces the failed one. The households are better able to weather shocks. One household lost its house, furniture and clothing in a fire, but it had access to credit (hire purchase) in order to replace them. The resources of households in this group enable them to put social assets to better use. People within their networks send remittances and/or provide information about jobs (structurally poor households also report this exchange of information, but the non-poor networks seem to be more fruitful). Organisational memberships often involve income generation. Home and community gardening contribute to subsistence of the non-poor, as well. Although fundamentally it is access to stable work and pensions that keep these households out of poverty, social networks enable fortification of household well-being through the spreading of opportunities. The ability to afford participation in organisations provides additional (if not large) forms of support.

(b) Comparing Qualitative and Quantitative Mobility Findings

Table 3 compares the results of the qualitative analysis with the quantitative analysis from Section III. The columns define the predicted long-term mobility of a household based on its 1998 estimated asset index and the livelihood dynamics predicted in the prior section. The rows display mobility outcomes for the 1998–2001 period as determined by the qualitative analysis.

The cells in Table 3 are clustered into four groups based on an initial prediction, the direction and type of mobility experienced over the 1998–2001 period. Group 1 (grey shading) includes households that appear to be trapped in poverty, either remaining poor in both periods, falling structurally downward into a worse position and staying there, or stochastically better or worse but not structurally different. Group 2 (horizontal stripe shading) are those households that started out structurally poor, or poor and falling in the first period, but managed to move structurally upward in the second period. Group 3 (vertical stripe shading) represents households that were structurally non-poor in the first period, but then moved structurally downward in the second period. Group 4 (no shading) represents households that were non-poor in the first period, and whose position appears to be stable; that is, they either remained non-poor in the second period, moved structurally further upward, or moved stochastically downward, but nevertheless were stable.

The finding of the quantitative analysis in the prior section has three major implications that can be tested against the qualitative information on 1998–2001 mobility. First, the existence of a low-level poverty trap equilibrium just below the poverty line suggests that many of the poor (especially the 'better off' poor) should exhibit little change in their situation. Second, there should be very little structural upward mobility for the poor and near-poor households, as the Micawber dynamic asset poverty threshold is estimated to be two times the conventional poverty line.[18] Third, there should be substantial downward mobility among households that were non-poor but below the Micawber threshold.

Table 3 confirms each of these implications. Of the 13 households that appeared to be caught in the poverty trap equilibrium 1998, 11 of those remained in the same position or experienced a further deterioration in their structural position. Only two advanced structurally. Of the 18 households estimated to move downward toward the poverty trap equilibrium, ten appear to be structurally poor by 2001, another three experienced favourable shocks that improved their positions, and the remaining five avoided the predicted slippage towards poverty. Finally, of the 14 households predicted to be converging toward the higher-level equilibrium, only

Table 3. Qualitative and quantitative analysis of post-1998 mobility
Absolute numbers of observations (Per cent of column in parentheses)

		Predicted mobility class *(Quantitative prediction)*		
		Poverty trap equilibrium *(n=13)*	Downwardly mobile toward poverty trap *(n=18)*	Converging to non-poor equilibrium *(n=14)*
1998–2001 mobility *(Qualitative observation)*	Chronic structural poverty	6 (46%)	5 (27%)	1 (7%)
	Structurally downward	3 (23%)	5 (27%)	2 (14%)
	Stochastically downward	2 (15%)	–	1 (7%)
	Stochastically upward	--	3 (17%)	1 (7%)
	Structurally upward	--	--	1 (7%)
	Stable non-poor	2 (15%)	5 (27%)	8 (57%)

three moved downwards structurally, while the other 11 maintained their advantaged structural positions.

(c) The Role of Social Assets in Explaining Mobility and Stasis

The role of social capital in explaining poverty dynamics has several dimensions that emerge from the qualitative research. The main way in which social capital influences well-being is by mediating access to work (see Adato et al. B, forthcoming). Friends or relatives provide information about jobs in the city, contacts with employers, and advice on how to get a job. They sometimes also provide transportation fees and accommodation for job seekers. Better-off households tend to have more effective networks for these purposes, since those who have work also have better connections and information.

Remittances are highly important and often the main or only source of income. Remittances would be even more important if work were not so scarce in urban as well as rural areas (Adato et al., 2003). However, to the extent that the main paths through which social relationships provide economic benefits are through information about work and remittances, the high unemployment rate in the province, and country as a whole, means that these paths are more often than not closed off to those who are poor and marginalised.

The qualitative research revealed approximately 20 additional ways in which social assets are used. Some of these have an effect on livelihoods, though not necessarily offering protection from poverty. Others have no effect. Categories of socially-mediated assistance most frequently reported by households are (in descending order from 70 per cent to 18 per cent): assistance in looking for work; burial societies; cash (loan or gift); stokvels, savings and borrow groups; and community gardens. A smaller number of households mentioned lending tools/equipment and helping with work, religious groups, and sports and music groups.

The qualitative research also uncovered ways in which social relationships *negatively* influenced household economic advance. One mechanism is where people who know a small business owner pressure him or her to provide goods on credit, which is not repaid; another is where jealousy and competition undermine the success of a fledgling small business (Adato et al. B, forthcoming). In addition, one-third of households report problems of conflict and distrust within and between families that also make economic improvement difficult.

Looking across the different groups represented in Table 2, we see interesting patterns emerge in the functioning of social capital between structurally poor and non-poor groups. Providing assistance in looking for work emerges frequently in poor and non-poor households. Yet, this assistance does not necessarily mean that work is obtained, and it is likely that the access provided by a working person is more fruitful than that of an unemployed person. Burial societies are equally common across the two groups, while saving groups are found almost entirely in the non-poor group. Respondents explained that lack of money was an obstacle to participation in the latter, while the cost of burial societies is more affordable and a high priority even if hard to afford. Cash assistance and in-kind assistance are more common among poor households (non-poor households probably need this less). Community gardens are used by both groups, but more so by poor households. Interestingly, conflict and distrust is equally prevalent across the groups. This has had negative economic consequences in many households, where conflict is directly associated with worsening economic conditions as both a cause and consequence. While non-poor households seem to be less negatively affected by conflict, it is not the primary explanatory variable of the status of either poor or non-poor households.

In summary, what is evident from the qualitative research is that social connections often attempt to help households look for work, get by in times of need, or cope with shocks. Yet, they are not connections that provide pathways out of poverty. Poor people do not have the resources to provide much to each other, and they are not connected with others who do. In fact, poverty causes conflicts over resources and other strains among family and among neighbours, further diminishing sources or potential sources of support. The results provide empirical confirmation of Mogues and Carter's (forthcoming) argument that social capital becomes more narrowly constructed and increasingly ineffective as a mechanism of capital access for poor people in a country facing a legacy of horizontal inequality and social exclusion.

V. Conclusion

The problem of chronic or persistent poverty has received increasing attention of late, punctuated by the publication of the *Chronic Poverty Report* (Chronic Poverty Research Centre, 2004). While South Africa has living standards that are on average significantly above those in countries where chronic poverty is assumed to be most severe, its peculiar polarised legacy of racially embedded inequality and poverty raises particular questions about the ability of South African poor to use social mechanisms of access to capital to engineer a pathway from poverty.

Drawing on new asset-based approaches to poverty and poverty dynamics, this paper has used panel data from the 1993–98 period to estimate patterns of asset dynamics. In sharp contrast to the expectation that the end of apartheid would signal the creation of an economy that worked for all South Africans, these estimates identify a dynamic asset poverty threshold. Households that begin with an asset base expected to yield a livelihood less than two-times the poverty line are predicted to collapse toward a low-level poverty trap with an expected standard of living equal to 90 per cent of the South African poverty line. Households that begin above that threshold are estimated to advance over time.

While these findings unavoidably reflect the broader confluence of factors that struck the South African economy across the 1990s including sluggish economic growth, rising unemployment and HIV/AIDS, this study employed a distinctive qualitative methodology to examine events at the household level from 1993 through 2001. The qualitative analysis found particular patterns underlying mobility dynamics, and broadly confirms the quantitative finding of a dynamic poverty threshold and a low-level poverty trap equilibrium. In addition, the qualitative analysis underwrites a close look at the role played by social networks and social relations in the evolving pattern of poverty and income distribution. While there is ample evidence of active social relationships, with the exception of a few atypical cases, social networks and relations at best seem to stabilise incomes, but provide little in the way of longer-term accumulation or economic advance. The broader problem of poverty alleviation seems unlikely to be resolved until deeper structural changes make time and markets work more effectively for the broader community of all South Africans.

Acknowledgement

The authors thank the MacArthur Foundation for financial support under a Collaborative Research Grant; Francie Lund, Phakama Mhlongo, Sibongile Maimane, Mamazi Mkhize and Zweni Sibiya for their important contributions to the collection of the qualitative data; and Jaqui Goldin and Chantal Munthree for assistance in processing data.

Notes

1. See the studies of Hoogeven and Ozler (2004), van der Ruit and May (2003); Meth and Dias (2004); Van den Berg and Louw (2003). In addition, using several national surveys undertaken subsequent to the 1993 survey, Leibbrandt and Woolard (1999) calculate a suite of consumption-based poverty measures that confirm this racial distribution of poverty.
2. Although debate still persists concerning the notion of social capital, this paper accepts that social networks of trust, support, cooperation and information are a form of capital that mediate economic transactions.
3. Fields et al. (2003), using income data from KIDS, find evidence of a more convergent income distribution process. While the contrast between the income and expenditure data is worrisome, the KIDS expenditure data produces poverty estimates that closely match those found in other South African datasets (for example, see Hoogeven and Ozler, 2004).
4. Note that measurement error will lead to an overstatement of transitorily poor households.
5. Carter and May estimate the asset poverty line by regressing livelihoods on asset holdings. Using those estimates, it is possible to calculate the expected level of well-being for each household given its assets. A household was deemed above the asset poverty line if it was possible to reject the hypothesis that their expected level of well-being was below the asset poverty line. Note that two thing influence the level of expected well-being: the household's asset holdings, and the general structure of the economy that determines returns to assets. Both factors potentially change over time.
6. Note that $\Lambda(A_c^*)$ is an equilibrium because it lies on the 45-degree line (where $\Lambda(A_t) = \Lambda(A_0)$) and hence an individual with an initial stock of A_0 would tend to remain at that asset and livelihood level over time.
7. Charles Dickens' character Wilkins Micawber (*David Copperfield*) extolled the virtues of savings with his statement 'Annual income twenty pounds, annual expenditure nineteen nineteen and six, result happiness. Annual income twenty pounds, annual expenditure twenty pounds ought and six, result misery'. The Micawber threshold divides those able to engage in a virtuous circle of savings and accumulation from those who cannot.
8. There is no significance to the fact that we draw that the upper equilibrium to be the same for both convergent and bifurcated dynamics – we were only trying to eliminate clutter in the graph.
9. This notation indicates the use of flexible regression techniques so that marginal livelihood contribution of an asset depends on the full vector of assets, A_i, controlled by the household.
10. There is, of course, no reason to think that everybody within a given society would be characterised by same asset dynamics. Indeed, the theory of poverty traps itself suggest that those individuals with poor access to capital would be on a divergent trajectory, while those with better access could be on the convergent trajectory. However, as discussed earlier, one of apartheid's legacies may be both thinly developed markets and ineffective social capital, exposing most individuals to the possibility of a divergent, poverty trap asset dynamics. In this situation, it may well be that most individuals lack both

market and socially mediated access to capital. In this paper's first effort to explore asset dynamics, we will in fact only try to characterise a single (dominant) trajectory.

11. Households were selected for inclusion in the qualitative study to assure coverage of each of the main cells in the transition matrix shown in Table 1.
12. This method was particularly effective in triggering recall to elicit retrospective data.
13. The survey defined the household as comprising individuals who lived in the dwelling for at least 15 days out of the year and shared food and other resources when co-resident.
14. These five types of assets are a categorisation found in the sustainable livelihoods framework (Ashley and Carney, 1999). Though this framework was not used in this research, this categorisation of assets was helpful in distinguishing different factors in the analysis.
15. These periods have an overlapping year – 1998 – because it was seldom possible for people to recall whether an event occurred early or late in the year. For the purpose of determining change across two periods from the qualitative data alone, this overlap is not a problem. However, in comparing the qualitative with the quantitative findings, the placement of 1998 can be important because the survey recorded people's status at a particular point in 1998.
16. A stream of income can be from an unstable source, for example, a one-time pay-out of a retrenchment package, or income from an informal business that may collapse at any time.
17. A food stokvel is an informal organisation where members make contributions for the purchase of food, serving either as a form of savings or rotating fund.
18. Note that the quantitative analysis does not rule out upward mobility for either the lucky few, or for those households who enjoy exceptional access to market or socially-mediated access to capital and other services.

References

Adato, M., Lund, F. and Mhlongo, P., forthcoming A, Methodological innovations in research on the dynamics of poverty: a longitudinal study in KwaZulu-Natal, South Africa, *World Development*.

Adato, M., Lund, F. and Mhlongo, P., forthcoming B, Capturing 'work' in South Africa: evidence from a study of poverty and well-being in KwaZulu-Natal, in M. Chen, R. Jhabvala, and G. Standing (Eds) *Rethinking Work and Informality* (Geneva: ILO Publications).

Adato, M., Mhlongo, P. and O'Leary, C. (2003) The changing nature of urban–rural livelihood linkages in KwaZulu-Natal, South Africa. Paper presented at the International Conference on Poverty, Food and Health in Welfare, Lisbon, Portugal, July, 1–4 2003.

Ashley, C. and Carney, D. (1999) *Sustainable Livelihoods: Lessons from Early Experience* (London: DfID).

Bhalla, A. and Lapeyre, F. (1997) Social exclusion: towards an analytical and operational framework, *Development and Change*, 28, pp. 413–33.

Bracking, S. (2003) The political economy of chronic poverty, Institute for Development Policy and Management Working Paper No. 23, University of Manchester, Manchester.

Carter, M. R. and Barrett, C. B., this volume, The economics of poverty traps and persistent poverty: an asset-based approach, *Journal of Development Studies*, 42, 2.

Carter, M. R. and May, J. (2001) One kind of freedom: poverty dynamics in post-apartheid South Africa, *World Development*, 29, 1987–2006.

Chronic Poverty Research Centre, *Chronic Poverty Report, 2004–2005* (Manchester: University of Manchester).

Cleveland, W., Devlin, S. and Grosse, E. (1988) Regression by local fitting: methods, properties and computation algorithms, *Journal of Econometrics*, 37, 87–114.

Dercon, S. (1998) Wealth, risk and activity choice: cattle in Western Tanzania, *Journal of Development Economics*, 55, pp. 1–42.

De Haan, A. (1998) 'Social exclusion': an alternative concept for the study of exclusion? *IDS Bulletin*, 29, pp. 10–9.

Durlauf, S. and Fafchamps, M., forthcoming, 'Social capital,' in P. Aghion and S. Durlauf (Eds) *Handbook of Economic Growth*.

Fields, G., Cichello, P., Freije, S., Menendez, M. and Newhouse, D. (2003) For richer or for poorer: evidence from Indonesia, South Africa, Spain and Venezuela, *Journal of Economic Inequality*, 1.

Figueroa, A., Altamirano, T. and Sulmont, D. (1996) Social exclusion and inequality in Peru, International Institute for Labour Studies Research Series, No. 104, International Labour Organisation, Geneva.

Hoogeven and Ozler, B. (2004) Not separate, not equal, *World Bank Economic Review*.

Klaasen, S. (1997) Poverty and inequality in South Africa: an analysis of the 1993 SALDRU Survey, *Social Indicators Research*, 41, pp. 51–94.

Leibbrandt, M. and Woolard, I. (1999) A comparison of poverty in South Africa's nine provinces, *Development Southern Africa*, 16, pp. 37–54.

Manuel, T. (2003) Africa and the Washington Consensus: finding the right path, *Finance & Development*, 18–20 Sept.

May, J., Carter, M. and Padayachee, V. (2004) Is poverty and inequality leading to poor growth? *South African Labour Bulletin*, 28(2): pp. 18–20.

May, J., Woolard, I. and Klasen, S. (2000) The nature and measurement of poverty and inequality, in J. May (Ed.) *Poverty and Inequality in South Africa: Meeting the Challenge*, pp. 19–48 (Cape Town: David Philip).

Meth, C. and Dias, R. (2004) Increases in poverty in South Africa, 1999–2002, *Development Southern Africa*, 21, pp. 59–86.

Mogues, T. and Carter, M. R., forthcoming, Social capital and the reproduction of inequality in polarised societies, *Journal of Economic Inequality*.

Moser, C. (1997) Poverty reduction in South Africa: the importance of household relations and social capital as assets of the poor, unpublished report, The World Bank, Washington, DC.

Sen, A. K. (1985) *Commodities and Capabilities* (North Holland: Amsterdam).

Stewart, F. (2001) Horizontal inequalities: a neglected dimension of development, Annual Lectures, No.5, World Institute for Development Economics Research, Helsinki.

Townsend, P. (1985) A sociological approach to the measurement of poverty – a rejoinder to Professor Amartya Sen, *Oxford Economic Papers*, 31, pp. 659–68.

UNDP (2003) *South African Human Development Report, 2003* (Pretoria: United Nations Development Programme).

Van de Ruit, C. and May, J. (2003) Triangulating qualitative and quantitative approaches to the measurement of poverty: a case study in the Limpopo Province, South Africa, *IDS Bulletin*, 34, pp. 21–33.

Van der Berg, S. and Louw, M. (2003) Changing patterns of South African income distribution: towards time series estimates of distribution and poverty. Paper to the Conference of the Economic Society of South Africa, Stellenbosch, 17–19 Sept., 2003.

Williamson, J. (2003) From reform agenda: a short history of the Washington Consensus and suggestions for what to do next, *Finance & Development*, 10–13 Sept.

Woolard, I. and Klasen, S. (2004) Determinants of income mobility and household poverty dynamics in South Africa. IZA Discussion Paper Series, No. 1030, Institute for the Study of Labour, Bonn.

Zimmerman, F. J. and Carter, M. R. (2003) Asset smoothing, consumption smoothing and the reproduction of inequality under risk and subsistence constraints, *Journal of Development Economics*, 71, pp. 233–60.

Welfare Dynamics in Rural Kenya and Madagascar

CHRISTOPHER B. BARRETT, PASWEL PHIRI MARENYA,
JOHN MCPEAK, BART MINTEN, FESTUS MURITHI,
WILLIS OLUOCH-KOSURA, FRANK PLACE,
JEAN CLAUDE RANDRIANARISOA, JHON RASAMBAINARIVO, &
JUSTINE WANGILA

I. Introduction

All development policy is based implicitly on a conceptualisation of why people are poor and what interventions, if any, are needed to facilitate or accelerate their climb out of poverty. But the poor are a heterogeneous lot. Some people fall into poverty temporarily and are soon able to climb back out, while others are poor from birth or suffer a serious setback of some sort and stay poor for a long time thereafter. The latter two types of poor people may be ensnared in a poverty trap, while the former type retains economic mobility. Appropriate interventions may differ fundamentally according to the nature of the target subpopulation's poverty.

Under prevailing theories of economic growth and development, the poor enjoy higher marginal returns to productive assets than the rich do, so capital should flow disproportionately to the poor, enabling them to catch up economically. This follows logically from the standard simplifying assumption that there are diminishing marginal returns to assets in production. Moreover, this assumption implies that shocks cause merely temporary setbacks and that everyone enjoys the same latent opportunities. Under the prevailing orthodoxy, economic mobility should be enjoyed by all and persistent poverty should reflect merely a slow climb up from a low initial welfare level.

Under the poverty traps hypothesis, however, there exists a positive correlation – locally, albeit not necessarily globally – between wealth and rates of return on assets. This positive correlation is generated by (locally) increasing marginal returns to assets, in contrast to the standard assumption of globally diminishing marginal returns that underpins the prevailing orthodoxy. Regions of locally increasing marginal returns to assets can only exist if some mechanism excludes some people with low initial conditions from accessing more remunerative livelihoods. Typically, exclusion occurs through restricted access to (formal or informal) finance necessary to build assets through investment and to protect them against loss, or through socially exclusionary processes that limit certain groups' or individuals' access to preferred employment, credit or land. Latent opportunities are not identical for all. Furthermore, shocks can have permanent consequences when wealth is positively correlated with return on assets.

The policy implications of the poverty traps hypothesis therefore differ from those associated with mainstream models of welfare dynamics. In the presence of poverty traps, asset transfers, protection against shocks to productive asset holdings and removal of barriers that restrict the opportunities enjoyed by historically disadvantaged groups may matter as much as or more than exogenous improvements in productivity due to the endogenous productivity growth that may result from changes in asset holdings and accumulation and livelihood opportunities. Hence the importance of careful empirical research into the nature of persistent poverty.

This paper contributes new micro-level evidence to the debate over the nature of economic growth and poverty dynamics. We use detailed panel data from several sites in rural Kenya and Madagascar to explore the nature of poverty in novel ways.[1] By focusing on households' assets, the possibility of locally increasing returns to assets, and asset dynamics, we show that multiple equilibria indeed exist in at least some places. We explore some reasons why this might be.

The remainder of the paper proceeds as follows. Section II provides a brief background on Kenya and Madagascar, and then describes the data we use and the settings from which they were collected in rural Kenya and Madagascar. The sampling strategy was designed to generate informative variation in agro-ecological and market access conditions so as to explore the possibility of geographic poverty traps. Section III then presents standard evidence on economic mobility and poverty dynamics in our survey villages. Section IV then uses more innovative empirical methods to explore the possibility that poverty traps indeed exist, as reflected in structural income and asset dynamics. Section V then investigates some possible explanations as to why poverty traps appear to exist in some of our sites. Section VI briefly draws out a few key policy implications of these findings.

II. The Settings and the Data

(a) Poor Countries with Liberalised Markets

Kenya and Madagascar are both poor, rural African nations that underwent relatively dramatic market-oriented reforms beginning in the latter half of the 1980s. They had followed nearly-opposite post-independence trajectories for the 20–25 years prior to the onset of economic liberalisation. Kenya had long been considered the most vibrant economy in east Africa, a former British colony that was home to the largest urban market (Nairobi) between Cairo and South Africa and to a wide range of modern agricultural and industrial producers who took advantage of the country's climate, soils, physical and social infrastructure that were well above sub-Saharan African norms. Madagascar, on the other hand, was a former French colony that enjoyed 12 years of relatively successful, liberal economic rule similar to Kenya's before a Marxist dictatorship took over in 1972, imposing a state-controlled, inward-looking economic system explicitly modelled on the Democratic People's Republic of Korea.

The differences between the two countries mask, however, important similarities. Both countries encompass remarkable variation in agro-ecological conditions, from desert to humid rainforests to rugged highlands, from which the ruling elites of both countries have hailed. Natural disasters – drought, floods and cyclones – ravage parts of both countries regularly and disease is widespread, confronting poor populations with considerable risk. Moreover, in spite of the stark differences in their early post-independence histories, both countries suffered serious balance of payments, external debt and fiscal deficit problems in the 1980s that necessitated reforms under the aegis of structural adjustment programmes underwritten by the International Monetary Fund and the World Bank. In spite of 10–20 years of sometimes halting reforms, the consensus among domestic and foreign observers is that getting the macro economy 'right' has failed to stimulate broadly based, sustainable economic growth. Poverty has increased in both countries over the past decade. The variation in their histories and their shared recent experience of market-oriented policy reforms that appear not to have made an appreciable dent in poverty, make Kenya and Madagascar as a pair a reasonable microcosm for much of sub-Saharan Africa.

(b) Data Description

The data we use were collected through the Rural Markets, Natural Capital and Dynamic Poverty Traps in East Africa project of the USAID BASIS CRSP.[2] We opportunistically constructed household-level panel data sets in five different sites in rural Kenya and Madagascar, building on previous surveys conducted by our team. In order to control for the possibility of exogenous variation in welfare status and dynamics due to agricultural potential, access to commercial markets, or both, sites were selected to cover each cell of a matrix reflecting better or worse market access on one axis and a better/wetter or worse/drier agroecology on the other. Between-sites variation in observed welfare dynamics thus helps us explore the possibility of geographic poverty traps. Meanwhile, the within-site variation according to endogenous household attributes such as wealth enables us to explore the possibility of poverty traps associated with multiple equilibria at household level.

Our highest potential sites enjoy sufficient water to sustain sedentarised livestock and high-value horticulture and tree crops year-round and good enough access to markets to be able to engage in high frequency (daily or semi-weekly) commercial transactions. We have one such site in the central highlands of Madagascar: the Vakinankaratra region around Antsirabe and Betafo, about three hours' drive from the capitol city, Antananarivo, on a macadam highway (Figure 1). There we resurveyed 94 households previously surveyed in 1997.

Our sites with greater agro-ecological potential, but limited market access likewise have adequate rainfall to sustain multiple crops over the course of the year, but while access to secondary cities is adequate, it is a drive of a day or more to the nation's principal commercial markets. In western Kenya, we resurveyed 89 households that had originally been surveyed in 1989 in Madzuu location in Vihiga District. The 'wetter-worse' site in Madagascar is in the southern highlands, in Fianarantsoa province, where we resurveyed 58 households previously visited in 1997.

We had no Malagasy sites with poor agro-ecological potential for which we also had suitable baseline data on which to construct a panel. So our 'drier' sites are all in northern Kenya. In lower Baringo District, a semi-arid region that nonetheless enjoys reasonable water access through Lake Baringo and the Pekerra River and the national irrigation scheme along the River before it empties into the Lake, we surveyed 30 households on a quarterly basis from March 2000 through June 2002,

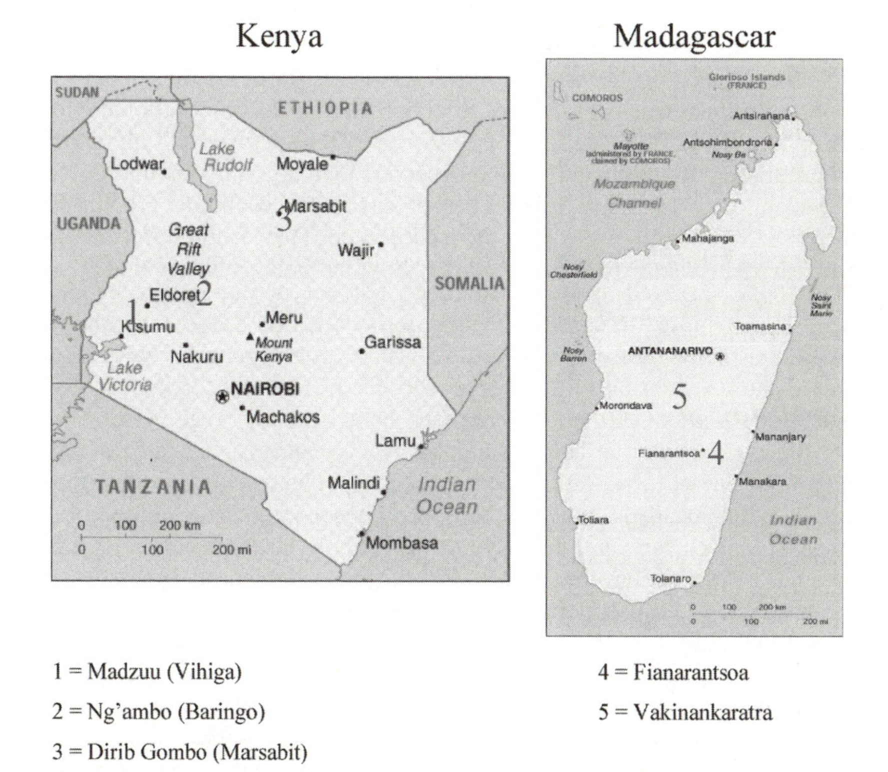

Figure 1. Survey sites in rural Kenya and Madagascar

in Ng'ambo location. This site is less than two hours by all-season road from the secondary city of Nakuru and only half a day's drive from Nairobi. Our most remote, semi-arid site is Dirib Gombo, eight kilometres from Marsabit town in the eponymous dryland Marsabit District of northern Kenya, 540 kilometres from Nairobi, roughly half of that distance without a macadam road. The sample size and survey instruments and frequency were identical in Ng'ambo and Dirib Gombo, as they were part of a broader survey of six sites in northern Kenya (and five in southern Ethiopia) begun by the Pastoral Risk Management (PARIMA) project of the USAID Global Livestock CRSP. Agro-pastoralism predominates in both Ng'ambo and Dirib Gombo, with extensive grazing combined with rain-fed crop cultivation (and limited irrigated agriculture in Ng'ambo) and some non-agricultural activities, especially for Ng'ambo with its superior market access.

Each site's baseline survey was designed for a different purpose and thus the data are imperfectly comparable across sites, although we took great care to ensure consistency across survey periods within each site. The Ng'ambo and Dirib Gombo sites are the only ones for which we have many periods' observations, so they are the only ones for which we can study high-frequency intertemporal variation. Because of these inconsistencies across data sets, the comparisons made in Sections III and IV are necessarily partial between sites and we focus mainly on intra-site variation among households. We use income data for comparative quantitative analysis because good expenditure data are not available for all five sites.[3] But we intentionally use multiple quantitative and qualitative methods as a check on robustness, as a way to tailor the measure to the question at hand, and to play to what we perceive as the relative strengths of different data sets.

The resurveying interval varies markedly across sites as well. As we discuss in the next section, this variation, from the high frequency, short 2000–2002 panel in northern Kenya, through the intermediate five-year panels in Madagascar to the low frequency, 1989–2002 panel in western Kenya, enables a suggestive look at how time affects economic mobility and inference about the persistence of poverty. Each site's panel suffered attrition as households that were in an early round disappeared, were unwilling to be surveyed again or otherwise fell out of the sample by the later round(s). We attempted to control for prospective attrition econometrically in each site's data, but could not establish any robust statistical pattern, suggesting that concerns about attrition bias do not seem serious in these data.[4]

Our meta-data set of 301 households also spans the full range of rural poverty rates in the two countries. The Vakinankaratra site lies in the highest potential region and has one of the lowest poverty rates in Madagascar. In contrast, the Dirib Gombo and Fianarantsoa sites are located in resource scarce areas of the two countries, and have headcount poverty rates well above 80 per cent (Kenya Ministry of Planning, 1998; Minten and Zeller, 2000). The intermediate potential sites in Baringo and Vihiga Districts lie between these extremes.

Finally, we followed up the panel survey data collection with qualitative poverty appraisals in each site. This involved both community-level focus group meetings and key informant interviews to establish local conceptualisations of poverty and community-level phenomena that affected households' observed trajectories. We followed up these group meetings with in-depth case studies of selected households so as to construct social-historical profiles of distinct household types characterised by observed welfare transitions. We constructed household-level per capita income transition matrices for each site in order to establish which households had been poor in each survey period, which had exited poverty from one round to the next, which had fallen into poverty between survey rounds, and which had consistently stayed non-poor. We then further broke down the subsamples in each site who remained poor in both periods and those who were non-poor in both periods according to the direction of change in their income between periods: those with significant per capita income losses between periods, no significant change, and those who enjoyed significant per capita income gains from one survey round to the next. We did intensive household level oral histories for two sample households from each site in each of those eight transition matrix groups. In those interviews – and subsequent closing community meetings – we focused especially on understanding the historical context underpinning local households' strategies to improve their welfare and the pathways by which certain households collapse into or escape from poverty.

III. Income Mobility and Poverty Dynamics in Rural Kenya and Madagascar

We begin the empirical analysis by offering simple descriptions of intertemporal income mobility and poverty transitions by site, what Carter and Barrett (this issue) refer to as second generation poverty analysis, before we move into asset-based poverty measures, or what Carter and Barrett term fourth-generation poverty measures, in the next section.

Per capita income transition matrices offer perhaps the simplest way of depicting economic mobility, in that they summarise intertemporal movement relative to an income poverty line. In order to be able to compare households across periods and countries, we established a common poverty line. We use an ultra-poverty line of US$0.50 per capita per day in real 2002 US dollars. This ultra-poverty line is reasonably close to (and roughly equidistant from) the relevant official poverty lines. Kenya's rural poverty line of KSh1,238/month per capita is equivalent to about US$0.53/day, while the official Malagasy poverty line of FMG988,600 equals about US$0.43/day per person.[5] We converted each period's local currency observations into US dollars using the period-specific exchange rate and, lacking proper deflator series for these rural communities, used the US GDP deflator to convert all nominal figures into real terms under the maintained hypothesis of constant real exchange rates. Table 1 presents the resulting real daily per capita income transition matrix.[6]

The sample proportions that were poor in each survey period are greatest in the 'drier-worse' site of Dirib Gombo (northern Kenya), where every household's per capita daily income fell below $0.50 in each period, and least in the 'wetter-better' site of Vakinankaratra (Madagascar's central highlands), where only 58.5 per cent fell below the ultra-poverty line in each survey period. The population shares that were poor in both the initial and subsequent period also decrease as one moves in either the direction of better agroecology or better market access. Similarly, the population share that was non-poor in both the initial and subsequent survey periods increases as one improves agro-ecological conditions, market access, or both. Overall, more than 70 per cent of our aggregate sample fell below the $0.50 daily per capita income ultra-poverty line in each survey period, and less than one

Table 1. Ultra-poverty transition matrices
As measured against $0.50/day per capita real income ultra-poverty line

	Poor in subsequent period		Non-poor in subsequent period	
Poor in initial period	2000–2002 Dirib Gombo 100.0% **70.8%**	1989–2002 Madzuu 60.7% 1997–2002 Fianarantsoa 82.8%	2000–2002 Dirib Gombo 0.0% **11.2%**	1989–2002 Madzuu 20.2% 1997–2002 Fianarantsoa 10.3%
	2000–2002 Ng'ambo 86.5%	1997–2002 Vakinankaratra 58.5%	2000–2002 Ng'ambo 9.0%	1997–2002 Vakinankaratra 7.4%
Non-poor in initial period	2000–2002 Dirib Gombo 0.0% **11.3%**	1989–2002 Madzuu 10.1% 1997–2002 Fianarantsoa 6.9%	2000–2002 Dirib Gombo 0.0% **6.8%**	1989–2002 Madzuu 9.0% 1997–2002 Fianarantsoa 0.0%
	2000–2002 Ng'ambo 0.0%	1997–2002 Vakinankaratra 22.3%	2000–2002 Ng'ambo 4.5%	1997–2002 Vakinankaratra 11.7%

Note: Within each transition matrix cell, the sites are presented in a two-by-two matrix, with the upper left reflecting sites with poor agro-ecological conditions and market access (Dirib Gombo), those on the upper right having poor market access but favourable agro-ecological conditions (Fianarantsoa, Madzuu), that on the lower left having favourable market access but poor agro-ecological conditions (Ng'ambo), and those on the lower right having favourable agro-ecological conditions and market access both (Vakinankaratra).
Bold underlined number is the weighted average across all sites.

quarter crossed the poverty line between survey rounds, with overall ultra-poverty remarkably stable at 82 per cent since 11.3 per cent fell into poverty while an almost identical 11.2 per cent climbed out. There is mobility around the poverty line, but it is essentially offsetting in that one household is replacing another.[7] The overwhelming majority of households in our sites are persistently ultra-poor.

This simple transition matrix suggests two key results, although one must be cautious about over-interpretation since these data are not statistically representative of either nation, much less of broader aggregates of low income countries, and because the time periods of the surveys do not coincide perfectly. First, there is non-trivial entry into and exit from poverty. Even in very poor places, some people commonly escape while others fall into poverty, consistent with the mounting evidence on the extent of transitory poverty (Baulch and Hoddinott, 2000). Second, there seem to be distinct geographic patterns, with sites with poorer agro-ecological conditions and market access exhibiting greater and more persistent poverty than sites in more favourable settings. This is consistent with the idea of geographic poverty traps.

IV. Stochastic versus Structural Welfare Dynamics

(a) Stochastic and Structural Income Dynamics

As Carter and Barrett (this issue) explain, these second generation approaches to studying economic mobility cannot distinguish whether a household exits poverty because they accumulate productive capital, because the productivity of their assets permanently improves – either of which would suggest a structural transition and that they should remain non-poor thereafter – or if they merely enjoyed a transitory windfall, in which case they would probably soon fall back below the poverty line. Yet it matters whether someone entered poverty due to permanent asset loss (due to injury, death of prime-age worker, loss of land or livestock), or because of transitory events (such as a job change, temporary illness). To address this distinction, one must study the structural underpinnings of poverty and poverty transitions directly.

Transitory variation – for example, due to seasonality or short-lived shocks – and measurement error loom large in income (or expenditure) data. As a result, much of any period's observed income is stochastic. That necessarily clouds inference about the structural patterns of welfare dynamics. This can perhaps be seen most easily by considering a simple decomposition of income for household i at time t:

$$Y_{it} = A_{it}'[r_{it}(A_{it}) + \varepsilon_{it}^{R}] + U_i + \varepsilon_{it}^{T} + \varepsilon_{it}^{M} \qquad (1)$$

where Y is measured income,[8] A is a vector of productive assets (labour, land, livestock, and so forth) used to generate earned income, r is the corresponding vector of expected returns per unit asset held, which may depend systematically on the household's asset holdings, ε^R reflects period and household specific returns (that is, yield and price) shocks, U captures household-specific but time invariant unearned income flows (for example, the time invariant component of pensions or transfers), ε^T represents transitory unearned income (for example, period-specific deviations from mean transfer volumes) , and ε^M is measurement error. Each of the stochastic components, ε^M, ε^R and ε^T is zero mean and independently and identically distributed over time. Expected period-specific income – or what Carter and May (2001) or Carter and Barrett (this issue) term 'structural income' – is therefore just:

$$E\{Y_{it}\} = A_{it}`r_{it}(A_{it}) + U_i \tag{2}$$

Assets vary in importance among households. In rural Africa, the poorest households typically rely heavily on unskilled agricultural labour markets; labour power comprises the vast majority of their productive asset stock (Barrett et al., 2001, Jayne et al., 2003). Wealthier households commonly rely more heavily on earnings from land, livestock and skilled employment (for example, salaried labour or skill- or capital-intensive non-farm enterprises). Hence the importance of thinking about A in equations (1) and (2) as a vector of assets.

Growth in observed income can be represented by totally differentiating equation (1):

$$dY_{it} = dA_{it}`[r_{it}(A_{it}) + \varepsilon^R{}_{it}] + A_{it}`[dr_{it}/dA_{it} + d\varepsilon^R{}_{it}] + d\varepsilon^T{}_{it} + d\varepsilon^M{}_{it} \tag{3}$$

Taking the expectation of equation (3) determines the expected change in income, or the structural income dynamics of the household:

$$E\{dY_{it}\} = E\{dA_{it}\}`r_{it}(A_{it}) + A_{it}`E\{dr_{it}/dA_{it}\} \tag{4}$$

Equation (4) highlights that structural income growth depends on changes in productive asset holdings and on changes in rates of return on assets. A household's assets evolve according to its accumulation behaviour and asset shocks. Expected returns on assets evolve according to exogenous changes in prices and productivity and changes in one's asset holdings.

The latter point is central to poverty traps based explanations. The existence of multiple equilibria implies nonlinear returns on assets. Multiple dynamic equilibria can only exist if there exist locally increasing returns at some point(s), that is, $dr/dA_{|A=A^*} > 0$ at some asset level(s) A^*. This points us towards a natural empirical test for poverty traps that we undertake later.

The preceding equations equip us to investigate the implications of the considerable stochasticity of income in these sites. If we simply regress the period-on-period change in income, dY_{it} on beginning period income, Y_{it}, then we necessarily incorporate intertemporal change in transitory unearned income, in the stochastic component of returns on assets, and in measurement error. Each of these will necessarily generate a regression-to-mean effect, a negative correlation between income change and beginning period income, controlling for the effects due to dA_{it} and dr_{it}/dA_{it}, which could be either negative or positive. In other words, if the stochastic components are serially independent, good draws in one period are typically offset by poorer draws in subsequent periods and vice versa. Just as the stochastic component of income tends to exaggerate income inequality in cross-sectional analyses, so too does it generate spurious economic mobility in longitudinal analyses.

The best approach to studying long-term dynamics, therefore, is to focus on structural income dynamics and the underlying dynamics of households' assets.

One way to do this is to regress the change in income on structural income. This approach necessarily focuses on just the structural (non-stochastic) components of income and income dynamics.[9] These structural income dynamics reflect that portion of income on which one needs to focus to understand persistent poverty, not on total income dynamics that necessarily include measurement error and transitory shocks that one would expect to be reversed in time.

To demonstrate the difference between the two methods, we estimated both total income dynamics and structural income dynamics regressions for each site. If economic opportunities are open to all and returns on assets are globally diminishing, as prevailing theories hold, then one should find a negatively sloped relation between income change and base period income, with the curve crossing the zero change threshold just once, at the point towards which all households converge. By contrast, under the poverty traps hypotheses, the regression relationship need not be monotonically negatively sloped. Rather, it will cross the zero income change line around each dynamic equilibrium toward which households converge, with the stable (unstable) equilibria occurring where the regression line crosses the zero expected change point with negative (positive) slope.

Figure 2 presents these income change regressions for each site.[10] The dashed lines reflect the nonparametric regressions[11] of the total income change on beginning period income. For each of the five sites, the estimated slope is negative over most or all of the conditioning domain and the regression line intersects the (horizontal) zero change line from above at just a single point, as prevailing theory hypothesises.

However, when one strips out the noise due to the stochastic component of income and looks at the estimated structural income dynamics of these households, the results change strikingly. To estimate household-level structural income dynamics, we estimated equation (2) via a simple ordinary least squares regression of income on a vector of assets appropriate to each site and period-specific dummy variables for each survey village, pooling observations across periods.[12] The coefficients on the individual assets reflect the expected rates of return, r, while the coefficients on the site- and period-specific dummy variables summarise the exogenous change in expected rates of return holding asset stocks constant, dr, and the conjectured time-invariant level of unearned income, U. We study the resulting estimates of r in more detail in the next section. We generate expected change in income by using households' assets stocks in the first and last periods of the panel data to predict structural income in each period, then take the difference between them.

The solid lines in Figure 2 reflect the nonparametric structural income dynamics regressions. Unlike the total income dynamics regressions, these lines are not monotonically negatively sloped. Except for Dirib Gombo – where no household graduated from poverty in our survey period (Table 1) – each of the site-specific structural income dynamics regressions exhibits multiple dynamic equilibria, as reflected by points where the regression line crosses the zero change line from above. In each site, one such equilibrium lies below the ultra-poverty line of $0.50/day per capita, suggesting no expectation of a graduation out of poverty if one relies merely on the natural dynamics of the extant system. These regressions of expected income changes on base period structural income are consistent with the poverty traps hypothesis.

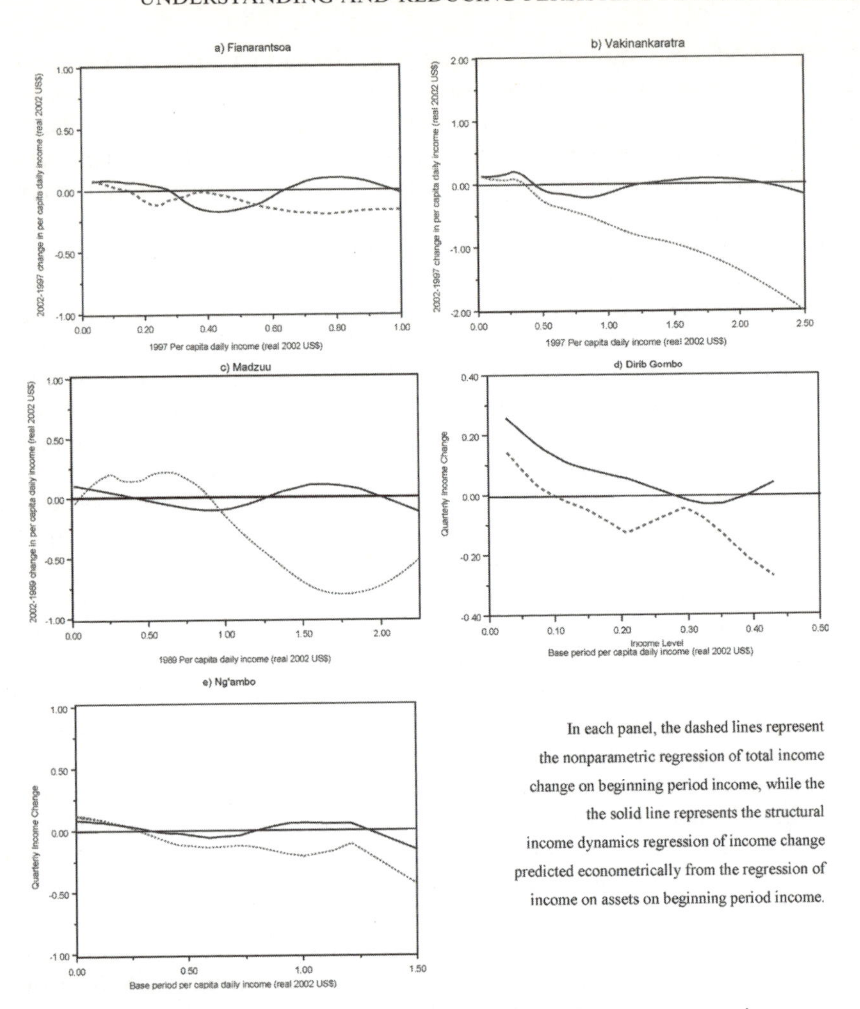

Figure 2. Site-specific filtered and structural income change regressions

Our qualitative studies echo this general impression that there exist multiple equilibria. In our Kenya sites, community focus groups told us repeatedly that poverty has increased in our survey communities and that the time it takes for a household to recover from an adverse shock or to exit poverty has increased over the past 10–20 years. Although local definitions of poverty vary across sites, in both community focus group interviews and in depth oral histories of individual households, respondents in Dirib Gombo, Madzuu and Ng'ambo all explained increased poverty and reduced economic mobility as arising due to greater environmental variability and lower average rainfall, poorer quality soils due to less frequent fallowing and reduced manure application, decreasing per capita holdings of land and livestock, increasing difficulty finding remunerative employment for educated adults, and the decline of informal support networks to help respond to temporary health and income shocks (Mango et al., 2004).

Interestingly, those who were continuously non-poor or who were poor but exited poverty commonly offer stories consistent with prevailing theories of economic growth. Meanwhile, the current poor – whether they became poor during the survey period or had always been poor – describe poverty dynamics in a fashion far more consistent with the hypothesis of poverty traps. Inference from above the poverty line plainly differs from the perspective from below.

The currently non-poor frequently emphasise individual attributes – most notably work ethic and drunkenness – as leading to fundamentally different stations in life. By their view, those without the discipline to refrain from excessive alcohol consumption and to work hard stay poor, while more self-disciplined peers exit poverty and then remain non-poor. This is essentially a story of convergence to a group-specific equilibrium, with little hope of people changing groups.

By contrast, the currently poor emphasise the difficulty of asset accumulation and the central role of asset losses in explaining patterns of mobility. Every one of the households we interviewed who were poor in the most recent period could trace their poverty ultimately to some asset shock, whether before or after the first round of our surveys. Serious human health shocks causing permanent injury or illness or death were the most frequently cited reasons for households falling into poverty (Mango et al., 2004; Randrianjatovo, 2004).[13] Some adverse effects are direct, as when economically active household members fell ill and subsequently had to stop working or even died and their earnings were lost or their absence came at a critical time in the cropping cycle, causing them significant seasonal losses from which they have been unable to recover. Other effects respondents mentioned frequently are indirect, as when children had to be pulled out of school for want of school fees due to the high costs of treating illness or funeral expenses, or when the family lost productive draught power, manure or milk production when it had to undertake ritual slaughter of livestock for a funeral.

The poor routinely point to certain activities – for example, zero-grazing dairy production with improved (cross-bred) cows, commercial tea cultivation, salaried employment based on above-average educational attainment and social connections – as higher-return activities that lie beyond their reach for want of start-up capital to buy improved cattle or tea bushes, or due to a lack of education or the connections to land a good job. Several people mentioned the importance of migration as an escape route. Young, educated people who can move to better land or to cities where they can find a good job enjoy some prospect of escaping the persistent rural poverty toward which they otherwise seem headed. Parents frequently invest heavily in educating their children in the hope that they can indeed win the skilled employment lottery in a city and eventually provide financial support back home. But the personal connections necessary to land a good job and the capital necessary to start small businesses are perceived as major obstacles to be overcome by poorer families. The poor's perception is that barriers to entry into more remunerative activities dampen their labour, land and livestock productivity relative to their non-poor neighbours. Meanwhile, their considerable exposure to risk of asset loss – due to human or livestock disease, theft or natural disasters – leaves them reluctant to undertake activities that might further increase those risks. We return to this risk management theme below.

The qualitative descriptions offered by our respondents to explain their own welfare dynamics mirror the quantitative evidence. Between site variation in ultra-poverty rates suggest that poverty is lower where market access and the basic agroecology are more favourable. This creates significant migration incentives. There nonetheless remains considerable intra-community variability in welfare status.[14] One needs to guard against geographic determinism in explaining patterns of persistent poverty. Furthermore, within sites, where we focus, there appear to be multiple equilibria toward which household incomes converge, providing empirical support to the hypothesis that poverty traps exist.

(b) S-Shaped Asset Dynamics

Because assets generate income, asset dynamics underpin structural income dynamics. We therefore also study asset dynamics in order to understand structural income dynamics better in these rural Kenyan and Malagasy communities. If the return on assets increases with ex ante wealth over at least some portions of the wealth distribution, then one would naturally expect this to lead to asset accumulation. Then, as the returns on asset diminish, accumulation slows, leading to a stable dynamic equilibrium where asset stocks remain stable over time. When returns on assets are increasing only locally, however, there may be multiple stable dynamic equilibria, consistent with the notion of a poverty trap.

Multiple stable dynamic equilibria imply nonlinear asset dynamics, more precisely S-shaped dynamics when one plots future assets against current assets. Lybbert et al. (2004) found such patterns in southern Ethiopian pastoralist communities very similar to the northern Kenya sites in our study. There seem to be multiple stable dynamic herd size equilibria in our northern Kenya sites, as well. Figure 3 depicts the nonparametric regression of herd size (the solid line without markers), measured in tropical livestock units (TLU)[15] per capita, a useful scalar measure of wealth in pastoralist communities, on the previous quarter's herd size, pooling the Dirib Gombo and Ng'ambo observations together to improve precision.[16] The dashed diagonal line depicts dynamic equilibria. The expected asset dynamics exhibit stable equilibria – points at which the regression line crosses the dashed diagonal line from above – at approximately 0.2 and 10 TLU per capita. Translated into somewhat more concrete units, a median household of six persons faces both a low-level equilibrium herd size of about one cow or 10–12 goats or sheep, or a higher stable equilibrium herd size on the order of 50–60 cattle.

There exists one unstable dynamic equilibrium between these two stable dynamic equilibria. This nonparametric regression suggests that household-level herd dynamics bifurcate at 5–6 TLU per capita. Above that level, the herd size naturally grows toward the higher equilibrium of 10 TLU per capita. But below the unstable equilibrium, household herd sizes tend to collapse toward the low-level equilibrium of less than one TLU per capita. This suggests that 5–6 TLU per capita demarcates a critical threshold that northern Kenyan pastoralist households and those interested in their welfare need to defend vigorously.[17]

We need to be careful, however, about investing too much in the estimates that result from the simple bivariate autoregression depicted in Figure 3. This necessarily assumes away statistically significant differences in other characteristics, thereby

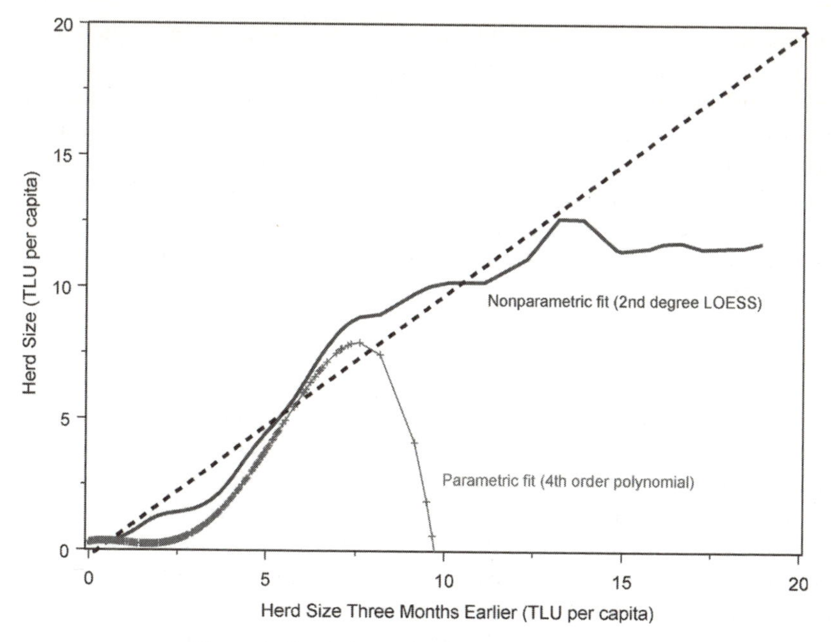

Figure 3. Herd dynamics in Northern Kenya

raising the real possibility of omitted relevant variables bias. On the other hand, parametric methods of estimating these recursion diagrams must use high order polynomials of the lagged asset holdings, along with proper controls for life-cycle effects that naturally influence observed asset dynamics – people accumulate assets during their working adult lives and then begin divesting assets in their latter years – and for community- and period-specific effects, in order to allow for multiple equilibria.[18] Such estimation is simply not feasible in most panel data sets. And even when it is, it can still be very difficult to fit complex nonlinear dynamics parametrically, as we show momentarily.

As a check on the robustness of the basic pattern, we therefore also estimated herd dynamics in Dirib Gombo and Ng'ambo parametrically. More precisely, we regressed the year-on-year change in household i's per capita herd size on a fourth order polynomial in one-year lagged herd size:

$$A_{it} = \alpha_1 Y_{it} + \alpha_2 Y^2_{it} + \beta_1 A_{it-1} + \beta_2 A^2_{it-1} + \beta_3 A^3_{it-1} + \beta_4 A^4_{it-1} + \boldsymbol{\delta}_t + \boldsymbol{\lambda}_i + \varepsilon_{it} \quad (5)$$

where Y is the household head's age in years, entering quadratically to control for life cycle effects, and the bold-faced vectors $\boldsymbol{\delta}$ and $\boldsymbol{\lambda}$ represent period- and household-specific effects, respectively. The regression results (available from the authors by request) imply a modest, statistically significant steady increase in herd size as a household head ages, peaking at age 53 before declining again. Of more immediate interest to the present analysis, the regression point estimates suggest stable dynamic equilibria at 0.35 and 7.83 TLU per capita and an unstable equilibrium at 6.08 TLU per capita. The lower estimated equilibrium herd size is strikingly similar to that derived through the simpler, bivariate nonparametric regression shown in Figure 3.

The unstable equilibrium is statistically significantly higher and the higher-level stable equilibrium is statistically significantly lower than the counterpart estimates from the nonparametric regression. But as the plot of the parametrically fitted expected herd dynamics in Figure 3 (depicted by the line with + markers) shows, even a fourth order polynomial seems to over-smooth the estimated asset dynamics in the upper tail of the wealth distribution, underscoring the value of nonparametric statistical methods in studying potentially complex nonlinear asset dynamics. Clearly, more work needs to be done to identify such thresholds confidently with an appropriate balance between flexibility of functional form and control for other covariates. Nonetheless, the hypothesis of multiple herd size equilibria among these pastoralists, consistent with the poverty traps hypothesis, appears robust.

One advantage of studying such patterns among pastoralists is that one can reduce wealth to herd size without doing much violence to the underlying reality.[19] In order to replicate this analysis in our other sites, where more favourable agroecology leads to more diversified crop and animal agriculture and where higher population densities lead to greater propensity to own nonagricultural assets and businesses, we need an alternative method for summarising assets.

The asset index introduced by Sahn and Stifel (2000) provides one method for doing precisely this.[20] The Sahn-Stifel asset index reflects a latent 'wealth' variable common to most assets, providing a summary statistic of general wealth manifest in a range of assets. This method conserves degrees of freedom relative to including a long laundry list of assets and lends itself to graphical presentation in a way multi-dimensional asset measures do not.

We computed Sahn-Stifel asset indices separately for each site, pooling data across sample periods so as to be able to apply a consistent set of weights across periods, but adding period-specific dummy variables so as to account for temporal changes that might otherwise influence asset weights. We then used the resulting factor weights to compute household- and period-specific asset indices. These are unitless measures with unconditional site-specific means equal to zero due to the normalised weights of the asset index. So we cannot compare levels across sites, since the weighting schemes and normalisations are not comparable. We can, however, study household-specific asset dynamics using these asset indices just as we studied herd dynamics among northern Kenya pastoralist households.

Figure 4 presents the nonparametric autoregressions of household-specific asset indices for the three other sites. The two Malagasy sites do not appear to exhibit multiple equilibria in asset index dynamics. But in Madzuu, our western Kenya site, multiple dynamic equilibria appear to exist, with one at the upper reaches of the current wealth distribution and another around the mean of the current wealth distribution. If we run the simple ordinary least squares regression of real per capita daily income on the asset index and then calculate the predicted value at the dynamic asset equilibria, we find that these dynamic asset equilibria correspond to expected real per capita daily incomes of $0.51 in the lower equilibrium, just beneath Kenya's rural poverty line, and $1.48 in the upper equilibrium, hardly wealthy but nonetheless nearly three times higher than the lower equilibrium and the relevant poverty line. Again, the data appear consistent with the poverty traps hypothesis.

If multiple dynamic equilibria exist, households should converge toward these equilibria, leading to a mode in the cross-sectional distribution around the stable

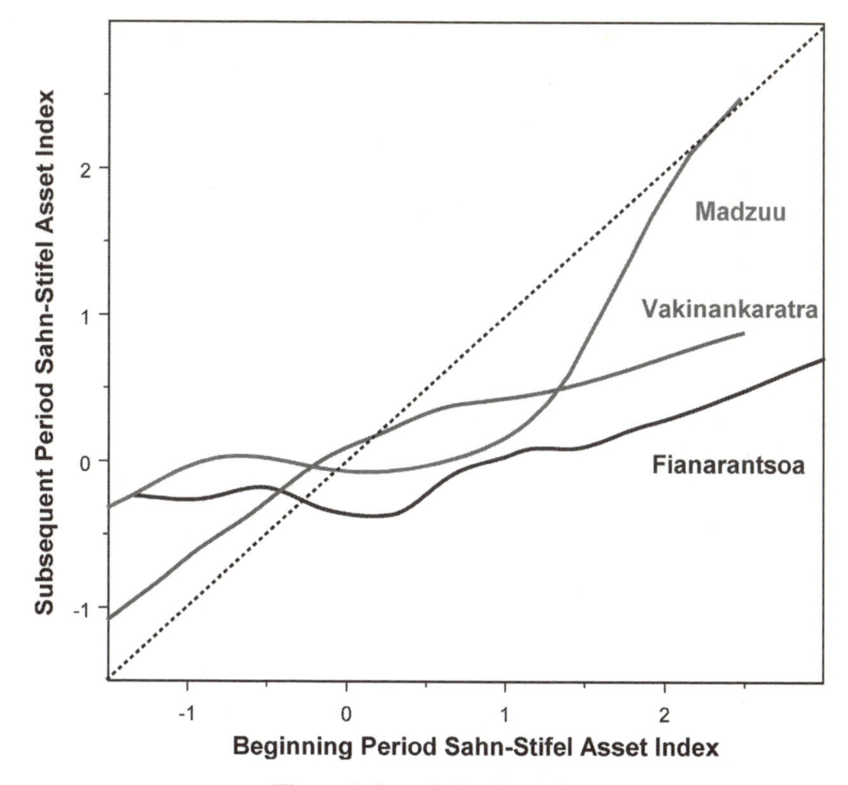

Figure 4. Asset index dynamics

dynamic equilibria (Barrett, 2005). Because households should not remain long at or near unstable equilibria, observed density at those points should be less than at the nearest stable equilibria. If there are multiple equilibria, then there should therefore appear more than one local mode in the cross-sectional income distribution, Quah (1996) referred to as 'twin peaks', although there could in principle be more than two such local modes.[21] We see precisely this pattern of multi-peaked income distributions in Figure 5, whose peaks match up reasonably well against the incomes implied by the asset index dynamics (Figure 4). It certainly appears that multiple equilibria exist in Madzuu, with less than one-quarter of the population clustered around the higher dynamic equilibrium and the rest distributed around, and presumably converging toward, the lower level equilibrium beneath the poverty line.

As suggested in Figure 4, the chronically poor in Madzuu hold limited assets. Table 2 shows household mean asset holdings by categories from the poverty transition matrix (Table 1). Those who were poor in both two survey rounds, on average, had smaller asset bases – land, improved or crossbred dairy cattle or access to off-farm employment earnings—than either the transitorily poor or, especially those households who were consistently non-poor, although the differences are only statistically significant between the chronically poor and the consistently non-poor. This reinforces the impression that initial asset conditions affect poverty dynamics, consistent with the poverty traps hypothesis.[22]

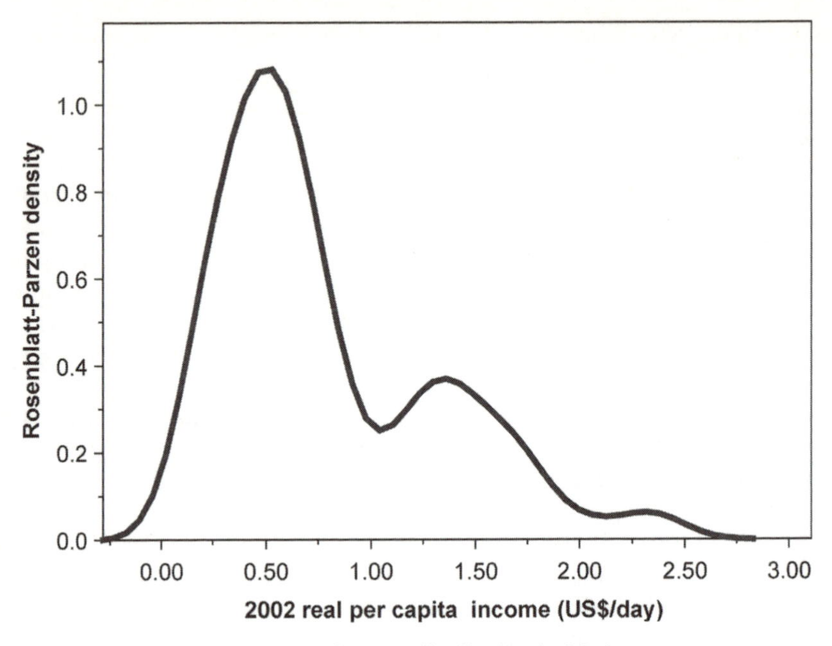

Figure 5. 2002 income distribution in Madzuu

Table 2. 1989 Mean asset holdings, Madzuu

	Chronically poor	Transient: poor to non-poor	Transient: non-poor to poor	Non-poor
Farm size (acres)	0.81	1.00	0.97	2.41*
Head of improved, cross-bred dairy cattle	0.06	0.11	0.11	0.25*
Household includes secondary school graduate (1 = yes, 0 = no)	0.44	0.44	0.44	0.88*
Family has off-farm employment earnings at least 10 months/year (1 = yes, 0 = no)	0.26	0.22	0.33	0.38

*Statistically significant differences at 5 per cent level.

V. Does Income Immobility Signal Poverty Traps?

So why do there appear to be multiple structural dynamic equilibria in at least the rural Kenya sites? In this section we explore this question further. We look in turn at whether there might exist measurable differences in risk management strategies by ex ante household wealth, and whether there might be locally increasing returns on assets due to discrete shifts in livelihood strategies or production technologies, both phenomena suggested by the qualitative evidence.

(a) Wealth-Differentiated Risk Management

The considerable short-term income volatility manifest in the data series from each of our sites raises important questions about poor households' capacity to undertake consumption smoothing. This is of interest for its own sake, as consumption smoothing is intrinsically valuable for households exhibiting risk aversion. But understanding more about households' management of income volatility also offers us a window into prospective sources of differential expected returns on assets, as is implied by a poverty traps explanation of persistent poverty.

A small literature demonstrates that in the presence of highly stochastic income, risk preferences, subsistence constraints or both can induce poorer households to trade off expected income growth for reduced income volatility, relative to wealthier households (Rosenzweig and Binswanger, 1993; Carter, 1997; Bardhan et al., 2000; Zimmerman and Carter, 2003). Of course, if this means that poor households eschew the risks inherent to investment, this can lead households to precisely the sort of low-level equilibrium posited by the poverty traps hypothesis. If this wealth-differentiated portfolio choice phenomenon is true, then we should see a lower coefficient of variation (CV)[23] of income among poorer households than among wealthier households, corresponding to the risk-return tradeoffs predicted by standard economic assumptions about preferences characterised by decreasing absolute risk aversion. Poor households should have lower expected returns on assets and a disproportionately lower variability in those returns.

Furthermore, poor households may be more likely to destabilise consumption as part of their strategy to cope ex post with uninsured and unmitigated income risk, precisely so as to avoid having to divest scarce productive assets on which future wellbeing – or even survival – depends. This implies that poorer households may have higher coefficients of variation in consumption (expenditure) than do richer households. Richer households will have more savings (in cash and in kind, including in the form of productive assets) and more access to credit, so they will have more opportunity to smooth consumption ex post of stochastic income realisations than do poorer households.

The combination of these two hypotheses raises an interesting possibility. If income variability increases with wealth but consumption variability decreases with wealth, that implies that consumption smoothing increases in expected income. If consumption smoothing increases welfare due to risk aversion, and if poorer households indeed smooth consumption less than wealthier households – that is, if consumption smoothing is a normal good, increasing in income or wealth – then standard, static expenditure measures will tend to understate welfare differences because they omit the positive value of smoother consumption.

To the best of our knowledge, the hypothesis that wealth has opposing effects on the volatility of consumption and of income has not yet been empirically tested perhaps because this requires sufficiently high frequency data to establish the volatility of both income and expenditures. Fortunately, with ten quarterly observations per household, our northern Kenya data are suitable for this task.

The data cannot support testing this hypothesis in our other sites. Using data from all six of the PARIMA sites in northern Kenya, we computed 177 household-specific coefficients of variation for quarterly income and expenditure series.[24]

Figure 6 plots the nonparametric regression of these CVs on initial period household herd size, expressed in per capita TLU. The positive correlation between wealth and income risk is apparent in the upward slope of the thinner solid line depicting income CV. Bootstrapped confidence bands (not shown) indicate that the positive slope to this regression line is indeed statistically significant over most of the conditioning domain. Poorer households indeed appear to systematically suppress income variability. One would expect this to come at a cost of lower expected marginal returns on assets. As we show in the next sub-section, these data support that hypothesis as well.

The thicker solid regression line reflects the regression of the CV of household expenditure and wealth. This slopes modestly downward, although bootstrapped confidence bands (not shown) indicate that the differences are only statistically significantly different between the tails of the wealth distribution. The gap between the income and expenditure CV regressions reflects consumption smoothing behaviour. While richer households take on greater income risk than poorer households do, they nonetheless enjoy lower intertemporal variability in expenditures. Consumption smoothing indeed appears to be a normal good among these households, increasing in wealth in spite of prospectively greater absolute risk aversion among the poor.

The dashed curve, which should be read against the right-hand vertical axis, depicts the empirical wealth density depicting the asset distribution among surveyed households. Among the poorest households – up to roughly the median of the wealth distribution – mean intertemporal income variability is actually less than mean

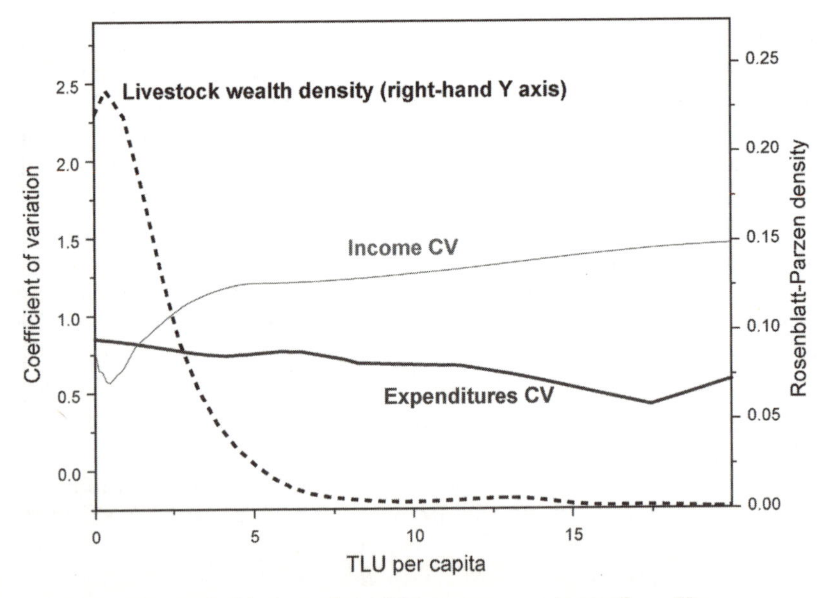

Figure 6. Wealth-dependent risk management in northern Kenya

expenditure volatility, signalling that the most vulnerable households indeed seem not to smooth consumption at all, but to destabilise consumption in order to protect crucial productive assets on which their future survival depends. This underscores the dynamic welfare cost of uninsured risk borne by vulnerable households. Consumption smoothing appears to increase relatively rapidly as one moves above the median of the wealth distribution among these northern Kenya pastoralists.

(b) Locally Increasing Returns on Assets

If poorer households trade lower risk for lower returns, this should appear as well when we plot expected income against assets. Figure 7 presents the nonparametric kernel regression of per capita daily income per capita herd size using the same 177 northern Kenya households. The increasing slope of the income function over most of the wealth distribution signals increasing returns per unit wealth, as would be expected if households are indeed taking on higher risk – higher reward portfolios of activities and assets as their wealth increases. Of course, this creates multiple dynamic equilibria based on initial wealth, consistent with the S-shaped asset dynamics identified in the previous section. The marginal rate of increase in expected income (the slope of the income function) does not begin to decrease until about the 96th percentile of the wealth distribution – corresponding with the higher stable dynamic equilibrium in Figure 3. Over most of the wealth distribution, there appear to be increasing returns to asset holdings.

This raises the obvious question: if expected returns are increasing in livestock holdings over most of the wealth distribution in the northern Kenya pastoralist sites

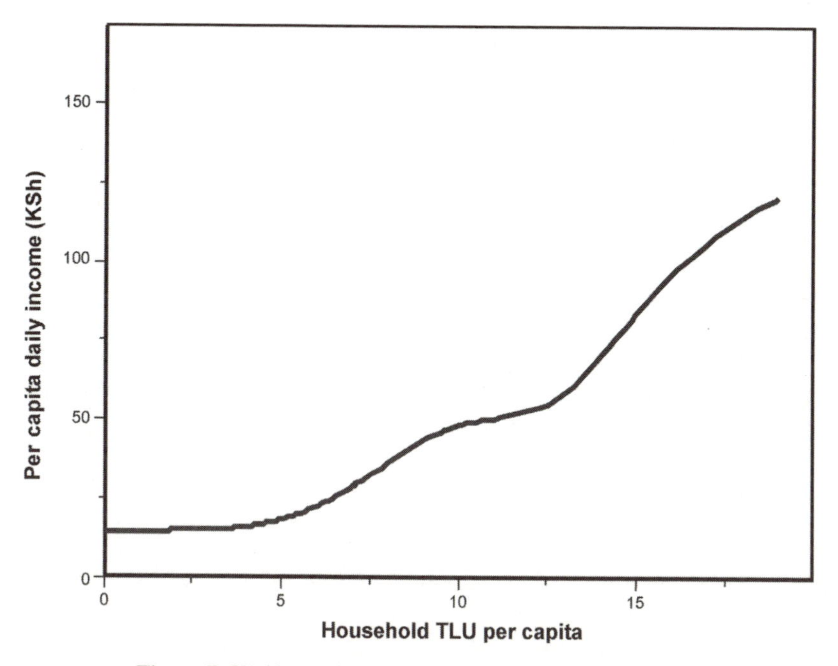

Figure 7. Welfare – herd size relation in northern Kenya

we study, why do poorer households not accumulate assets so as to increase expected income? It would seem that there must be some barrier(s) to accumulation. The explanation already discussed concerns portfolio choice based on risk preferences that differ across the wealth distribution. The data appear consistent with that claim. But there may be alternative or supplementary explanations.

One candidate explanation would be subsistence constraints that limit households' ability to reduce current consumption in order to increase savings and thus asset accumulation. Unfortunately, we have no good way to test directly for subsistence constraints in our data. The data do show, however, that all of these households received food aid in at least some period and that many suffer acute food insecurity manifest in coping behaviours such as reduced frequency of meals, in many households to just one a day.

Another plausible, complementary explanation arises from the lack of liquid savings and credit. Although there are bank services in the larger towns of northern Kenya and there have been efforts at promoting microfinance institutions in several of the survey communities, fixed fees at KCB make real rates of return negative on small accounts and loan limits at existing microcredit institutions preclude purchasing fertile large ruminants for herd building (Osterloh, 2004). Less than 15 per cent of the survey households hold bank accounts and access to credit is negligible. Given scant cash holdings or credit, very few households purchase animals; herd accumulation involves almost exclusively biological reproduction (Barrett et al., forthcoming). To a certain extent, then, households' asset holdings may be constrained to follow the natural population dynamics of their livestock assets.

The phenomenon of locally increasing returns on assets appears in all of our sites for at least some assets, but with variation in degree across years and locations. To get at the hypothesis in a different way, we ran the ordinary least squares regression of household income on a range of household assets for each location and year separately using a generalised quadratic, second-order flexible functional form to allow for nonlinearities and interaction effects among assets,[25] then computed the estimated marginal returns on assets and ran the nonparametric LOESS regression of those estimated marginal effects on the asset stock. The results underscore a pattern of locally increasing returns to several key assets in many of our sites.

Consider, for example, Figure 8, which depicts the nonparametric regression of estimated marginal returns to labour force (measured as working age adults in the household) and to the amount of rice land area a household owns on household stock of labour and rice land, respectively.[26] These regressions depict the potentially endogenous returns on assets, as permitted in equation (1). The upper left panel of Figure 8 shows that the estimated marginal returns on household labour stock are increasing significantly around the middle of the labour distribution in Fianarantsoa, the poorer of our Malagasy sites, where illness and migration limit labour availability for many poor households, commonly impeding expansion into higher return, labour intensive activities such as dairy production or SRI rice production.[27] Few households in Fianarantsoa have cash savings, access to credit or steady cash income from salaried employment to use to hire unskilled workers when they (perhaps temporarily) suffer labour shortages that might impede adoption of an improved technology or that might cause agricultural yield losses due to mistiming

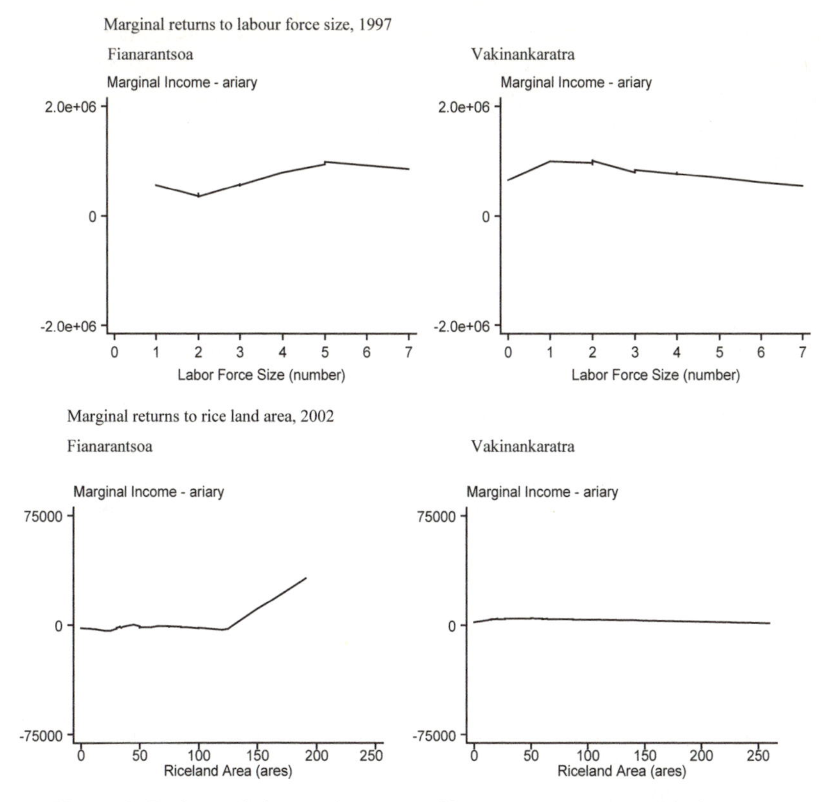

Figure 8. Estimated site- and year-specific returns on assets, Madagascar

of field operations (for example, due to a spell of malaria). Liquidity constraints make labour availability a critical determinant of household livelihood strategies. Those households that lose an adult to death or migration (without compensating remittances) thus lose not only a productive worker, but also suffer average productivity losses among the remaining adults, reflecting the endogenous asset returns characteristic of poverty traps. Interestingly, this effect is not present in the wealthier Vakinankaratra site, where widespread off-season cropping and salaried employment and better access to markets and credit enable households to hire labour more freely in response to latent demand. The result is diminishing returns to labour, as shown in the upper right panel of Figure 8.

The marginal returns to rice land likewise exhibit locally increasing returns in Fianarantsoa. It is almost exclusively the households with the largest lowland rice area who adopt SRI, apply fertiliser or manure or use animal traction. Estimated marginal income per unit area of rice land owned is thus sharply increasing in the upper third of the land distribution as the largest farms enjoy the highest rice yields. The locally increasing returns evident in the poorer Fianarantsoa site are again absent in the better-off Vakinankaratra region, where even small farmers are commonly able to secure off-season contract farming that provides fertiliser inputs and where water management is relatively reliable, maintaining reasonable yields even on smaller farms.

The argument we advance here is subtle. We do not claim that there exist globally increasing returns to any particular asset, nor even that locally increasing returns exist everywhere. Rather, our point is that there exist places where market failures – perhaps especially in the finance necessary to undertake investment or to cope with shocks without liquidating productive assets – can lead to sharp differences in productivity among reasonably similar households and thus to poverty traps. In less-favoured areas such as the rangelands of northern Kenya and the southern highlands of Madagascar, such phenomena seem to exist, while we do not find evidence of similar patterns in the more favoured area of Madagascar's central highlands.

This quantitative evidence corresponds with the qualitative evidence from our in-depth interviews with a sub-sample of farmers and participatory focus group discussions about local definitions, dynamics and responses to poverty. The prevailing view within the community is that those who manage to complete their secondary education and secure salaried employment through social connections or good fortune – education is merely a necessary condition to finding a decent job, but by no means is it sufficient – can then build and sustain a reasonable livelihood, with improved dairy cattle and tea bushes on several acres of land in addition to – and in large measure because of – steady non-poor cash income. Each of the households we interviewed who were non-poor in both 1989 and 2002 emphasised non-farm employment as playing a crucial role in their achievement and maintenance of an adequate standard of living.

Equally important, an adequate livelihood is vulnerable to shocks in Madzuu. Overwhelmingly, health shocks were the most frequent reason given for households falling into poverty, cited by nearly every Madzuu household we spoke with that was poor in 2002.[28] Health and mortality shocks may cause a loss of permanent salaried employment or self-employment, ending a household's steady cash flow and often necessitating distress sale of productive agricultural and household assets to pay for medical expenses. Even transient health shocks – most commonly malaria in this area – can lead to significant yield losses because they prevent the application of labour at crucial periods during the rainy, growing season, when illnesses are most common. These yield losses can reduce consumption over the subsequent year, leaving the household more vulnerable to further disease, thereby igniting a vicious cycle of disease and destitution.[29] In other cases, the death of a close family member – a father, brother or spouse – imposed funeral expenses on a household that wiped out its assets, causing it to pull children from school and thus breaking the household's long-term access to remunerative employment.[30]

Retrenchment in Kenya's off-farm labour market, due in considerable measure to reduced public sector employment and to infrastructure decline that has hurt rural non-farm industry throughout the country, has affected the accessibility of the higher-level equilibrium. Madzuu residents repeatedly told us that 15 or 20 years ago, secondary school leavers could almost always find remunerative employment. That is no longer true. The result of lower off-farm skilled labour demand relative to supply has had multiple adverse effects in communities such as Madzuu. First, there are the obvious, direct labour market effects: greater unemployment and lower real wages, both skilled and unskilled (the latter because skilled workers who fail to find salaried employment commonly join the unskilled labour market, expanding supply there as well). The indirect impacts have likewise proved important, according to the households we interviewed. Less off-farm employment has reduced outmigration from Madzuu, leading to increased on-farm population density. The result has been farm partitioning, manifest in sharp declines in average farm sizes, reduced fallowing and as a direct consequence, accelerated soil nutrient depletion. Uniformly, respondents report that farms in Madzuu are now smaller and less fertile than they were a generation ago. Perhaps more remarkably, Madzuu residents routinely make the sophisticated connection between land and labour markets, observing that adverse changes in local land quality follows in large measure from the lack of growth in off-farm labour demand for a growing rural population.

VI. Conclusions and Policy Implications

In order to make progress in combating persistent poverty, policymakers must have a clear and accurate conceptualisation of the causal mechanism that keeps people poor indefinitely. In particular, the increasingly popular term 'poverty traps' implies a quite different mechanism behind poverty than do prevailing economic theories of growth and development. This paper offers a novel attempt at establishing empirically whether there might really exist poverty traps in the form of multiple dynamic equilibria, with households attracted toward low-level equilibria when they start with limited initial wealth or when they suffer a serious shock to the stock or productivity of their assets.

The results are striking. Our data from rural Kenya and Madagascar offer consistent support for the poverty traps hypothesis, finding that structural income and asset dynamics exhibit multiple stable dynamic equilibria in several sites, especially in lower potential and remoter regions. Both quantitative and qualitative evidence support these inferences.

Why might poverty traps exist? We offer a few tentative results in the direction of explaining this phenomenon, but we cannot confidently establish causality. We find evidence that marginal returns on assets are positively correlated with initial wealth in some places and over some ranges of asset holdings. Such locally increasing returns also lead to divergent growth patterns and to poverty traps for those facing locally diminishing marginal returns on their meagre asset stocks. This seems to occur because households with fewer productive assets tend to be excluded from higher-return livelihood strategies due to cash liquidity constraints, social exclusion, or both. We likewise find evidence that considerable risk exposure leads to wealth differentiated risk management, with the relatively wealthy able to smooth consumption and take on higher risk-higher return livelihoods. Meanwhile, poorer households have to destabilise consumption so as to protect scarce, crucial productive assets and they choose lower risk-lower return livelihoods. This predictably leads to observable divergence in household-level asset and structural income dynamics.

So what are the key policy implications of these findings? First, macroeconomic and sectoral reforms alone are probably insufficient to put poorer populations on a sustainable growth trajectory. Less-favoured areas and the poorest households need more direct intervention to build and protect assets and to improve the productivity of households' existing asset stocks, or to remove the barriers (for example, access to credit, insurance and savings products) that exclude the poorest households and regions from accumulation processes. Such interventions can induce natural asset accumulation and income growth. The most appropriate assets to build will depend on local context. In the northern Kenyan rangelands, livestock are (not surprisingly) the key asset and our evidence suggests a critical threshold at 5–6 TLU per capita. In that context, it seems critical to build herds to that size, perhaps most cost-effectively by lowering the critical threshold through, for example, improved veterinary care, physical security of herds and herders, and dry season water availability. In the southern Madagascar highlands, it would appear the persistently poor could be helped considerably by improving preventive and curative health care so as to prevent households from losing precious adult workers, relieving seasonal liquidity constraints that impede uptake of improved rice production methods, and facilitating adoption and marketing of higher-value fruits, vegetables and dairy products.

Second, bifurcation in accumulation and risk management patterns must originate in one or more exclusionary process that prevents poorer households from choosing more remunerative livelihood strategies. Some of this exclusion may be geographic, as certain production strategies are infeasible in particular areas due to soil and hydrological conditions, available infrastructure, access to markets, and demand for skilled labour. In other cases, the exclusion may result from household-level barriers to entry associated with limited access to credit or insurance, educational attainment or other critical assets. We cannot probe these issues adequately here. Our objective, rather, is to call attention to the emerging evidence that poverty traps indeed seem to exist and we must redouble efforts to understand and combat them where they exist.

Third, effective safety nets to protect the assets households accumulate can prevent inadvertent backsliding. Such safety nets need to be located strategically just above the critical asset thresholds at which expected income dynamics bifurcate. This calls for a somewhat broader conceptualisation of safety nets than simply the nutrition-focused, food aid-based safety nets prevalent in policy discussions today. Protecting human health through adequate nutrition and ensuring children stay in school (for example, through food-for-education projects) is indisputably important and may suffice where one need only maintain access to labour markets in order to grow out of poverty. But in the rural sites we study, health shocks largely unrelated to nutrition – for example, HIV/AIDS, malaria, tuberculosis – are the most common reason households become and stay poor, underscoring the importance of preventive and curative health care quite apart from support for adequate access to food. Moreover, labour is not the only critical productive asset. A number of recent studies have pointed, in particular, to the importance of losses of livestock in explaining households' decline into poverty (Freudenberger, 1998; Krishna et al., 2004, Kristjanson et al., 2004), results echoed in our own qualitative and quantitative results. This underscores the importance of developing insurance and other means to help poor households manage risk due to theft, climate and civil strife.

Much remains to be learned. Our results are by no means definitive. But they offer some innovative ways to investigate the causal mechanism underpinning chronic poverty in Africa and how communities, governments and donors can most effectively combat persistent poverty.

Acknowledgements

The authors thank Erin Lentz, Andrew Mude and Amare Yirbecho for valuable data assistance, Michael Carter, Angelique Haugerud, Ravi Kanbur, Peter Little, an anonymous referee and seminar participants at Cornell University and the BASIS CRSP Washington policy conference on Combating Persistent Poverty in Africa for helpful comments, and our field assistants and survey respondents for their invaluable assistance in data collection and in helping us to understand the nature and dynamics of poverty in their villages. This work has been made possible, in part, by support from the United States Agency for International Development (USAID), through grant LAG-A-00-96-90016-00 to the BASIS CRSP, grants DAN-1328-G-00-0046-00 and PCE-G-98-00036-00 to the Pastoral Risk Management (PARIMA) project of the Global Livestock CRSP, and the Strategies and Analyses for Growth and Access (SAGA) cooperative agreement, number HFM-A-00-01-00132-00. The views expressed here and any remaining errors are the authors' and do not represent any official agency.

Notes

1. Several recent studies use an explicit growth model to study household-level dynamics (Ravallion and Jalan, 1996; Gunning et al., 2000; Elbers et al., 2002; Jalan and Ravallion, 2002, 2004; Deininger and Okidi, 2003; Dercon 2004). Yet none seeks to test among competing hypotheses of the underlying growth mechanism. Most simply impose a variant of the classic Solow model. Our approach imposes no model of the underlying growth mechanism.
2. For more information, see the project website at http://afsnrm.aem.cornell.edu/basis/ or the BASIS CRSP website at http://www.basis.wisc.edu
3. Different metrics – expenditure, income, anthropometric status – can yield different measures of chronic and transitory poverty. See Place et al. (2003) for a demonstration of this point using data from western Kenya.
4. We used probit and logit models to estimate the probability of attrition from the survey conditional on households' initial characteristics. For a range of different explanatory variables, we could never come up with a regression specification that yielded a p-value of less than 0.09 on the test of the null hypothesis that the full set of regressors is uncorrelated with sample attrition. Alderman et al. (2001) and Falaris (2003) similarly found that attrition bias is not a serious concern in other developing country panel data sets.
5. Prevailing exchange rates in 2002–3 are roughly 75 Kenya shillings and 6,200 Malagasy francs per US dollar.
6. Income measures were constructed the same way for each site. Income equals net cash income (wages, salary, earnings from farm and non-farm enterprises, transfers, remittances, interest on savings and rental income from properties owned), plus the cash value of home-consumed food production (including milk and meat from slaughtered animals), valued at prevailing annual average, village-specific market prices for the goods in question.
7. Krishna et al. (2004) similarly find symmetry between entry into and exit from poverty (around 19 per cent for each category) over a 25-year span in their study of western Kenya.
8. One can substitute expenditures for income and repeat the analysis exactly, except that one then must account for endogenous savings. The income-based version is simpler and yields qualitatively identical results.
9. Carter and May (2001) explain and demonstrate the importance to poverty analysis of this distinction between the stochastic and structural components of income.

10. Note that the axes are not scaled identically across sites, given differences in ex ante income distributions.
11. A locally-weighted scatter plot smoother (LOESS) regression generates a series of conditional means over a fine grid on the conditioning domain by fitting a weighted linear regression, where the weights decrease with distance from the point of interest. We connect these predicted values to produce a (potentially highly nonlinear) curve. The key parameters affecting the estimated regression curve are the span or bandwidth, which determines how many nearby observations are used in predicting the dependent variable at a given point, and the degree of the regression, whether it is locally linear or quadratic. We use second degree (quadratic) LOESS estimators with optimal, variable span (based on cross-validation) on this and all subsequent nonparametric regressions.
12. With enough household-specific observations over time, one could properly estimate U_i, the time-invariant household-specific component of income from equations (1) and (2). In practice, we typically have not enough longitudinal observations on single households to retain sufficient degrees of freedom in estimation if we include these household fixed effects. We therefore opt here for village-specific fixed effects. In Madzuu, the assets used as regressors are farm size, improved dairy cattle, unimproved dairy cattle, non-dairy cattle, small ruminants (sheep and goats), poultry, farm and business equipment, household demographic composition (size, ages, gender), dummies for educational attainment categories for the household head and for the most educated member of the household, distance to nearest market, bicycles owned, and dummy variables for receipt of credit, being native to the village, and for 2002 (to capture period-specific shocks to aggregate returns). The equation fitting income on a linear function of these asset variables had an adjusted $r^2 = 0.34$. In the two Malagasy sites, we used the same regressors as in Madzuu, minus small ruminants and poultry, but adding number of hogs, bank savings and dummy variables for extension service access and villages, and breaking total farm land into lowland rice fields and all other agricultural lands. In Dirib Gombo and Ng'ambo, we used the Madzuu regressors, dropping improved dairy cattle (irrelevant in these sites) and whether the respondent was native to the village (the variable is absent from the northern Kenya data sets). The adjusted r^2 on the Fianarantsoa, Vakinankaratra, Baringo and Marsabit regressions were 0.43, 0.44, 0.37 and 0.28, respectively. The modest explanatory power of these regressions, given small sample sizes that would typically yield high r^2 statistics, reinforces the point that much household-and-period-specific income appears stochastic rather than structural.
13. This echoes other qualitative work on poverty dynamics undertaken in the eastern escarpment of Madagascar (Freudenberger, 1998), western Kenya (Krishna et al., 2004; Kristjanson et al., 2004) and India (Krishna, 2004).
14. Jayne et al. (2003) find similar patterns using nationally representative data from several eastern and southern African countries. Mistiaen et al. (2002) have similar findings in their poverty mapping study of Madagascar.
15. The TLU represents a standardised measure of metabolic liveweight in animals, enabling aggregation across species according to the formula 1 TLU = 1 cattle = 0.7 camels = 10 goats = 11 sheep.
16. We also ran these regressions separately for each site and found no statistically significant difference between the two sites in herd dynamics, thus justifying combing the data from the two sites.
17. Previous animal science and ethnographic research similarly suggests 4.5 TLU per capita as a threshold for the minimum herd necessary to provide adequate nutrition for an individual surviving on livestock in arid lands, based on productivity estimates and approximate caloric needs (Pratt and Gwynne, 1977; Fratkin and Roth, 1990).
18. A third order polynomial in the lagged asset stock is an absolute minimum to allow for the possibility of multiple stable equilibria; and that only permits two stable equilibria on the tails of the sample data.
19. Nonetheless, with increasing voluntary sedentarisation of educated and employed pastoralists (McPeak and Little, forthcoming), using herd size as a proxy for overall wealth is becoming increasingly suspect even in pastoral areas with little crop agriculture or nonagricultural industry.
20. The Sahn-Stifel method uses factor analysis to find a single common factor that explains the covariance of a vector of assets under the assumption that these assets reflect a common, latent wealth variable that we cannot directly measure. The resulting factor loadings then represent data-driven weights on the assets. The product of these weights and a given household's asset holdings yields an intuitive, unitless asset index.

21. Quah (1996) first remarked on this in the context of empirical macroeconomics, referring to the phenomenon of 'twin peaks' reflecting two distinct dynamic equilibria. More generally, 'multi-peakedness' provides prima facie evidence of multiple dynamic equilibria inconsistent with the hypothesis of unconditional convergence.
22. Gamba et al. (2004) likewise find that initial assets, particularly land holdings and educational attainment, are negatively related to the likelihood of being poor in multiple periods in their rural Kenya panel data.
23. Coefficient of variation, a unit-less measure or risk, equals the standard deviation divided by the mean.
24. Because we have to compute household-specific estimates of income and expenditure coefficients of variation, we lose the time series variation on which site-specific regression estimation depends in our northern Kenya locations of Dirib Gombo and Ng'ambo. So for this analysis we pool the data with those from households in the four other northern Kenya PARIMA survey sites, which are described in Barrett et al. (2004a).
25. Detailed regression results and diagnostics are available from the authors by request.
26. In Madagascar, 'rice land' (*bas fond* or *tanimbary*) is irrigable lowland suitable for cultivation of rice. It is distinct from the upland (*tanety*) that is purely rainfed. The underlying regression coefficients for the variables discussed are statistically significantly different from zero at the 5 per cent level. Marginal returns were then estimated for each household using the point estimates from the second order generalised quadratic specification – normalised to produce an exact second-order approximation at the sample means – and the household-specific asset stock values. Here, we report only the 1997 results. The 2002 data yield qualitatively identical patterns.
27. The system of rice intensification (SRI) was developed in Madagascar in the late 1980s and has demonstrated tremendous potential for yield growth without requiring any new seed, chemical fertiliser or other purchased inputs. SRI generates these effects through a suite of changes in agronomic practices in plant spacing, timing of seedling transplanting and soil moisture management. However, SRI requires additional initial labour investment that typically puts it out of reach of the poorest and smallest households. Moser and Barrett (2003) document these effects, while Barrett et al. (2004b) document that SRI increases yields on average by more than 80 per cent, holding farmer and plot characteristics and other inputs constant, while also increasing yield risk, providing a link to the preceding sub-section on wealth-differentiated risk management strategies.
28. Krishna et al. (2004) and Kristjanson et al. (2004) similarly find health shocks to be overwhelmingly the most common explanation for households falling into poverty in their study of a broader cross-section of western Kenya.
29. Tegemeo/MSU (2001) study on health shocks and productivity and income find qualitatively identical patterns using a far larger panel data set from 24 rural districts in Kenya.
30. Freudenberger (1999) offers a hauntingly similar narrative of a vicious cycle wrought by local custom regarding funeral expenses. Based on participatory poverty assessments in forest communities in Fianarantsoa, she found that ritual slaughter of livestock in Betsileo culture had driven many families from stable livelihoods into destitution, as the loss of cattle reduced draught power and manure, both essential inputs to the intensive terraced rice cultivation practiced in these communities.

References

Alderman, H., Behrman, J., Kohler, H. P., Maluccio, J. A. and Watkins, S. (2001), Attrition in longitudinal household survey data: some tests for three developing-country samples. *Demographic Research*, 5, pp. 78–124.

Bardhan, P., Bowles, S. and Gintis, H. (2000) Wealth inequality, wealth constraints and economic performance, in A. B. Atkinson and F. Bourguignon (Eds) *Handbook of Income Distribution, Volume 1* (Amsterdam: Elsevier Science).

Barrett, C. B. (2005) Rural poverty dynamics: development policy implications, in D. Colman and N. Vink (Eds), *Reshaping Agriculture's Contributions to Society* (Oxford: Blackwell).

Barrett, C. B., Bellemare, M. F. and Osterloh, S. M. (forthcoming) Household-level livestock marketing behavior among Northern Kenyan and Southern Ethiopian pastoralists, in P. D. Little and J. G. McPeak (Eds), *Livestock Marketing in Eastern Africa: Research and Policy Challenges* (London: ITDG Publishing).

Barrett, C. B., Gebru, G., McPeak, J. G., Mude, A. G., Vanderpuye-Orgle, J. and Yirbecho, A. T. (2004a) Codebook for data collected under the improving pastoral risk management on East African Rangelands (PARIMA) Project. Cornell University working paper.

Barrett, C. B., Moser, C. M., McHugh, O. V. and Barison, J. (2004b) Better technology, better plots or better farmers? Identifying changes in productivity and risk among Malagasy rice farmers, *American Journal of Agricultural Economics*, 86, pp. 869–88.

Barrett, C. B., Reardon, T. and Webb, P. (2001) Nonfarm income diversification and household livelihood strategies in Rural Africa: concepts, dynamics and policy implications, *Food Policy*, 26, pp. 315–31.

Barrett, C. B. and Swallow, B. (2006) Fractal poverty traps, *World Development*, in press.

Baulch, B. and Hoddinott, J. (2000) *Economic Mobility and Poverty Dynamics in Developing Countries* (London: Frank Cass).

Baumol, W. J. (1986) Productivity growth, convergence, and welfare: What the long-run data show. *American Economic Review*, 76, pp. 1072–85.

Carter, M. R. (1997) Environment, technology and the social articulation of risk in West African Agriculture, *Economic Development and Cultural Change*, 45, pp. 557–90.

Carter, M. R. and Barrett, C. B. (this issue), The economics of poverty traps and persistent poverty: an asset-based approach, *Journal of Development Studies*.

Carter, M. R. and May, J. (2001) One kind of freedom: the dynamics of poverty in post-apartheid South Africa, *World Development*, 29, 1987–2006.

Deininger, K. and Okidi, J. (2003) Growth and poverty reduction in Uganda, 1992–2000: panel data evidence, *Development Policy Review*, 21, pp. 481–509.

Dercon, S. (2004) Growth and shocks: evidence from rural Ethiopia, *Journal of Development Economics*, 74, pp. 309–29.

Elbers, C., Gunning, J. W. and Kinsey, B. H. (2002) Convergence, shocks and poverty, Tinbergen Institute Working Paper.

Falaris, E. (2003) The effect of survey attrition in longitudinal surveys: evidence from Peru, Cote d'Ivoire, and Vietnam, *Journal of Development Economics*, 70, pp. 133–57.

Fratkin, E. and Roth, E. A. (1990) Drought and economic differentiation among ariaal pastoralists of Kenya. *Human Ecology*, 18, pp. 385–402.

Freudenberger, K. S. (1998). USAID Landscapes Development Initiative project report.

Gamba, P., Jayne, T. and Mghenyi, E. (2004) Rural poverty dynamics, agricultural productivity and access to resources. Tegemeo Institute of Agricultural Policy and Development working paper.

Gunning, J. W., Hoddinott, J., Kinsey, B. and Owens, T. (2000) Revisiting forever gained: income dynamics in the resettlement areas of Zimbabwe, 1983–1997, *Journal of Development Studies*, 36, pp. 131–54.

Jalan, J. and Ravallion, M. (2002) Geographic poverty traps? A micro model of consumption growth in rural China, *Journal of Applied Econometrics*, 17, pp. 329–46.

Jalan, J. and Ravallion, M. (2004) Household income dynamics in rural China, in S. Dercon (Ed.) *Insurance Against Poverty* (Oxford: Oxford University Press).

Jayne, T. S., Yamano, T., Weber, M. T., Tschirley, D., Benfica, R., Chapoto, A. and Zulu, B. (2003) Smallholder income and land distribution in Africa: implications for poverty reduction strategies, *Food Policy*, 28, pp. 253–75.

Kenya Ministry of Planning and National Development (1998) *First Report on Poverty in Kenya*. Two Volumes, Central Bureau of Statistics, and the Human Resources and Social Services Departments, Nairobi, Kenya.

Krishna, A. (2003) Escaping poverty and becoming poor: Who gains, who loses, and why? accounting for stability and change in 35 North Indian villages, *World Development*, 32, pp. 121–36.

Krishna, A., Kristjanson, P., Radeny, M. and Nindo, W. (2004) Escaping poverty and becoming poor in twenty Kenyan villages, *Journal of Human Development*, 5, pp. 211–26.

Kristjanson, P., Krishna, A., Radeny, M. and Nindo, W. (2004) Pathways out of poverty in Western Kenya and the role of livestock, Working paper for the FAO Pro-Poor Livestock Policy Initiative.

Lybbert, T. J., Barrett, C. B., Desta, S. and Coppock, D. L. (2004) Stochastic wealth dynamics and risk management among a poor population, *Economic Journal*, 114, pp. 750–77.

Mango, N., Cheng'ole, J., Kariuki, G. and Ongadi, W. (2004) Social aspects of dynamic poverty traps: cases from Vihiga, Baringo and Marsabit Districts, Kenya. BASIS CRSP research report.

McPeak, J. (2003) Analyzing and addressing localised degradation in the commons, *Land Economics*, 79, pp. 515–36.

McPeak, J. G. and Barrett, C. B. (2001) Differential risk exposure and stochastic poverty traps among East African pastoralists, *American Journal of Agricultural Economics*, 83, pp. 674–79.

Minten, B. and Zeller, M. (2000) *Beyond Market Liberalization: Welfare, Income Generation and Environmental Sustainability in Rural Madagascar* (Aldershot, UK: Ashgate).

Mistiaen, J., Ozler, B., Razafimanantena, T. and Razafindravonona, J. (2002) Putting welfare on the map in Madagascar, Africa Region Working Paper 34, World Bank.

Moser, C. M. and Barrett, C. B. (2003) The disappointing adoption dynamics of a yield-increasing, low external input technology: the case of SRI in Madagascar. *Agricultural Systems*, 76, pp. 1085–1100.

Osterloh, S. (2004) Microfinance in adverse environments: the case of KDA in Kenya. M.S. thesis, Cornell University.

Place, F., Hebinck, P. and Omosa, M. (2003) Chronic poverty in rural Western Kenya: its identification and implications for agricultural development, Paper presented at Conference on Chronic Poverty, University of Manchester.

Pratt, D. and Gwynne, M. (1977) *Rangeland Management and Ecology in East Africa* (London: Hodder and Stoughton).

Programme Ilo (2002) Impact de la crise politique sur le bien-être des ménages: les résultats d'une évaluation par des focus groups communaux, Crise Politique policy brief no. 3.

Programme Ilo (2003) Bien-être et sécurité alimentaire: perceptions postcrise par des focus groups communaux, Juillet 2002, Policy brief Post-crise, no. 3.

Randrianjatovo, J.-F. (2004) Analyse descriptive de l'aspect qualitatif de la dynamique de pauvreté. FOFIFA report.

Ravallion, M. and Jalan, J. (1996) Growth divergence due to spatial externalities, *Economics Letters*, 53, pp. 227–32.

Quah, D. (1996) Twin peaks: growth and convergence in models of distribution dynamics, *Economic Journal*, 106, pp. 1045–55.

Rosenzweig, M. R. and Binswanger, H. (1993) Wealth, weather risk and the composition and profitability of agricultural investments, *Economic Journal*, 103, pp. 56–78.

Sahn, D. E. and Stifel, D. C. (2000) Poverty comparisons over time and across countries in Africa. *World Development*, 28, pp. 2123–55.

Zimmerman, F. and Carter, M. R. (2003) Asset smoothing, consumption smoothing and the reproduction of inequality under risk and subsistence constraints, *Journal of Development Economics*, 71, pp. 233–60.

Persistent Poverty in North East Ghana

ANN WHITEHEAD

I. Introduction

This paper explores local poverty and wealth inequality in the Bawku District of the Upper East Region of northern Ghana in the period from 1975–89. This region has been one of the poorest for several decades: living standards, literacy levels, health and nutritional status are all very low and worse than the rest of the country. All the three Regions of Ghana's northern savannah contribute disproportionately to national poverty[1] and there have been a number of different approaches to the depth, persistence and causes of this poverty. Regional underdevelopment, low colonial and postcolonial state spending, high rates of labour migration, low underlying agro-ecological potential, lack of access to markets, diminishing rainfall and increasing environmental degradation have all been offered as explanations. This paper describes the historical background to the underdevelopment of Ghana's north and then situates the research site in southeastern Bawku within the region, emphasising the significant variability between different localities. Based on data collected from six contingent communities, the paper describes key household characteristics associated with poverty and security, changes in the wealth status of households between 1975 and 1989 and some household trajectories over this period. In exploring the nature of poverty dynamics, it makes three central arguments: first, that in this situation where land was not scarce, so that financial resources and labour were key factors in farming enterprises, the social management of household membership and labour was very critical; second, that this social management was not independent of wealth status, so that there was a virtuous circle between wealth and household labour supply and a vicious circle between poverty and small household size; and third, that poverty traps existed so that those with too little labour and too little wealth engaged in strategies which entrenched them in poverty.

II. Colonial and Post-Colonial Underdevelopment: The Bawku District in Ghana's North

Regional inequality in Ghana has long been and remains pronounced. Discussions of it are dominated by accounts of north–south differences – a discourse that has a geographical and political foundation (Ewusi, 1976; Shepherd and Gyimah-Boadi, 2004). Geographically, the low soil fertility and harsh climate of the savannah, marked by pronounced seasonality, a short growing season and periodic drought, are in profound contrast with the abundant natural fertility and rainfall of much of the south (Dickson and Benneh, 1988). The north–south discourse also has a clear political foundation in Ghana's pre-colonial, colonial and post-colonial history. Naturally less well-endowed than the ancient southern forest states and with economies markedly lacking in their complexity and surpluses, the Northern Territories were not brought under British colonial government until 1902 (Lund, 2003; Roncoli, 1994). Scholarly accounts of early colonial policy cite the very limited investment in the Northern Territories (Staniland, 1975; Bening, 1976; Lentz, 1998), but differ in evaluating these policies as benign neglect or the deliberate creation of a source of migrant labour to the farms and mines of the south (Plange, 1979; van Hear, 1982; Konigs, 1986). Despite this underdevelopment, there were nevertheless economic and other impacts throughout the north. Economic policies in the first decades of the twentieth century concentrated on trade, which included controlling and enhancing revenues from the north (Saharan) to south (forest region) trade routes and encouraging local trade through a vast extension of market places and greater integration of markets (Whitehead, 1996; Chalfin, 2004). Many farmers in the Bawku District introduced groundnuts to their farming cycles from the 1930s on and these were almost exclusively traded (White, 1956; Whitehead, 1996). Both Bawku District and Bawku town, which were crisscrossed with existing trade routes, benefited from these spurs to trade and markets and attracted many immigrants from nearby Togo and Burkina Faso (Chalfin, 2004).

Contrasting agro-ecological constraints gave rise to rather different colonial trajectories in the northern Regions, most starkly shown in the evolution of very different population densities. The Upper East is the driest and most prone to drought, but also had somewhat better soil fertilities and an abundance of rivers and streams and became much more densely settled than the remainder of the north. Its high population densities exacerbated the underlying proneness to periodic food insecurity, borne out when the Region suffered a severe and widespread famine in 1946–47 (Devereux, 1993; Roncoli, 1994). However, another key feature has been the marked variation between the localities of the Upper East in the levels of population density and land availability.[2] The Bawku District remained a food surplus area much longer than other more densely populated neighbouring Districts and sold cereals to them at times of food shortage (Roncoli, 1994; Whitehead, 1996). When a mixed farming scheme was set up in the 1940s, introducing bullock ploughing and expanding groundnuts as a cash crop, the Bawku District, with its existing experience of trading groundnuts and areas of land abundance, had the highest take-up rate (Whitehead, 1996). Another indicator of variability in levels of impoverishment, of land availability and of economic opportunity is to be found in the rates and character of labour migration. The more heavily populated areas of the region around Bolgatanga became sources of seasonal labour for southern cocoa farms from very early on (Fortes, 1971; Hart, 1971). High rates of migration from the Bawku District did not begin to show up in census records until 1960, when population pressure leading to land and environmental degradation in some communities resulted in food insecurity (Cleveland, 1980; Roncoli, 1994). By the time of Ghana's independence in 1957, Upper East communities had been very differentially placed to take advantage of new opportunities for income and for limited technological and agricultural innovation.

The research communities are some 20 miles southeast of Bawku town and were predominantly farming villages. They are all within reasonable walking distance of Garu, a large village that lies straddled across the dirt road south from Bawku, which provides alternative access to the Northern Region. Garu is the main market and service centre for this area. (See Figure 1 for a map of the region.)

The Tempane Gagbiri communities had been well placed to benefit from the limited state spending of the Nkrumah government. The Bawku District is ethnically mixed, composed of Kusasi and Mamprussi, as well as ethnic groups from Burkina Faso and Togo. Kusasi political leaders had supported the Convention People's Party (CPP) in the run up to independence, in opposition to their historic enemies, the Mamprussi (Davis, 1984), who like most traditional state societies in the north,

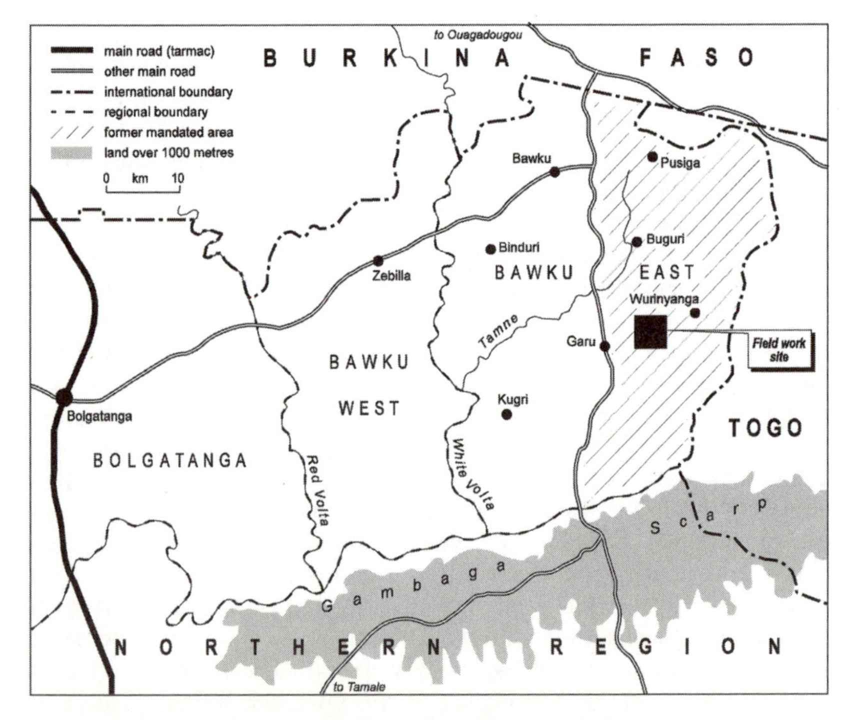

Figure 1. Bawku map, with research site

supported the Northern People's Party (NPP).[3] The research communities were composed of mainly Kusasi households, who had provided most of the chiefs and headmen when the CPP formed the first Ghana government. Although the agricultural policies of the Nkrumah government did very little to improve livelihoods in the Bawku District, independence did bring some state spending, especially on education, on roads and on local administration. In Tempane Gagbiri, this government spending had improved school enrolment, opened up some labouring jobs and brought new money into the local economy from wages and salaries. Access to ploughs, through the Kusasi Agricultural Development Cooperative, established in 1952 with a large grant from the National Agricultural Loans Scheme, had been particularly important (Dickson, 1972; Benneh, 1973; Devereux, 1989; Whitehead, 1996). Together with better roads and transport and locally generated income for investment, this allowed some families to expand their farming and trading in the early years of independence.

III. Research in 1975 and the 1989 Follow Up

This limited economic development was cut short as the national economy soon began a period of slow and painful decline, depressing local markets and creating inflation and consumer shortages. When I undertook anthropological fieldwork in the area between 1974 and 1976, the rhythm of household economies revolved around the farming cycle. Millets and sorghums were the main cereal crops, with groundnuts and rice, beans, some cotton and vegetables grown for sale. Compound households were built with a permanently cultivated and manured field around the house and had 'away' fields that needed to lie fallow to regain their fertility. Although studies elsewhere in the Bawku District have shown that increasing population pressure had resulted in loss of fallowing (Cleveland, 1980, 1981; Roncoli, 1994), it was still being practised on a reduced scale in Tempane Gagbiri. Sufficient land had been available for the approximately one-third of household heads that had invested in their own ploughs and ploughing cattle to increase their farm sizes.

Farming took place during a single rainy season that normally lasted between six and seven months. Farming was rain-fed, consequently yields were very variable year to year, and rainfall could be too sparse or too maldistributed to grow and harvest enough cereals. Prices of cereals in local markets showed a sharp annual cycle, rising steeply during the hungry season before crops were harvested, with the extent of the rise a good indicator of the success, or otherwise, of the previous harvest. Only a minority of households aimed to meet all their food needs through consuming their own production and food shortfall was met by investing in and then later selling small livestock and increasingly using the income from cash-crops to buy food staples. (Whitehead, 1989).[4] The area also offered some limited opportunities for off farm income. The farming system and household livelihood strategies contained many adaptations to risks and low economic potential, including labour migration for young to middle aged men. In 1975, two thirds of households had at least one adult male away on labour migration.

This paper is based on the original fieldwork and a 1989 restudy, which traced the links back to the earlier households. In 1975 I had collected qualitative data and carried out quantitative surveys in six communities, totalling 404 households.

The restudy was specifically designed to compare the poverty and well-being of the set of households first surveyed in 1975 and collected quantitative data from a sample of 136 households. There were about 10 per cent more households in 1989 than in 1975: some of these had moved in and others were sons or brothers of 1975 household heads who had built new compounds. There were only nine households of the over 400 present in 1975 whose fate was not known in 1989. This paper looks at male headed households only: 378 out of 404 surveyed households in 1975 and 127 out of 136 surveyed households in 1989. Female headed households were not only statistically rare, but their profile of economic activities and farming differed markedly from that of male headed households as did the dynamics of household change.[5] In the discussion that follows the longitudinal component consists of two quantitative snapshots taken at different times, with the known linkages between households providing the potential to examine changes in poverty status and qualitative accounts of individual household trajectories.

A number of significant changes had affected Tempane Gagbiri between the two study years. By the early 1980s Ghana's economic decline had become a full-blown crisis that had precipitated a change of government in 1979 and had been accentuated by a national drought in 1983–84. Economic reforms comprising structural adjustment introduced by the Rawlings government included many measures that were bound to impact negatively on the Upper East, such as the removal of agricultural subsidies. Tempane farmers interviewed in 1989, who said that things had got very much worse over the previous five years, complained that poverty, hunger and the problems of farming had increased. They also said the rainy season had 'got shorter', that rains were more unpredictable, that the land was 'exhausted' and that yields were 'declining'. My investigations suggested that fertiliser use had declined as prices had leapt, that millet yields had declined and that farmers were having to go further and further afield to find bush land (Whitehead, 1996). Rainfall data from the whole Bawku District found mean amounts to have fallen over for the 30-year period from 1961 to 1990 compared with the previous thirty years (Ofori-Sarpong, 2001). The most important agricultural innovation between the two study years had been market led: farmers had begun to grow significant amounts of onions in stream beds during the dry season, which were traded and conveyed by lorry to Southern Ghana.

IV. Socio-economic Inequality and Household Labour Supply

Visible levels of socioeconomic inequality were quite marked in 1975. Walking around the area in the dry season soon revealed a contrast between small dilapidated compounds containing little by way of obvious stored crops, economic activity or livestock, and large well kept households, with several granaries and a livestock herd containing small cattle as well as goats and sheep. Buzzing with many economic activities, visitors came and went all day in these households, especially if one of the wives had brewed beer, when her yard would be filled with noisy conversation and a heaped stack of visitors' bicycles. Underpinning these conspicuous differences was a considerable range in the amount of land being farmed by individuals and households. Fields were only measured in one of the six communities and only in 1975. Amounts of land farmed can be quite high (Table 1) – certainly for rainfed

Table 1. Land inequality in 1975: farm sizes of Tempane male household heads

Acreage	No. Households	%
Under 5	11	21
5.1–10	24	46
10.1–20	9	17
20.1–40	7	13.5
40+*	1	2
Totals	52	99.5

*Actually 55 acres.

farming system – and higher than the average figures for Bawku as a whole (Whitehead, 1996). Almost half of household heads (46 per cent) farm between five and ten acres; one-third of household heads farm more than ten acres and one-fifth of household heads farm less than five acres. The total land base of households is known in only a very small number of erratic cases.[6] These suggest that: (a) there can be large differences in the total amount of land farmed by households; (b) adult married male dependents can also be farming extensively; (c) there is little regularity in the relation between the amount farmed by household heads and the additional land farmed by other adult males; and (d) that the amounts of male land farmed per adult capita ranges widely.

The range of possessions that most people owned was very limited. Only a few of these were sufficiently durable, valuable and resalable to constitute savings or liquid assets. These include poultry, small and large livestock and ploughs, zinc roofs, bicycles and radios. My investigation of economic inequality centred on the extent of the household head's livestock as the key measure of current savings easily available for investments and emergencies. There are some weaknesses in the data available to measure household resources. I have information on the livestock and poultry of household heads, but not for other household members, who did also own livestock and poultry, although to a much lesser extent. A point value was assigned to each kind of livestock on the basis of their local prices (see appendix) and used to calculate the livestock points of the head of the household. The decile distribution of these is shown in Table 2. At the lower end of the scale household heads owned very little. A household head with one livestock point had some poultry, or a goat and a few poultry; someone with seven livestock points owned less than ten sheep or goats and poultry; anyone with ploughing bullocks had at least 14 livestock points. Although the amount of livestock owned remains modest until the top percentiles, there was significant inequality in both 1975 and in 1989. In 1975 the top 10 per cent of households had a mean livestock points four times greater than the other 90 per cent of the population. Similarly, comparing the livestock means of the bottom 50 per cent with the top 10 per cent, in both 1975 and 1989 the top 10 per cent had 22 times as many. An asset index was derived from adding the livestock points to the points assigned to the household's zinc roofs, ploughs and bicycles and Table 2 also shows the decile distribution of this indicator.

This information on differences in livestock owned and land farmed by male household heads raises acutely a problem posed with particular force by Hill in her

Table 2. Mean livestock and asset points male household heads: 1975 and 1989

	Livestock points		Asset points	
Decile	1975	1989	1975	1989
10.00	0.420	0.105	0.765	0.245
20.00	1.145	0.900	1.145	1.530
30.00	2.505	1.705	2.645	2.645
40.00	3.387	2.645	4.305	4.000
50.00	7.105	4.533	7.723	6.505
60.00	12.145	8.550	14.005	12.005
70.00	18.766	14.745	21.800	21.085
80.00	27.024	24.645	30.530	31.245
90.00	38.13	36.275	42.445	50.950
100.00	148.55	97.25	175.00	152.00

study of an agricultural community in Northern Nigeria (1972). Land scarcity in rural Kano was not a problem, but measuring poverty by the extent of food insecurity there were quite big differences between households. Wealth and poverty were associated with the size of households and households went through cycles of economic well-being and poverty as they grew and waned through the developmental cycle. Male labour was extremely important in the farming cycle in Northern Nigeria, with women also playing a part in production. Hill drew attention to family labour as a key asset and the locally specific ways in which household form affected its labour supply. Fathers and sons worked together through a specific form of domestic economic organisation, gandu labour, and obligations between a father and his adult married son(s) centred on common household residence. The normative composition of Hausa households was a three generational one, and the developmental cycle of these households included a phase of fission that occurred at some point after the father's death, and not on a son's marriage. The wealth of most households increased with the age of the head, but the new households formed by sons after a father's death shared out his resources and hence were no longer wealthy. Although Hill identified several ways in which households escaped poverty – by improving the household labour supply, by hiring on the local labour market and exploiting relations between rich and poor households in other ways – her core argument was that economic inequality between households was not inherited because of the central role of demographic and resource dispersal after a household head had died. Clough contains a detailed refutation of Hill's analysis suggesting that in the dispersal phase of households sharing between sons did not reduce the land holdings of the sons of rich fathers down to the smaller amounts which sons inherited from poor fathers (1995).

To explore the same issues in Tempane Gagbiri, male headed households were divided into three different poverty categories on the basis of the distribution of livestock points. The division into poverty categories was based solely on features of the distribution shown in Table 2 and does not refer to any other aspect of the households, such as whether they are food secure or insecure, or whether they are plough owning or not. Approximately the top 10 per cent of the population were, in local terms, considerably better off than the rest of the population. In 1975, there is a major jump in the mean livestock points of the penultimate decile – at 38 – to the mean for the last decile, which is 148 and there is a similar steep jump in 1989. The break between the 'secure' poverty category and the 'vulnerable' is put at households with livestock points over 35 and up to 200. At the other end of the scale was a minority of households that were effectively without resources. These 'destitute' households had one livestock point and below and usually had just a few hens. The much larger middle rank of 'vulnerable' households had livestock points between 1.1 and 35.

The numbers and proportions in each category are shown in Table 3. 12.4 per cent of the 1975 research population was destitute, 74.9 per cent of households were in the vulnerable category and 12.7 per cent of the population were secure. In 1989 the proportion that was destitute had grown to 21.9 per cent, the vulnerable were 68 per cent and the secure were 10.2 per cent. No attempt has been made to calculate the per capita livestock holdings of households, not least because information is confined to those claimed by the household head.

The most significant difference between these three poverty categories was household size. The Upper East is part of a large belt of West African Savannah societies in which domestic production units and reproducing units are nested within compound structures formed around a core of agnatically related men. Inheritance, kinship affiliation and social identity are patrilineal and wives moved to live in their husbands' compounds and communities on marriage. The normative Kusasi household developmental cycle was one in which, because groups of sons had remained living with their fathers once they had married, it was not uncommon for married brothers also to remain living together after their father's death. Households could have several adults living in them and these adults included closely related married and single men, as well as polygamously married wives and the elderly widows of former male household members. This complex compound was an asset holding and cooperative work unit, although its physical, economic and social organisation allowed for the possibility of overlapping circles of individual and collective responsibilities (Whitehead, 1981, 1996). As a result, living units accommodated married couples living together within the same compound, so that some compounds attained a large size. In this study, because farming was organised by compound heads who also owned and managed livestock, the term household refers to the full nested set of units that comprise a compound. Rarely in 1975 and slightly more often in 1989, the constituent units could decide not to farm together under the household head, but to become separate farming units within the compound.

Table 3. Distribution and resources of poverty categories 1975 and 1989

	Distribution		Mean livestock points		Mean asset points	
Poverty categories	1975	1989	1975	1989	1975	1989
Destitute	12.4%	21.9%	0.23	0.19	0.47	1.62
Vulnerable	74.9%	68.0%	11.94	11.55	13.48	15.66
Secure	12.7%	10.2%	58.55	59.41	64.19	81.72

The median number of people per household in 1975 was 9.7, while in 1989 it was 12.05. In 1975, although a majority of households clustered around 5 to 15 persons (about 60 per cent), one quarter of households had four or fewer members, while one in 10 had over 15 persons. There were 73 people in the largest household. By 1989 households had got on average larger, with a doubling of the numbers of households with over 15 members. In each year approximately 40 per cent of landlords were living with married sons or married brothers, while those living with unmarried adult sons or brothers were 19 and 29 per cent respectively.[7] Polygamy was another source of household members, with the numbers of wives per married men 1.5 and 1.6 respectively in 1975 and 1989. Birth rates and infant mortality rates were high, so that individual mothers had a wide range of living children.

The size of these complexly organised households was a key factor associated with socio-economic differentiation and poverty. Table 4 shows a positive relationship between greater wealth, measured by the livestock held by the household head, and larger household size. In 1975, the average total size of secure households was three times as high as the destitute group and in 1989 nearer four times as high (14.75 compared with 4.95 and 6.85 compared with 24.15). The differences between the vulnerable and the destitute were smaller, but they are nevertheless noteworthy. In 1975 the ratio of household size of vulnerable households compared to destitute households was 1.75 and in 1989 it was 1.6 (8.76: 4.95 and 5.16: 3.06). In both years the mean household size for the most economically secure group is high – at 14.75 in 1975, and an astonishing 24.15 in 1989.

A number of investigations were undertaken with respect to the influence of numbers of children, of the elderly and the balance between men and women on household poverty status. These suggest that current available male labour per non productive household member was not a critical difference between the resource secure and poorer sets of households. Absolute size and the number of men, married women and adult women, excluding mothers, were all positively associated with the increasing economic security of households in both years. In Table 4, the mean number of adult men per household goes up from 1.47, through 2.18 to 3.48 through the poverty categories in 1975, and from 1.57 through 2.45 to 4.92 in 1989. Although they had greater numbers of men in absolute terms, the economically better off households had relatively less male labour power per child, and per female household member. It was household size that was positively associated with socioeconomic standing.

Table 4. Household size and household memberships by poverty category 1975 and 1989

	Total household size		No. adults		No. adult men	
Poverty category	1975	1989	1975	1989	1975	1989
Destitute	4.95	6.85	3.06	3.39	1.47	1.57
Vulnerable	8.76	10.85	5.14	5.43	2.18	2.45
Secure	14.75	24.15	9.07	12.38	3.48	4.92
All	9.7	12.05	5.2	6.3	2.2	2.9

V. The Social Management of Households and Family Labour

A link between larger household size and better endowments is reported elsewhere in the West African savannah (Toulmin, 1992) and described in Ghana's Upper East by Fortes (1949). Tallensi adult married sons remained living and farming with their fathers until he died and then formed new households (Fortes, 1958). A similar process was found in Binduri by Roncoli (1994), but in Tempane Gagbiri, fission into new households occurred much later, with married brothers remaining together after their father had died.

Illustration 1 – Not enough sons – cannot solve his problems: In 1975, Abagare was the head of an economically secure household, farming large tracts of land and owning a plough, a horse, three bullocks, a bicycle, five other cattle, three pigs and 18 sheep and goats. His married junior brothers farmed with him, working on their private farms in the afternoons. Abagare complained that he had given birth to all daughters. His brother had a son of labour age, but he was attending school. Three foster sons provided additional labour, as did communal labour parties which had brought in 68 men-day's work in the previous farming season.

By 1989 their economic fortunes had gone steadily downhill: they were unable to farm all their land and they were disposing of substantial numbers of livestock. Abagare, aged between 70–80, was still living with his two junior brothers, although each was farming separately. There was no other adult male labour in the household. There were 14 children aged under 14 and two of the brothers had adult sons working in the South. Their millet yields were modest, but not extremely low. The junior brothers had no livestock, while the landlord had one cow and seven sheep and goats. In the previous year Abagare had sold a cow for hungry season food and a goat and a sheep to pay for an operation; his junior brother had killed goats for his wife's funeral and had sold a horse to buy millet, to meet substantial hospital expenses for his wife and for house repairs.

In 1989, the brothers had more land than they could farm and Abagare's earlier efforts to make up the labour shortfall, through fostering and communal labour, had not succeeded in staving off declining fortunes. Although Abagare's explanations used the language of demography ('too many daughters', 'too few sons') there are more complex issues in play. Household livestock resources were being used up very quickly, often in response to events such as illnesses, deaths, or thunderstorm damage, but the question of why two married sons had not returned from working away begs to be answered.

In 1975, Azong was in a very similar situation to Abagare: married four times, even so he had very few sons. He had added a 'servant' and a junior brother's son to his household male labour, he had developed cooperative farming relations with close kin living nearby, and had called several communal labour parties. He had also pursued a successful policy of diversification, for himself and for his wives and the unmarried sons and daughters in his house, investing in their education and giving them scope and start-up capital for independent income generation. His senior wife was one of the most economically active women in Tempane Natinga and Azong freely admitted that the household depended upon her earnings and those of his other wives during the lean period. In 1989 the household economic position was unchanged. Azong had recently provided land for a son who had returned from labour migration and encouraged his 'private' income generation, while the range and depth of his wives' economic activities remained important. Azong provides an example of a successful economic manager. Fathers and senior brothers as household heads wanted to keep their married sons and brothers within the house and these relations had to be socially and economically managed. A senior who was 'too strict' or did not allow 'enough time for our private farming' risked that 'junior' men might 'escape' to the south or move to build out. In Azong's case, his own intermittent income from carpentry might have helped his strategies to invest in his household 'dependants', but it was also by responding judiciously and flexibly to their individual aspirations that he had secured their commitment to household farming and a relatively economically and socially viable household. In contrast, Abagare appears to have been a poor manager: perhaps he was a comparatively inactive or uninterested farmer, or perhaps not very entrepreneurial, or unable to manage his social ties.

VI. Poverty Trends and Poverty Dynamics

Three kinds of data provide information about poverty trends and dynamics: direct comparisons between the distribution of resources (Tables 2 and 3), a poverty matrix to show whether and how households have changed their poverty status and qualitative case examples of household trajectories. Table 5 shows the changes in poverty status of all those households that we were able to track of the 1989 random sample of 136 male-headed households – about 80 per cent.[8]

Seventy of the households (62 per cent) were in the same poverty category in 1989 as they had been in 1975 with most stability in the vulnerable households. Two-thirds of the 1975 destitute have moved up into the vulnerable category, but most movement has been in the secure category, where more than four-fifths have moved down into the vulnerable or destitute category. The dynamics in Table 5 suggest a definite but slight decline in wealth holdings: of the 43 (38 per cent) households that have changed their poverty status over that period, 15 have moved up and 28 have moved down confirming a trend visible in Table 3.

Table 5 suggests the need to look more closely at the two ends of the poverty continuum, where there is most movement. Within those that were destitute in 1975, a majority had moved up into the vulnerable category in 1989, although there is a significant invisible category of 1975 destitute households that have died out completely. The greatest visible dynamic has been at the other end of the scale:

Table 5. Changes in poverty status between 1975 and 1989: male headed households from 1989 random sample

1975–1989	Destitute	Vulnerable	Secure	Totals
Destitute	5	14	3	22
Vulnerable	9	59	11	79
Secure	0	6	6	12
Totals	14	79	20	113

remaining secure seems quite difficult, with only 30 per cent of the 1975 secure also secure in 1989, when they made up 50 per cent of the total of secure households, with another 50 per cent that have moved up from the vulnerable category.

VII. Becoming and Being Destitute

The 1989 destitute comprise about one-third households who were destitute in 1975 and the remainder are households who have moved into destitution, mainly from being vulnerable. The three households that have moved from being secure to destitute arise out of special circumstances, since they are a result of headmen's or chief's households, which had been large and secure in 1975, splitting up into subunits of brothers, when the office holder had lost their political positions. Holding minor political office had contributed to wealth in Tempane Gagbiri communities, but over the long term, politics was also a source of shocks and the position of the adult male dependants in these households had become insecure. The economic basis of political households such as these was complex, but they had often been heavily hierarchical, with junior married men at the beck and call of the powerful senior, who kept resources tightly under his control. When these households split, as political fortunes waned, resources were rarely shared out. The economic well-being of the new units depended very much on the extent to which their heads had been able to build up an independent economic portfolio within the original household.

Of the 1975 vulnerable, 14 out of 79 (18 per cent) have dropped into destitution. Some downward spirals into destitution had occurred when household savings were insufficient to deal with what were fairly ordinary kinds of shock such as illness and death.

Illustration 2 – Apillu's decline into destitution: In 1975, Apillu then in his 40s, headed a household composed of two married brothers, each with one wife and he had three youngish children. Apillu had been away on labour migration in the south of Ghana and had come back some years before. The household had assets in the form of two adult cattle, one sheep, two goats, seven chickens and a dog. Apillu had cultivated four fields, two to grow millet and one each for groundnuts and rice as cash crops; he had gone out to about six labour parties during the farming season and had called three in return to work on his farms. Someone had ploughed for him and he had repaid the ploughing-team owner in labour-days. His previous year's food supply had lasted only nine months and then he sold off some goats bit by bit for millet.

By 1989, the household was very small, composed of Apillu, his wife and a daughter aged 17. They had no livestock and much land was being left fallow, as Apillu had a paralysed arm and leg and had 'hardly been able to farm.' He had no money or resources to call communal labour, or to hire it, or indeed to buy millet. Instead he had incurred debts for food and had borrowed seed as they had eaten all the previous year's groundnuts. 'I have no money to buy millet, it was only my wife who sells water. When she had money at the end of the day she bought just a little for consumption, I actually starved during the hungry season.'

Apillu's trajectory shows how a poor and vulnerable household can be precipitated into destitution by an extreme form of illness shock. In 1975, he was a young household head with no senior relatives either in the house, or living nearby, and a limited labour supply. His farming and the whole domestic economy were on a modest scale and he had a shortfall in his annual staple requirements. About five years after this he had spent three months in hospital, using up most of their animals to pay for treatment, while others had been stolen whilst he was away. After he had become disabled, the household had become increasingly destitute in a slow downward spiral. His brother had moved out to live and work in Garu and they had heard nothing from the oldest child, a son, who had left for work in Cote d'Ivoire in 1987. Apillu was 'hardly able to farm', being 'kept alive' by his wife and daughter's work selling bags of water in Garu market.

Children and adults in Tempane Gagbiri were frequently ill and health shocks to household members were made more severe by the poor medical services. The generally high levels of illness and disease pulled down aggregate agricultural production, but had a range of effects at the household level. Larger and more well resourced households were able to carry an adult ill during the farming season, but small households lost much needed food production. Illness episodes could become catastrophic for vulnerable households with low levels of assets. As well as lacking any senior relatives living near to him, a significant feature of Apillu's circumstances was that he had become a household head at a young age. Men who had the misfortune to become household heads at a young age (under 40) found it difficult to hold on to or manage their livestock and community and kinship relations and the mean age of destitute households was younger than other poverty categories.

VIII. Poverty Traps

Illustration 2 also shows some of the very poorest caught in poverty traps: they were engaged in strategies to cope with poverty that further entrenched them in poverty (Gore, 2003). Selling bags of water on market days was the most graphic instance of one such trap – working for very poor returns to labour in activities with no start-up costs. A common poverty trap occurred when men and women worked for others, leaving their own farms uncultivated or poorly weeded. Tempane Gagbiri communities were crisscrossed by an enormously complex web of labour transactions between households that arose out of socio-economic inequality, as well as contributing to it. Small or poorly resourced households used a good deal of their labour working for others, either because they were working off debts, or because they hired themselves out for 'by day' (wage) farm work, or by going out to many labour parties. With no, or extremely restricted, access to formal credit, most people turned to relatives and neighbours to borrow for a wide range of purposes: to farm, (for seeds or for ploughing and by women for hiring labour), for hungry season food and for a whole range of household emergencies. Such debts were often repaid in labour.

Labour debts and other changes in labour use had also become more important with the rise of bullock plough technology, used mainly for ridging the land for planting, which allowed households to cultivate much more land. Although only a minority of households had them (one third in 1975; slightly more in 1989) ploughs were widely used beyond this and plough owners benefited from a variety of hiring arrangements. These included hiring the ploughing team out in return for labour days and many 'helping' arrangements where the fields of kinsmen, in-laws, and occasionally neighbours were ploughed 'for free'. These often also resulted in returned labour days. Further labour effects were the knock-on demand for male hand hoe weeding labour and women's planting and harvesting labour. As well as increasing incentives for heads to find ways to keep adult men within households, these demands had led to an expanded use of labour parties and 'by-day' hiring. 'Communal labour', where a farmer brought together a group of relatives and neighbours to work for a day in return for food drink, cigarettes and kola, was widespread, not only for men's weeding, but also for women's planting and harvesting work. These labour parties were far from reciprocal, with some farmers calling in many more man-days to their farms and other farmers going out for a large numbers of days to work in such parties.[9] Plough owners tended to use the community's labour supply disproportionately through making considerable use of labour parties. Going out to many communal labours, or by day work, could also be a poverty trap for the poorest households.

Illustration 3 – Farming curtailed by labour debts and 'by-day' farm labour: In 1989 Akakeeb, who was between 45 and 50 years of age, had no other adult males living in a household that included his wife, six children and his mother. He was a returned labour migrant and had several brothers and sons working away. He had fallowed some land and had farmed three fields, two of staples and one of dry season onions. He had bought additional millet during the year using income from selling his onions and also from going out to 'by-day' labour. He had done some 51 days waged work and a few days for a close patrilineal relative, who had ploughed for him. Owning only two sheep and one chicken, he had borrowed money to repair his house and to buy medicines and food.

Akakeeb is just over the line between destitute and vulnerable households, but he has hardly any savings to smooth out essential consumption. His main strategy for additional income is to work for others, which he is successfully doing, but he can only do this while he remains able bodied and energetic and as his strength declines, this may become a poverty trap. Some of the 1975 households that have moved out of destitution include young and able bodied heads that have used these work opportunities to build up some savings.

A final poverty trap was labour migration. All manner and kind of households, richer and poorer, small and large, had adult men working away, but the decision making processes and the effects of labour migration varied between households. In larger more well resourced households, with polygamous marriages and an age pyramid of sons, a succession of men could leave on labour migration and return without denuding the household of male family labour. Younger men in smaller, poorer households went off to work with reluctant permission, or with no permission at all, knowing that they were leaving their families in very vulnerable circumstances. In neither study year was labour migration a well-rewarded option, with many labour migrants struggling to survive themselves and unable to send remittances.[10] In poorer households labour migration gave some household members access to different livelihood options, but at the cost of reducing the security of those left behind. These labour migrants tended to stay away for longer and, as the home household declined, so there was less incentive to return.

This process, whereby the labour migration of adult male labour impoverished the households left behind, is one example of a negative feedback loop between poverty and smaller household size. Destitute households also included some with very elderly heads whose male family labour was all away on extended labour migration.

IX. The Vulnerable and Poverty Thresholds

'Vulnerable' households, who were neither 'destitute' nor 'secure,' were the largest category. Households at the bottom end of the asset range were hardly different from the destitute, but there was a fairly wide continuum from those with one or two goats and sheep to those with a few cattle, goats and sheep and a plough and ploughing bullocks. All these vulnerable households had too few resources to do other than adopt defensive strategies in the face of the multiple risks. Illness and disability were only one of a number of the regularly occurring, though unpredictable, potential shocks, which included animal theft, diseases and pests and rainstorm damage. A significant and recurring community level shock was the failure of rains, or their maldistribution, which undermined food security and reduced farm incomes. Animals were regularly sold to meet food shortfall, although by 1989 increased cash cropping was being used to buy staple food. Communities and households were also subject to market shocks, being heavily dependent on prices received for a narrow range of crops and products and adversely affected by rises in fertiliser prices. Those who made petty incomes from trading also faced risks that the local market for particular goods and services could easily become saturated.

Vulnerable and secure households also differed in their off farm income sources. Recent literature emphasises the significance of off farm sources to African rural incomes (Barrett et al., 2001; Ellis, 1998; Reardon et al., 1998) frequently citing Reardon's finding that they make up around 47 per cent of rural income (Reardon, 1997). Many individuals in Tempane Natinga had economic activities other than growing crops. Non-farm incomes for women were usually beer brewing and petty trading, while men earned incomes by labouring 'by day', by forms of craft production, by casual or more formal forms of wage employment and by trading. While it is clear that entry costs to these activities varied considerably, as did returns to labour, this research has no solid information on what these were. Nevertheless, making and selling grass pads to cushion head loads was a very different scale of economic activity than sending a clutch of cattle on a lorry to the south of Ghana, or working as a well digger for the local council.

Although the diversification literature describes these off-farm incomes as responses to high levels of risk, Barrett et al. argue that risk mitigation 'cannot satisfactorily explain observed patterns of off farm activity' (2001: 322) and that those with the least agricultural assets and incomes 'are least able to make up the deficiency through off farm earnings' (2001: 324). The non-farm sector bifurcates into low-entry low-returns set and a high-entry higher-returns set that are survival strategies for some and accumulation strategies for others (Hussein and Nelson, 1998; Bryceson, 1999; Whitehead and Kabeer, 2001). Non-farm economic activities, with their different entry costs and returns, play different roles in richer and poorer rural households (see, for example, Dercon and Krishnan, 1996) and in the livelihood strategies of men and women (Whitehead and Kabeer, 2001).

The economic contribution of women to Tempane Gagbiri households had changed between 1975 and 1989. In both years most married women had small fields and grew rice and groundnuts, but the fields and the incomes realised were quite small.[11] In 1989 80 per cent of married women had annual incomes of less than 7,000 cedis (about 28–30 dollars) from such farming. Meanwhile, women's non-farm work had also increased.[12]

Illustration 4 – Women's non-farm incomes in a conservative farming household: In 1989, Atila who was over 65, had four fields, but was only growing millet on three, using the labour of his two wives, his son, and his son's two wives. Atila owned some small livestock, 11 sheep and goat, but had sold his last remaining cow to buy millet for two months during the hungry season. His married son Kwesi also grew some millet, as well as rice and groundnuts as cash crop and had gone out to five communal labour parties that year.

The off-farm incomes were brought in by the married women, although each of them was working on a very different scale. Kwesi's first wife was very active, brewing pito to buy clothes, some millet and soup ingredients. His second recently married wife was heavily pregnant and had done little independent work that season.

Both Atila's wives were in their 50s. Yawa, the younger, was mainly farming. She had called one communal labour party and used her farm income for soup ingredients, clothes, millet, and medicine and hospital costs. The elder, who grew only very small amounts of rice and groundnuts, sometimes went out 'to rich women' to 'help them a little for a little money to pay for soup ingredients.'

This pattern is typical of the vast majority of women's off farm incomes which were quite small and used for basic consumption, rarely enabling women to build up savings over a life time. There was, however, a small minority of women whose economic activities were on a much bigger scale. Six per cent of married women had incomes of between 60,000 and 70,000 cedis (between 240 and 300 dollars) per annum in 1989. These married women were all members of secure households in which men too had more income from off farm activities. It was only these households, as described below, that were able to go beyond consumption uses of the livestock herd or non-farm incomes and invest in accumulation strategies.

Savings in the form of livestock were potentially a source of working capital, but because of the high and multiple forms of risk, households with low levels of livestock endowment either did not have enough livestock resources to provide capital for farming, or were not able to risk running their livestock down. The breakpoint between the vulnerable and secure households observed in livestock endowments (Table 2) and used to assign to poverty categories may well represent a threshold between those who can use their livestock savings as productive capital and those that cannot (see also Dercon, 1998). The vulnerable represent a majority of Tempane Gagbiri households who, because of their poor resource endowments and the multiple risks in their physical and economic environments, have stabilised dynamically around exceedingly low levels of poverty.

X. Getting on: Searching for Security and Aspiring to Accumulate

By 1975 the Tempane Gagbiri communities had experienced a relatively long period of very slowly rising incomes, arising out of the introduction of plough technology, the growth of cash crops, limited new opportunities for education and formal employment and greater overall integration into the market. They were simultaneously experiencing a slow decline in the reliability and amount of rainfall and a reduction in available new land for farming. In 1975 and again in 1989, a small minority of households was much wealthier than the majority, although still quite poor by national standards. Locally these are households that 'can solve their problems'. It is these that have benefited from restricted access to these new opportunities, including public sector wage employment, which was highly prized because of the security and regularity of income. In 1975 6.9 per cent of male household heads and 4.1 per cent in 1989 combined wage employment with farming and they used their wages to invest in farming, including for labour. Others have benefited from access to ploughs and agricultural credit.

Illustration 5 – Akologo: an elder with two ploughs: In 1975, this was a large household built round a core of four married men who farmed together under the household head, Akologo, who was in his 60s. The household had a livestock herd, two ploughs and bullock teams and a bicycle. The huts in the compound had wooden doors and window frames, some had zinc roofs and four granaries stood outside it. Altogether there were 11 cattle and about 30 sheep and goats in this household and although Akologo had disposal rights over them all, some belonged to his junior brother Apaame. Akologo's main items of expenditure had been two bags of hungry season millet, animals for bridewealth and funerals, rafters for the new room of a son and school fees, school uniforms and medicine for the children. He had also bought plough parts, hoes, sacks and storage baskets.

Akologo, who had close agnatic links with numerous households in Tempane, was a highly respected elder and related to the chief. Akologo's household farming was not extensive consisting of only three fields of staple millets and beans comprising 7.6 acres. He had handed over one of his fields over to his wives and another to two unmarried sons who had returned from labour migration. The ploughs were also used on all the farms of the other men in the house and had been used to 'help' people outside the household. All the married men in his household had extensive independent farming and many of the women had heir own small farms and also brewed and traded. Apaame in particular was a farming and trading entrepreneur.

This household shows some of the key strategies identified earlier – use of bullock ploughs, investing in communal labour, women's non-farm incomes, the social management of dependents – but it also shows an interesting contrast between Akologo and his brother Apaame. Akologo was not a very active farmer and spent a good deal of his time on local kinship and community politics. The household was economically secure because of his management strategies: these had allowed for considerable independent economic activity of different adult married men and flexibility in the use of resources (for example, ploughs). The livestock herd had been important in other ways: as bridewealth for men in the house and in social and ritual activities which maintained the household's standing in the community. Akologo was able to pursue these strategies successfully because he and his brother had inherited a reasonable livestock herd and a plough. Apaame however had used these resources somewhat differently, developing his cattle trading slowly from the inherited stock and using this income for farming inputs, including mobilising considerable amounts of labour for his six fields of crops. He had notably also taken entrepreneurial risks in his farming: breeding pigs and investing in fruit trees. Trading and off-farm entrepreneurial activities were one recognised major route to farming investment. Apaame was also investing in the education of some of his sons, with one of them, Charles attending secondary school. By 1989 Apaame and Akologo had died. The new household was still large although there were now three farming separately units within it. One of these was headed by Charles who had inherited a plough and bullocks and livestock from his father. He too was a cattle trader and entrepreneurial farmer and he had also worked as an agricultural extension agent.

There is a strong positive feedback loop here between initial wealth endowments and long-established strategies for ensuring security and for limited accumulation that were well recognised within the communities. These depend on investing in entrepreneurial activities and managing a wide range of social and political relationships. In part these make up for a dearth of formal credit, always extremely limited in the Bawku District (Roncoli, 1994) and confined to the very limited agricultural innovation schemes, which recruited only a small minority of farmers. One such example is Atongi, who in 1975, farmed very seriously, growing 12 acres of food staples and 11 acres of groundnuts, rice and kenaf as cash crops. His livestock herd was not large and he relied instead on investing and re-investing in farming, partly through the market and partly through parastatals. He had begun his cash cropping through growing rice, basically in response to market demand, but had also taken advantage of the activities of extension agents from the mission-run agricultural station and state crop development boards to get inputs on credit and to introduce specific cash crops.

This household is a success story within the time span of my research in which Atongi's used his own physical strength and that of his wives and sons and limited credit to invest effectively in cash cropping. By 1989, his son had inherited 12 fields and his strategy was similar to his father's, investing in cash-crop farming, by getting inputs on credit or purchasing them out of crop income. He owed the Global 2000 scheme for two bags of fertiliser, but had also made a considerable outlay on hiring a plough and bullocks, on fertiliser, on bags and tools and on labour. He had also diversified: investing in a grinding mill and opening up a maize farm much further south that two of his wives had gone to farm.

Akologo and Atongi illustrate how investment and accumulation could occur, but they also emphasise the importance of initial resource endowments to take the risks involved. These endowments included savings in the form of livestock, physical strength and a favourable social and political network, including access to extension agents. Even so, these endowments and strategies did not guarantee success and the term 'secure' for these households in some senses is a misnomer: only about a third of 1975 secure households had remained secure in 1989 (Table 5). There are many risks in entrepreneurship and in this locality they include the difficulty of managing large households economically and socially. The ethnographic evidence suggests that household heads have to put in a good deal of daily effort to manage large households where many adult men and women have highly differentiated livelihood strategies. As individual sub units pursued different strategies, for example by investing heavily in off farm business, or by taking wage employment that required educational qualifications, they tended to farm separately.

XI. Persistent Poverty in North East Ghana: Concluding Remarks

In Ghana's Upper East, where levels of well-being are shockingly low and levels of poverty exceedingly high, poverty was persistent for a large proportion of households, with only a small minority having enough resources 'to solve their problems' and to invest. Historically, farming households had adopted new crops, had increasingly spent labour time on non-farm incomes and some had adopted new technologies leading to greater differentiation. Inequalities in the livestock assets of households were positively correlated with household size. Wherever possible household membership was managed and manipulated by household heads to produce larger households that were economically more secure. Their precise advantages probably lay in several different directions,[13] including more disciplined labour use, more intensive use of lumpy assets and different savings patterns. Important mechanisms linked household size to initial endowments. Households with more resources were better able to attract and retain household members and their greater wealth financed production activities for household members to spend their time on. Remaining secure however was not easy – as many households moved out of security as remained within in between 1975 and 1989. Entrepreneurial ventures failed, jobs and 'traditional' offices were lost, cattle died, people fell ill and household members found the discipline and thrift of good management hard to sustain.

The majority of vulnerable households had stabilised dynamically around exceedingly low levels of poverty. The dividing line between security and vulnerability is a heuristic one, but the 85–90 per cent of the households described here as vulnerable or destitute were smaller in size than the secure and their economic and social behaviours diverged. Illness, labour migration, consumption needs and farming inputs were resourced differently, they took up different positions in the labour relations between richer and poorer and had insufficient resources to invest in farming accumulation or to get into higher return non-farm activities. Women's non-farm incomes had become important in this group by 1989, but these were at only a low level of return for the time expended. Dependent on informal loans for farming inputs, to meet medical costs and small livestock for ceremonial kinship obligations, many such debts were paid off in the form of labour. While some vulnerable households had moved into security between 1975 and 1989, rather more had become destitute and there had been overall a slight but discernible downward shift in livestock assets. Livestock savings would, it can be conjectured, have declined even further were it not for the growth in the market for dry season onions, a crop that many households had added to their farming portfolios between 1975 and 1989.

Destitute households were small in size and their heads were either very elderly, or rather young. Some were trapped in poverty by having to work for very low returns or on other farms, so leaving their own fields uncultivated. Some of these households were also victims of a feedback loop between poverty and 'escaping' male dependents who 'ran away' and spent very long periods on labour migration, remitting little. The destitute households nevertheless included some that were able between 1975 and 1989 to climb into the vulnerable category. These are households headed by able bodied young men, who had worked exceedingly hard and been exceedingly lucky. Some destitute households had disappeared when some or all of their members had died and others had dispersed. These dynamics confirm the continuing significance of labour for using land resources in the period from 1975 to 1989, as does the network of labour transactions between households arising out of debt repayments, labour parties and by day hiring.

These findings suggest the urgent need to address regionally specific poverty traps. With such a high proportion of households in the Upper East in poverty, anti-poverty policy has to be based on geographic targeting rather than household targeting. Policy strategies also need to heed locally regarded significant pathways for agriculturally intensification and accumulation and the potential for expansion of meaningful rural employment. Because the area is relatively densely settled, rural health provision is likely to more cost effective here than in some other rural areas, leading to long-term beneficial effects. Yet, existing or incipient land pressure constrains the possibility of the Upper East benefiting from agricultural innovation based on extending cultivated areas, even though its farmers have adapted in numerous ways to opportunities as well as to agro-climatic and politically constructed risks.

Acknowledgement

The author gratefully acknowledges financial support from the ESRC (UK) for the 1975 fieldwork, ESCOR for the 1989 restudy and the British Academy for archival research (Whitehead, 1996). The author also thanks Elizabeth Harrison and Matthew Lockwood for assistance during this project and anonymous reviewers, the editors of this issue and Matthew Lockwood and Charles Gore for their comments on an earlier draft.

Notes

1. In the 1987–88 Ghana Living Standards Survey, Savannah households (the Northern, Upper West and Upper East Regions) had mean incomes of around 70 per cent of the national average. They made up over half of the national households in 'hard core' poverty, despite being only 12 per cent of Ghana's population. (Boateng et al., 1990). Later rounds show worsening Northern poverty (Ghana Statistical Service, 1995).
2. See Engmann 1975, Hilton 1968, Hunter 1967 and Cleveland 1981 for discussions of the population data for the Upper East.
3. The history of Mamprussi Kusasi relations which are one basis for present-day conflict in the Bawku area are described in Kelly 1974, Staniland 1975, Ladoucer 1979, Lund 2003.
4. Coping strategies adopted in another locality in Bawku District are described in Devereux 1989, 1991.
5. For discussions of gender relations and gender issues see Whitehead 1981, 1984, 1996.
6. I was not able to measure systematically the fields farmed by other male adults and by women household members.
7. These nested units are sometimes described as compounds in the West African savannah literature; I have called them households because of various features of their economic and social organisation and to correspond to local terminology. Veirich (1986) adopted the same usage in Burkina Faso.
8. Of the 136 households in the 1989 random sample the number of matched households was 113. Of the 23 households for which there are no matches, eight were not present in 1975, but had moved in by

1989, seven were households present in both 1989 and 1975, but missed in 1975 surveys and there were ten households for which there was not enough information.

9. Described in detail in Whitehead 1996. For elsewhere in West Africa see Saul 1983 and Geschiere 1995. See also Pottier's sustained account of work parties benefiting a rural elite that included local political officials and more commercial farmers in Zambia (Pottier, 1988).
10. An exception in 1989 was a few households who had educated sons and daughters in formal employment elsewhere who were more likely to send remittances to elderly parents.
11. Women's farming was not constrained because of their access to land, but because of their lack of resources for inputs.
12. Although women's' trading and petty income generation developed very early in Bawku town (Chaflin, 2004) and in some Frafra areas (Fortes 1971, Tripp 1978), they were slow to develop in the deep rural communities around Garu.
13. For an interesting discussion on a parallel theme see Lewis 1981.

References

Barrett, C. B., Reardon, T. and Webb, P. (2001) Off farm income diversification and household livelihood strategies in rural Africa: concepts, dynamics and policy implications. *Food Policy*, 26, pp. 315–31.

Bening, R. B. (1976) Colonial control and the provision of education in Northern Ghana, 1908–1951. *Universitas*, 5(2), pp. 58–99.

Benneh, G. (1973) Small-scale farming systems in Ghana. *Africa*, 43(2), pp. 134–46.

Boateng, E. O. et al. (1990) A Poverty Profile for Ghana 1987–88. World Bank Social Dimensions of Adjustment in Sub-Saharan Africa, Working Paper No. 5, Policy Analysis.

Bryceson, D. F. (1999) Sub-Saharan Africa betwixt and between: rural livelihood practices and policies. ASC working paper, No. 43, Africa Study Centre, De-Agrarianisation and Rural Employment Network, Leiden.

Chalfin, B. (2004) *Sheabutter Republic State: Power, Global Markets and the making of an indigenous commodity* (New York and London: Routledge).

Cleveland, D. A. (1981) Demographic change in Bawku District, Northeast Ghana: 1900 to 1978. Office of International Agricultural Programs and Department of Anthropology, University of Arizona, Tuscon.

Cleveland, D. (1991) Migration in West Africa: A Savannah village perspective, *Africa*, 61(2), 222–45.

Clough, P. (1995) The economy and culture of the Talakawa of Marmara, DPhil thesis, University of Oxford.

Davis, D. (1984) Continuity and change in Mampurugu: a study of tradition as ideology, PhD dissertation, Northwestern University.

Dercon, S. and Krishnan, P. (1996) Income portfolios in rural Ethiopia and Tanzania: choices and constraints, *Journal of Development Studies*, 32(6), pp. 850–75.

Dercon, S. (1998) Wealth risk and activity choice: cattle in Western Tanzania, *Journal of Development Economics*, 55(1), pp. 1–42.

Devereux, S. (1989) Household responses to food insecurity in North East Ghana, doctoral dissertation, Oxford University, Oxford.

Devereux, S. (1993) Goats before ploughs: dilemmas of household response sequencing during food shortages, *IDS Bulletin*, 24(4), pp. 52–9.

Dickson, K. B. (1972) Dynamics of agricultural innovation in Northern Ghana, *Ghana Journal of Social Science*, 2(2), pp. 212–27.

Dickson, K. B. and Benneh, G. (1988) *A New Geography of Ghana* (London: Longman).

Ellis, F. (1998) Household strategies and rural livelihood diversification, *Journal of Development Studies*, 35(1), pp. 1–38.

Ewusi, K. (1976) Disparities in levels of regional development in Ghana. *Social Indicators Research*, 3, pp. 75–100.

Fortes, M. (1949) *The Web of Kinship among the Tallensi* (London: Oxford University Press).

Fortes, M. (1971) Some aspects of migration and mobility in Ghana, *Journal of African and Asian Studies*, 6(1), pp. 1–20.

Geschiere, P. (1995) Working groups or wage labour? Cash-crops, reciprocity and money among the Maka of South Eastern Cameroon, *Development and Change*, 26(3), pp. 503–23.

Ghana Statistical Service (1995) Ghana Living Standards Survey Report on the Third Round (GLSS 3), Sept. 1991–Sept. 1992.

Gore, C. (2003) Globalization, the international poverty trap and chronic poverty in the least developed countries. Paper to Chronic Poverty Conference, University of Manchester.

Hart, J. K. (1971) Migration and tribal identity among the Frafra of Ghana, *Journal of Asian and African Studies*, 6(1), pp. 21–36.

Hill, P. (1972) *Rural Hausa: A Village and a Setting* (Cambridge: Cambridge University Press).

Hilton (1968) Population growth and distribution in the upper Regions of Ghana, in J. C. Caldwell and C. Okonjo (Eds) *The Population of Tropical Africa* (London: Longman).

Hunter, John M. (1967) Population pressure in a part of the West African savannah: A study of Nangodi, northeast Ghana, *Annals of the Association of American Geographers*, pp. 57, 101–14.

Hussein, K. and Nelson, J. (1998) Sustainable livelihoods and livelihood diversification. Working Paper 69, Institute of Development Studies, University of Sussex.

Kelly, R. (1974) Political consciousness and political parties in Northern Ghana, PhD thesis, University of Birmingham, Birmingham.

Konigs, P. (1986) *The State and Rural Class Formation In Ghana: A Comparative Analysis* (London: Routledge and Kegan Paul).

Ladouceur, P. A. (1979) *Chiefs and Politicians: The Politics of Regionalism in Northern Ghana* (London: Longman).

Lentz, C. (1998) The chief, the mine captain and the politician: legitimating power in northern Ghana, *Africa*, 68(1), pp. 46–67.

Lewis, J. V. D. (1981) Domestic labour intensity and the incorporation of Malian peasant farmers into localised descent groups, *American Ethnological Society*.

Lund, C. (2003) Bawku is still volatile: ethno-political conflict and state recognition in Northern Ghana, *The Journal of Modern African Studies*, 41(4).

Ofori-Sarpong, E. (2001) Impacts of climate change on agriculture and farmers' coping strategies in the Upper East Region of Ghana, *West Africa Journal of Applied Ecology*, 2, pp. 21–35.

Plange, Nii-k (1979) Underdevelopment in Northern Ghana: natural causes or colonial capitalism? *Review of African Political Economy*, 15/16, pp. 4–14.

Pottier, J. (1988) *Migrants No More: Settlement and Survival in Mambwe Villages, Zambia* (London: International African Institute).

Reardon, T. (1997) Using evidence of household income diversification to inform study of the rural non farm labour market in Africa, *World Development* 25(5), pp. 735–47.

Reardon, T., Stamoulis, K., Balisacan, A., Cruz, M. E., Berdegue, J. and Banks, B. (1998) Rural off farm income in developing countries, special chapter, in FAO, *The State of Food and Agriculture* (Rome: FAO).

Republic of Ghana Statistical Service (1989) Ghana Living Standards Survey First Year Report, Sept. 1987–Aug. 1986.

Roncoli, M. C. (1994) Managing on the margins: agricultural production and household reproduction in North Eastern Ghana, PhD dissertation, State University of New York at Binghamton.

Saul, M. (1983) Work parties, wages and accumulation in a Voltaic village, *American Ethnologist*, 10, pp. 77–96.

Shepherd, A. and Gyimah-Boadi, E. with Gariba, S., Plagerson, S. and Musa, A. W. (2004) Bridging the North South Divide in Ghana. Background Paper for WDR 2006 on Equity and Development.

Toulmin, C. (1992) *Cattle, Women and Wells: Managing Household Survival in the Sahel* (Oxford: Clarendon Press).

Tripp, R. B. (1978) Economic strategies and nutritional status in a compound farming settlement of Northern Ghana, PhD thesis, Columbia University.

Van Hear, N. (1982) Northern labour and the development of capitalist agriculture in Ghana, PhD thesis, University of Birmingham, Birmingham.

Vierich, H. (1986) Agricultural production, social status, and intra-compound relationships, in J. L. Moock (Ed.) *Understanding Africa's Rural Households and Farming Systems* (Boulder, CO: Westview).

White, H. P. (1956) Internal exchange of staple foods in The Gold Coast. *Economic Geography*, 32(2), pp. 115–25.

Whitehead, A. (1981) 'I'm Hungry Mum'; The politics of domestic budgeting in North East Ghana, in K. Young, C. Wolkovitz and R. McCullugh (Eds) *Of Marriage and the Market* (London: CSE Books).
Whitehead, A. (1984) Women and men: kinship and property: some general issues, in R. Hirschon (Ed.) *Women and Property – Women as Property* (London: Croom Helm).
Whitehead, A. (1989) The distributional effects of cash crop innovation: the peripherally commercialised farmers of Northeast Ghana, *IDS Bulletin*, 19(2), pp. 59–65.
Whitehead, A. (1996) Poverty in North East Ghana, Report to ESCOR, ODA.
Whitehead, A. and Kabeer. N. (2001) From uncertainty to risk: poverty, growth and gender in the rural African context. Working Paper No.134, Institute of Development Studies, University of Sussex.

Appendix. Weightings for assets

Livestock	Number of points
Ploughing cattle	7.0
Other adult cattle	4.0
Horses	2.0
Young cattle	1.5
Donkeys	1.5
Pigs	0.7
Sheep and goats	0.6
Fowl	0.035
Zinc roofs	4.0
Ploughs	2.0
Bicycles	2.0

Shocks and their Consequences Across and Within Households in Rural Zimbabwe

JOHN HODDINOTT

I. Introduction

In the last five years, researchers and policy makers have begun to consider poverty dynamics – as opposed to static representations of poverty status – in developing countries. This work is motivated in part by new empirical findings that stress that there can, in some societies, be a considerable amount of churning of households in and out of poverty with varying degrees of duration (Baulch and Hoddinott, 2000) and by findings that the temporary shocks that cause some households to fall into poverty can have permanent consequences if these shocks lead to irreversible asset losses. Dercon and Hoddinott (2004) and Barrett and McPeak (2005) review dimensions of this literature, with Barrett and McPeak (2005) noting that the micro-econometric evidence of poverty traps validates the hypotheses of Myrdal, Rosenstein-Rodan and others that different income-growth trajectories may arise given differences in initial asset endowments.

This literature on poverty dynamics has conceptual and empirical links to work on consumption smoothing (Deaton, 1991, 1992; Rosenzweig and Wolpin, 1993; Townsend 1994, 1995; Morduch, 1995; Jacoby and Skoufias, 1998; Rose, 1999;

Baulch and Hoddinott, 2000; Skoufias and Quisumbing, 2002; Harrower and Hoddinott, 2005). The churning of households in and out of poverty occurs because households are unable, or unwilling, to smooth consumption given income shocks. They may be unable because: (1) they lack assets that can be used to smooth out the consequences of these income shocks (Alderman and Paxson, 1992); (2) the price of the assets they hold plummets because, following an income shock, everyone tries to sell similar assets at the same time (Fafchamps and Gavian 1997); (3) the localities in which they live are characterised by incomplete financial markets for credit and/or insurance (Udry 1994); (4) private mechanisms such as gift exchange or remittances are insufficient to mitigate the income shock (Morduch 1999); and (5) public mechanisms such as cash or food transfers or public works schemes are insufficient to mitigate the income shock. However, it also reflects an unwillingness of households to sell assets given income shocks. Assets held at the household level often perform several functions; for example, they can be both a store of wealth *and* a means by which income is generated. Selling assets in response to shocks today risks permanently lowering future consumption. Given such a possibility, households may choose to 'smooth assets' rather than 'smooth consumption'. An older literature that focused on household behaviour under famine conditions made this point explicitly – while current circumstance might have been dire, to sell off the meagre assets a household possessed even when food consumption had fallen dramatically was to invite future destitution (Corbett, 1988; Devereux, 1993). Work by Fafchamps, Udry and Czukas (1998) implicitly supports this contention, finding that households do not draw down assets such as livestock holdings given in the face of income shocks. A limitation of this body of work, however, is the tendency to aggregate across households. As Zimmerman and Carter (2003) point out, the existence of poverty traps may induce differences in behaviour by asset levels. Households at the threshold of the poverty trap, or just below that threshold, may be far more reluctant to sell assets given an income shock. The first objective of this paper is to test empirically this proposition.

However, there are two limitations with much of the extant work on asset and consumption smoothing. First, the unit of analysis is almost always the household. Yet a growing body of evidence indicates that analysis of welfare at the household level can be a poor guide to the distribution of well-being within the household (Alderman, Chiappori, Haddad, Hoddinott and Kanbur, 1995; Haddad, Hoddinott and Alderman, 1997 and references therein). Applied here, variations in consumption may not be distributed equitably across all household members. Second, variations in consumption may have implications for health and nutritional status. Given the links between nutrition and productivity, see Behrman, Alderman and Hoddinott (2004) and Strauss and Thomas (1998), a distinction between 'asset' and 'consumption' smoothing may be too strong. Instead, the true distinction lies in households' choices regarding what type of capital – physical, financial, social, or human (and which human) – that they should draw down given an income shock. For example, if it is possible to draw down health stocks without incurring irreversibilities (that is, falling below some level of health stock from which it is impossible to recover, as in Dasgupta and Ray, 1986), this may be a rational strategy to follow. Note that how the household 'allocates' the shock amongst its members may be a function of individuals' relationships between health or human capital and productivity. Households may attempt to protect the health of the most 'productive' members in order to mitigate the impact of the shock on future income streams. Alternatively, households might allow the shock to fall most heavily on those members with the largest health endowments, effectively taxing these endowments in order to protect the human capital of other members.[1]

This paper speaks to these issues drawing on a unique data set from rural Zimbabwe. Specifically, it uses longitudinal data on households and individuals collected annually between 1994 and 1999. Household-level data include information on the key asset held in these localities, livestock. Individual-level data are available on anthropometric outcomes, body mass for adults and growth rates for children under six years of age. While these surveys were underway, Zimbabwe experienced, in 1994–95, a drought with rainfall levels lower than long-term averages by 20–40 per cent. This drought led to marked reductions in both crop and total household incomes. The longitudinal nature of these data, the presence of the drought midway through the data collection, and the existence of household and individual level data allow us to address the issues described above. We find that: (1) the 1994–95 drought was associated with a rise in the sales of livestock, particularly oxen and cows; (2) the likelihood of sales was strongly affected by pre-drought asset levels (households with one or two oxen or one or two cows were much less likely to sell than households with more than two of these animals); (3) as measured by their body mass index (BMI), men were unaffected by the drought whereas women's BMI fell (however, the fall was smaller in households that sold livestock *and* women's BMI recovered quickly the following year); and (4) children older than two were not affected by the drought. Children younger than two lost 15–20 per cent of their growth velocity. Children residing in poor households – including those that did not sell assets – are likely to have suffered a permanent loss in stature, schooling and earnings.

II. Setting

(a) Background

The households and individuals in this sample reside in resettlement areas of rural Zimbabwe. As their history is somewhat unusual, we begin with an extended introduction to their background.

Inequitable access to land was a major factor motivating armed rebellion against white minority rule prior to 1980. Upon gaining independence, the Government of Zimbabwe announced a wide-ranging programme of land reform, designed to redress these severe inequalities. A component of the land reform programme was the resettlement of households on farms previously occupied by white commercial farmers. Criteria for selection into these schemes included: being a refugee or other persons displaced by war, including extra-territorial refugees, urban refugees and former inhabitants of protected villages; being unemployed; being a landless resident in a communal area or having insufficient land to maintain themselves and their families (Kinsey, 1982). At the time of settlement, the household heads were also supposed to be married or widowed, aged 25–50 and not in formal employment. Families selected for resettlement were assigned to these schemes, and the consolidated villages within them, largely on a random basis. Generally, these criteria seem to have been followed. In this sample, some 90 per cent of households settled in the early 1980s had been adversely affected by the war for independence in some form or another. Before being resettled, most (66 per cent) had been peasant farmers with the remainder being landless labourers on commercial farms, refugees and workers in the rural and urban informal sectors.

Families settled on these schemes were required to renounce any claim to land elsewhere in Zimbabwe. They were not given ownership of the land on which they were settled, but instead were given permits covering residential and farm plots. Each household was allocated five hectares of arable land for cultivation, with the remaining area in each resettlement site being devoted to communal grazing land. In return for this allocation of land, the Zimbabwean government expected male heads of households to rely exclusively on farming for their livelihoods. Until 1992, male household heads were not permitted to work elsewhere, nor could they migrate to cities, leaving their wives to work these plots. Although this restriction has been relaxed, with male heads being allowed to work off farm (provided that household farm production is judged satisfactory by local government officials), in this sample agriculture continues to account for at least 80 per cent of household income in non-drought years.

The nature of the settlement pattern in these households deserves further comment. Unlike the homestead pattern of settlement found throughout much of rural Zimbabwe, households in these resettlement schemes live in small villages surrounded by cultivated fields. The small size of each village (12–60 households), together with their physical isolation, has precluded the development of small markets in these localities. Indeed, a striking visual feature of these places is the absence of shops or trading areas. Instead, each resettlement scheme has a centrally located 'rural service centre' where government offices, a health clinic and shops are found. Cattle sales are also held here.

(b) The Sample

Over the period, 1982–4, an initial survey of approximately 400 resettled households was undertaken. The initial sampling frame was all resettlement schemes established in the first two years of the programme in Zimbabwe's three agriculturally most important agro-climatic zones. These are Natural Regions II, III and IV and correspond to areas of moderately high, moderate and restricted agricultural potential. One scheme was selected randomly from each zone: Mupfurudzi in Mashonaland Central Province (which lies to the north of Harare in NRII), Sengezi in Mashonaland East Province (which lies south east of Harare in NRIII) and Mutanda in Manicaland Province (which lies south east of Harare, but farther away than Sengezi and in NRIV). Random sampling was then used to select villages within schemes, and in each selected village, an attempt was made to cover all selected households.

These households were first interviewed over the period July–September 1983 to January–March 1984. They are located in 20 different villages (two additional villages were added to the sample in 1993). Just over half (57 per cent) are found in

Mupfurudzi with 18 per cent located in Mutanda and 25 per cent found in Sengezi. They were re-interviewed in the first quarter of 1987 and annually, during January–April, from 1992 to 1999. There is remarkably little sample attrition. Approximately 90 per cent of households interviewed in 1983–84 were re-interviewed in 1999. There is no systematic pattern to the few households that drop out. Some were inadvertently dropped during the re-surveys, a few disintegrated (such as those where all adults died) and a small number were evicted by government officials responsible for overseeing these schemes.

These particular characteristics of the sample provide it with a number of desirable properties. First, there is no requirement to address biases brought about by *household* sample attrition. Second, as Rosenzweig and Wolpin (1988) have argued, examination of the impact of any locality level characteristic, such as quality of health care, access to drought relief and so on is hampered by considerations of selective migration. There are strong *a priori* grounds for believing that this will not affect these results. Relocation of these households preceded, by a significant period of time, the drought that occurred in 1994–95. Third, the availability of repeated observations makes it possible to control for any correlation between explanatory variables and fixed, unobserved characteristics. Fourth, because the survey was conducted at almost exactly the same time each year, the impact of seasonality considerations is minimised. Fifth, because the prohibitions on non-agricultural activities were only lifted after 1992, and because households had to be seen to be 'good farmers' if they were not to lose their access to this land, there was relatively little pre-existing non-agricultural activity in these localities and little opportunity to engage in such activities after the drought occurred. Consequently, unlike the households studied by Kochar (1999), there was little scope to mitigate the drought shock by engaging in other income-generating activities. Sixth, because there is no land ownership and financial institutions such as banks are not readily accessible; livestock represent the preferred means of accumulating wealth. Further, a span (two) of oxen is needed for ploughing and farmers state that in order to maintain herd size, they need a minimum of cows or heifers. This observation is supported by the data; Owens, Hoddinott and Kinsey (2003) find that crop incomes per hectare rise with the possession of pairs of oxen. Consequently, our observations on livestock will provide a good window into the extent to which there is asset smoothing while these minima (two oxen, two cows/heifers) provide the 'threshold'. Seventh, each survey round records deaths that have occurred in the previous 12 months and enumerators are instructed to probe carefully for all deaths. There are relatively few adult or child deaths in any given year, suggesting that these results are unlikely to be affected by selective mortality. Finally, it was not until after the 1991–92 drought that adult male heads were permitted to out-migrate. Rural–urban migration by males, together with temporary visits to rural areas, is an important mechanism by which HIV is passed from urban areas – where the disease is widespread – to rural areas. The presence of this prohibition, which appears to have been strictly enforced, provides an *a priori* reason for believing that HIV infection will play a much smaller part in explaining trends in adult health than might be the case in other parts of Zimbabwe or sub-Saharan Africa. Although we do not have direct evidence on HIV rates, there have been relatively few adult deaths from diseases such as tuberculosis, which are often HIV related, which is also suggestive of relatively low HIV prevalence in these areas.[2]

(c) Trends in Rainfall and Crop Income

Our rainfall data are taken from measurements made at the rainfall station nearest to the centre of these resettlement areas. In Mupfurudzi, this is located in the service centre. In Mutanda and Sengezi they are located about five kilometres away from the centre of the resettlement scheme. Both 1992–93 and 1993–94 were reasonably good years in terms of rainfall. The third year (1994–95) was a major drought year, which was followed by a recovery year (1995–96). 1996–97 was a year of exceptionally heavy rains leading to widespread flooding; this was followed by a slightly poorer-than-normal year (1997–98) in Mupfurudzi and Sengezi and a slightly better-than-normal year in Mutanda. These patterns are shown in Table 1 which records mean rainfall levels by agricultural year and resettlement scheme in terms of their departure from long term levels.

Two comments are in order. First, in examining these data, it is important to place them within the context of the seasonal cycles of these households. The Zimbabwean agricultural year runs from October to September. Planting typically occurs in October/November with harvesting occurring in May and June. Marketing occurs over the period June to September. The household survey takes place in February and March. The timing was deliberately chosen so as to interview households at the height of the hungry season. It does, however, mean that dating events can be somewhat confusing. For example, drought in the 1994–95 agricultural year implies that households potentially face severe food shortages in the year that *follows* as it is a full 12 months before the next harvest is ready. It should also be noted that the 1994–95 drought was somewhat unusual in that rainfall in the early part of the

Table 1. Trends in rainfall and income by agricultural year

	Per cent of long-term mean rainfall Agricultural year					
Resettlement scheme	1992–1993	1993–1994	1994–1995	1995–1996	1996–1997	1997–1998
Mupfurudzi	117.5	91.2	68.2	101.7	166.4	93.2
Mutanda	106.6	121.4	61.5	118	156.8	113.5
Sengezi	103.5	90.5	80.3	115.1	148.9	94.1
	Incomes by crop year					
Gross crop income	5815	4857	1817	6055	Not available	Not available
Total income	6982	6296	4051	8146	Not available	Not available

Note:
1. Income figures are expressed in constant (1992) Zimbabwe dollars.

season was consistent with long-term averages. The drought only began to manifest itself in February 1995 when mid- and end-season rains failed. Consequently, when examining the impact of this negative rainfall shock, the 'drought observation' will be 1996.

Second, Table 1 also records – for the four years for which it is available – gross crop income and total household incomes. These figures reveal two salient points: gross crop incomes fell as a consequence of the drought; and that use of other income sources only modestly offset these. Clearly, the drought shock generated an income shock.

III. Drought Shocks and Asset Sales

(a) Descriptives

We have ascertained that a drought shock occurred in 1994–95, that this led to a fall in household income and that livestock are the principal asset held by these households. We now examine whether households sold livestock in order to protect consumption levels following the drought.

Tables 2 and 3 provide descriptive statistics on oxen and cow/heifer ownership and sales. Ownership of both categories of livestock is widespread with a minimum of 72 per cent of households reporting ownership of oxen and 82.7 per cent reporting ownership of cows and heifers. The third and fourth rows provide information on the prevalence of sales of these assets. The percentage of households reporting oxen sales jumps from 15.3 per cent in 1995 to 36.3 per cent in 1996 before falling to 18.7 per cent in 1997. (Recall again that the observation for 1996 is the 'drought' year, reflecting the adverse consequences of the 1994–95 drought.) Similarly, the percentage of households reporting cow or heifer sales jumped from 16.3 per cent in 1995 to 21.5 per cent in 1996 before dropping to 17 per cent in 1997. Another way of expressing these data is in terms of off-take rates, the ratio of sales to prior levels of ownership. In the case of oxen, this ratio more than doubles – from 0.06 to 0.16 – between 1995 and 1996, before dropping back to 0.097 in 1997. For cows and heifers, it rises by nearly 50 per cent, from 0.043 in 1995 to 0.061 in 1996.

Households were also asked why they made these sales. In 1996, nearly half of all respondents indicated that they sold these assets in order to purchase food. This is in stark contrast to non-drought years when other reasons, such as the need to generate cash to pay school fees or purchase agricultural inputs, are considerably more prevalent.

The last rows of Tables 2 and 3 disaggregate sales by prior levels of asset ownership. We distinguish between three groups: households with no oxen, cow or heifer ownership; households holding one or two of these animals; and households owning more than two. The differences are striking. More than half the households owning more than two oxen sold at least one ox in the aftermath of the 1994–95 drought compared to 15 per cent of households owning only one or two oxen. Just over a quarter of households (27 per cent) owning two or more cows/heifers made at least one sale compared to 4.6 per cent of households owning one or two cows.

Table 2. Oxen sales by year

	Year observed					
	1994	1995	1996	1997	1998	1999
Percentage households with oxen	80.6%	79.8%	78.6%	75.1%	75.4%	72.3%
Mean number of oxen currently owned	2.30	2.34	2.17	2.38	2.35	2.29
Percentage households with oxen one year ago who sold in last 12 months	15.5%	15.3%	36.3%	18.7%	20.2%	20.0%
Mean number of oxen sold in last 12 months	0.18	0.15	0.38	0.21	0.20	0.20
Ratio: Oxen sold in last 12 months to number owned one year ago		0.065	0.162	0.097	0.084	0.085
Reasons for sales						
Consumption	67.4%	39.6%	76.1%	45.3%	38.1%	37.3%
Buy food	32.6	20.8	46.9	5.7	7.9	15.3
School expenses	21.7	12.5	14.2	24.5	14.3	11.9
Health expenses	6.5	2.1	1.8	5.7	6.4	5.1
Other consumption	6.5	4.2	13.3	9.4	9.5	5.1
Agriculture	17.4	50.0	15.0	41.5	33.3	27.1
Other	15.2	10.4	8.9	13.2	28.6	35.6
Percentage households selling oxen by lagged number of oxen owned						
Zero oxen owned one year ago	0	0	0	0	1.1	0
1–2 oxen owned one year ago	7.0	7.1	15.0	8.6	10.4	12.1
>2 oxen owned one year ago	23.4	23.0	52.8	26.7	27.0	25.6
F test on differences in oxen sales by number owned one year ago	14.77**	15.58**	49.75**	15.20**	17.00**	15.33**
Relevant agricultural year	1992–1993	1993–1994	1994–1995	1995–1996	1996–1997	1997–1998

(b) Econometric Analysis

These descriptive results are consistent with the argument that assets are used to buffer consumption following a drought shock, but that the threat of poverty traps means that only better-off households are likely to use such a mechanism. To confirm this possibility, we complement these descriptive statistics with an econometric analysis.[3] Doing so, however, is not completely straightforward. To see why, consider a simple model of livestock sales:

$$S_{ivt} = \beta_L \cdot L_{ivt-1} + \beta_R \cdot \mathbf{R}_{vt} \cdot \beta_X \cdot \mathbf{X}_{ivt} + \varepsilon_v + \varepsilon_i + \varepsilon_{ivt} \tag{1}$$

Table 3. Sales of cows/heifers by year

	Year observed					
	1994	1995	1996	1997	1998	1999
Percentage households with cows/heifers	82.7%	88.0%	88.9%	89.2%	86.4%	87.4%
Mean number of cows/ heifers currently owned	3.93	4.24	4.59	5.14	4.94	5.12
Percentage households with cows/heifers one year ago who sold in last 12 months	11.4%	16.3%	21.5%	17.0%	19.2%	20.4%
Mean number of cows/ heifers sold in last 12 months	0.11	0.17	0.26	0.20	0.24	0.23
Ratio: cows/heifers sold in last 12 months to number owned one year ago		0.043	0.061	0.044	0.047	0.046
Reasons for sales						
Consumption	64.1	56.9	69.4	37.9	42.0	43.6
Buy food	33.3	29.3	50.6	4.5	7.2	15.4
School expenses	12.8	15.5	10.6	12.1	17.4	12.8
Health expenses	10.3	3.4	2.4	6.1	10.1	5.1
Other purchases	7.8	8.6	5.9	15.2	7.2	10.3
Agriculture	15.4	31.0	22.4	40.9	39.1	34.6
Other	20.5	12.1	8.2	21.2	18.8	21.8
Percentage households selling cows by lagged number of cows owned						
Zero cows owned one year ago	0	0	2.4	0	0	0
1–2 cows owned one year ago	7.2	3.0	4.6	6.0	9.0	7.0
>2 cows owned one year ago	12.8	21.8	27.0	19.4	22.1	23.9
F test on differences in cow sales by number owned one year ago	4.23**	14.87**	13.06**	7.98**	7.77**	11.02**
Relevant agricultural year	1992–1993	1993–1994	1994–1995	1995–1996	1996–1997	1997–1998

Here S_{ivt} is the number of sales of oxen recorded for household$i$, residing in village v at time period$t$; L_{ivt-1} is the number of oxen owned in the prior period, $\mathbf{R_{vt}}$ is a vector of rainfall shocks – following Fafchamps, Udry and Czukas (1998) we distinguish between positive and negative rainfall shocks – and $\mathbf{X}_{ivt}$ is a vector of other household characteristics that might also affect oxen sales (sex of the household head, household size, wages and prices faced by the household,[4] illness shocks). Parameters and vectors of parameters to be estimated are given by β_L, β_R and β_X while ε_v and ε_i are fixed, unobserved characteristics of the village and household and ε_{ivt} is a white noise disturbance term. There are two problems, however, with estimating (1) using ordinary least squares.

First, lagged livestock holdings are likely to be correlated with both fixed village and fixed household characteristics. Two examples illustrate this. Ability to accumulate livestock might be constrained by availability of grazing land, a village characteristic, thus $E(L_{ivt-1}\varepsilon_v) \neq 0$. Individuals who accumulate livestock might do so because they are more diligent or harder-working than others, thus $E(L_{ivt-1}\varepsilon_i) \neq 0$.

While a fixed effects estimator could address the problem of correlation between observables and time-invariant unobservables, there is a second problem to consider. Livestock holdings in prior periods are not exogenous but in fact represent the outcome of, inter alia, prior sales. $L_{ivt-1} = f(S_{ivt-1})$ implies that prior livestock sales should also appear as a right hand side regressor, that is:

$$S_{ivt} = \beta_S \cdot S_{ivt-1} + \beta_L \cdot L_{ivt-1} + \beta_R \cdot \mathbf{R} + \beta_X \cdot \mathbf{X}_{ivt} + \varepsilon_v + \varepsilon_i + \varepsilon_{ivt} \qquad (1')$$

But this generates yet another econometric problem, namely that $E(S_{ivt-1}\varepsilon_{ivt}) \neq 0$. Arellano and Bond (1991) show that this can be resolved by estimating (1') in first differences using Generalised Methods of Moments (GMM) one-step and two-step estimators that remove this correlation by treating S_{ivt-1} as an endogenous variable. While the two-step estimator is more efficient, in finite samples Monte Carlo evidence suggests that their standard errors can be biased downwards whereas the standard errors from the one-step estimator are unbiased. Given all this, we report three sets of results, fixed effects estimates obtained from estimating,

$$S_{ivt} - (S_{iv}) = \beta_L \cdot (L_{ivt-1} - L_{iv}) + \beta_R \cdot (\mathbf{R}_{vt} - \boldsymbol{R}_v) + \beta_X \cdot (\mathbf{X}_{ivt} - \mathbf{X}_{iv}) + (\varepsilon_{ivt} - \varepsilon_{ivt}) \quad (3)$$

where mean values are written in italics, and the results of estimating (4) using the one- and two-step Arellano-Bond estimators.

$$S_{ivt} - (S_{ivt-1}) = \beta_S \cdot (S_{ivt-1} - S_{ivt-2}) + \beta_L \cdot (L_{ivt-1} - L_{ivt-2}) + \beta_R \cdot (\mathbf{R}_{vt} - \mathbf{R}_{vt-1}) + \beta_X \cdot (\mathbf{X}_{ivt} - \mathbf{X}_{ivt-1}) + (\varepsilon_{ivt} - \varepsilon_{ivt-1}) \qquad (4)$$

When estimating (4), the first lagged difference in sales, the first lagged difference in oxen/cow holdings standard errors are treated as endogenous as is log household size. All current and prior first differences and levels of exogenous variables serve as instruments. The Arellano-Bond one-step estimates are also corrected for hetero-skedasticity.

Table 4 reports the results of estimating (3) and (4). To conserve space, only the impacts of rainfall shocks are reported.[5] The full set of regressors for each model are listed in the notes underneath Table 4; it is worth noting that the results reported here are robust to alterations to the set of additional regressors used to derive these results.[6] Irrespective of the estimator used, negative rainfall shocks are associated

Table 4. The impact of rainfall shocks on oxen, cows and heifer sales

	Dependent variable: sales of oxen		
	Fixed effects specification	Arellano-Bond one-step estimator	Arellano-Bond two-step estimator
Positive rainfall shock, deviation from mean	0.199 (3.54)**		
Negative rainfall shock, deviation from mean	0.253 (4.05)**		
$\Delta_{t,\ t-1}$ Positive rainfall shock		0.264 (4.06)**	0.222 (4.22)**
$\Delta_{t,\ t-1}$ Negative rainfall shock		0.382 (4.89)**	0.324 (5.18)**
F test, fixed unobservables	1.31**		
Sargan over-identification test		40.57**	20.47
Arellano-Bond test for AR(2) in first differences		−0.05	0.23
Sample size	2325	1484	1484
	Dependent variable: sales of cows and heifers		
Positive rainfall shock, deviation from mean	0.111 (2.00)**		
Negative rainfall shock, deviation from mean	0.147 (2.41)**		
$\Delta_{t,\ t-1}$ Positive rainfall shock		0.114 (1.57)	0.078 (1.30)
$\Delta_{t,\ t-1}$ Negative rainfall shock		0.156 (1.91)*	0.112 (1.71)*
F test, fixed unobservables	1.58**		
Sargan over-identification test		63.98**	31.49**
Arellano-Bond test for AR(2) in first differences		0.48	0.06
Sample size	2325	1484	1484

Notes:

1. For fixed effects specification, variables included but not reported are deviations from mean values of: sex of household head, log household size, dummy equalling one if household head unable to work in previous 30 days, locality agricultural wage rate, locality consumer price of cooking oil. In oxen specification, lagged number of oxen owned is also included; in cows/heifer specification, lagged number of cows and heifers is also included.
2. For Arellano-Bond one- and two-step estimators, variables included but not reported are first differences of: sex of household head, dummy equalling one if household head unable to work in previous 30 days, locality agricultural wage rate, locality consumer price of cooking oil. In oxen specification, lagged number of oxen sold, lagged number of oxen owned and log household size are also included but are treated as endogenous. In cows and heifers specification, lagged number of cows and heifers sold, lagged number of cows and heifers owned and log household size are also included but are treated as endogenous.
3. Standard errors in Arellano-Bond one-step estimator robust to heteroskedasticity.
4. Absolute value of t statistics in parentheses. *Significant at the 5 per cent level.

with the sale of oxen. The fixed and one-step Arellano-Bond estimators also show that the sale of cows and heifers increases with negative rainfall shocks, but this relationship does not hold when the two-step estimator is used.

Table 5 adopts the same approach used in Table 4 but interacts negative rainfall shocks with two representations of prior levels of livestock ownership: owning one or two animals; and owning two or more animals.[7] The results for both oxen and cows are striking. Households with prior ownership of more than two animals were considerably more likely to sell in the aftermath of a negative rainfall shock than households with only one or two animals and the differences in the parameter estimates are always statistically significant. As such, these results reinforce the findings first observed in the descriptive statistics. Better-off households do indeed draw down assets following an income shock, but the threat of a poverty trap means that less-well off households do not do so.[8]

IV. Drought Shocks and their Impact on Adults

As discussed in the introduction, a limiting feature of the analysis presented above is that it abstracts from the effects of shocks on *individual* welfare. In this and the following section, we exploit information on individual health outcomes to redress this weakness.

Specifically, we have anthropometric data on adults and children under six years of age for the same period, 1994–99. In the case of adults, we express these data in terms of their Body Mass Index (BMI), defined as weight (in kilograms) divided by the square of height (in metres). Variations in an individual adult's body mass reflect variations in weight brought about by changes in energy intake, activities and therefore energy expenditures, or illness. When we examine the levels of BMI over time for men and women separately, an interesting finding emerges. For men, BMI is basically constant over the entire period running from 1994 to 1999, averaging around 21.5. There is no apparent correlation between men's BMI and the 1994–95 drought. By contrast, although women have slightly higher average BMI (22.1), their body mass falls by about 3 per cent in the aftermath of the 1994–95 drought. However, in the following year it recovers quickly.

To see if these results are robust to the inclusion of additional controls, we again estimate a dynamic panel data model with first differences in BMI as the dependent variable. All right hand side variables are also expressed in first differences. They are lagged BMI, absolute values of positive and negative rainfall deviations from their long-run averages, the value of livestock holdings, recent illness and locality level wages and prices.[9] We estimated this model using a variety of methods but, in order to save space, report only the most conservative findings, the Arellano-Bond one-step estimator with lagged body mass, livestock holdings and illness treated as endogenous and standard errors corrected for heteroskedasticity.

Results are reported in Table 6.[10] For men, rainfall shocks have no effect on BMI. For women, however, negative rainfall shocks do reduce body mass.[11] Also, women's BMI are higher in wealthier households. Given this, we interact negative rainfall shocks with whether the household sells cattle treating this variable as endogenous. The parameter is positive, though somewhat small in magnitude and not statistically significant. However, recalling that sales are more likely in wealthier households, we re-estimate this model, restricting the sample to women in households with livestock holdings in the second, third and fourth quartiles – that is, we exclude women living in the poorest quartile. When we do, as shown in the

Table 5. The impact of negative rainfall shocks on oxen, cows and heifer sales by previous holdings

	Dependent variable: sales of oxen		
	Fixed effects specification	Arellano-Bond one-step estimator	Arellano-Bond two-step estimator
Negative rainfall shock x dummy for owned 1–2 oxen at $t-1$, deviation from mean	0.043 (1.09)		
Negative rainfall shock, x dummy for owned >2 oxen at $t-1$, deviation from mean	0.151 (3.66)**		
$\Delta_{t,\ t-1}$ Negative rainfall shock x dummy for owned 1–2 oxen at $t-1$		0.109 (2.39)**	0.109 (3.00)**
$\Delta_{t,\ t-1}$ Negative rainfall shock, x dummy for owned >2 oxen at $t-1$		0.250 (2.56)**	0.275 (4.27)**
F test for equality of negative rainfall shocks	8.81**	3.95**	10.25**
F test, fixed unobservables	1.31**		
Sargan over-identification test		49.23**	18.59
Arellano-Bond test for AR(2) in first differences		0.46	−0.49
Sample size	2325	1484	1484
	Dependent variable: sales of cows and heifers		
Negative rainfall shock x dummy for owned 1–2 cows/heifers at $t-1$, deviation from mean	−0.017 (0.35)		
Negative rainfall shock, x dummy for owned >2 cows/heifers at $t-1$, deviation from mean	0.118 (2.74)**		
$\Delta_{t,\ t-1}$ Negative rainfall shock x dummy for owned 1–2 cows/heifers at $t-1$		−0.027 (0.59)	−0.051 (1.47)
$\Delta_{t,\ t-1}$ Negative rainfall shock, x dummy for owned >2 cows/heifers at $t-1$		0.083 (1.63)	0.088 (2.06)**
F test for equality of negative rainfall shocks	11.93**	4.62**	10.31**
F test, fixed unobservables	1.58**		
Sargan over-identification test		67.99**	30.94**

(*continued*)

Table 5. (*Continued*)

	Dependent variable: sales of oxen		
	Fixed effects specification	Arellano-Bond one-step estimator	Arellano-Bond two-step estimator
Arellano-Bond test for AR(2) in first differences		0.35	0.10
Sample size	2292	1484	1484

Notes:
1. For fixed effects specification, variables included but not reported are deviations from mean values of: sex of household head, log household size, dummy equalling one if household head unable to work in previous 30 days, locality agricultural wage rate, locality consumer price of cooking oil and positive rainfall shocks. In oxen specification, lagged number of oxen owned is also included; in cows/heifer specification, lagged number of cows and heifers is also included.
2. For Arellano-Bond one- and two-step estimators, variables included but not reported are first differences of: sex of household head, dummy equalling one if household head unable to work in previous 30 days, locality agricultural wage rate, locality consumer price of cooking oil and positive rainfall shocks.
3. For Arellano-Bond one- step estimator, in oxen specification, lagged number of oxen sold, lagged number of oxen owned and log household size are also included, but are treated as endogenous. In cows and heifers specification, lagged number of cows and heifers sold, lagged number of cows and heifers owned and log household size are also included but are treated as endogenous.
4. For Arellano-Bond two-step estimator, in oxen specification, lagged number of oxen sold and lagged number of oxen owned are included, but are treated as endogenous as are $\Delta_{t,\ t-1}$ Negative rainfall shock *x* dummy for owned 1–2 oxen one year ago, $\Delta_{t,\ t-1}$ Negative rainfall shock, *x* dummy for owned >2 oxen one year ago and log household size.
5. For Arellano-Bond two-step estimator, in cows and heifers specification, lagged number of cows and heifers sold and lagged number of cows and heifers owned are included but are treated as endogenous as are $\Delta_{t,\ t-1}$ Negative rainfall shock *x* dummy for owned 1–2 cows/heifers one year ago and $\Delta_{t,\ t-1}$ Negative rainfall shock *x* dummy for owned >2 cows/heifers one year ago and log household size.
6. Standard errors in Arellano-Bond estimator one-step estimator robust to heteroskedasticity.
7. Absolute value of t statistics in parentheses. *Significant at the 10 per cent level, **Significant at the 5 per cent level.

final column of Table 6, we do indeed see that sales following a negative rainfall shock do indeed boost women's BMI.

It is also worth noting changes in livestock, which when treated as endogenous, raise women's, but not men's, BMI. This deserves further comment in light of the findings of Fafchamps, Udry and Czukas (1998) that in the very different environment of semi-arid West Africa, livestock transactions do not appear to play a major role in household consumption smoothing. We hypothesise that livestock holdings are working through two channels. First, this may capture a wealth effect – livestock are a relatively liquid store of wealth whose real value has been maintained in the Zimbabwean context of persistent inflation. Second,

Table 6. Determinants of adult log body mass index

	Men		Women	
Rainfall shocks				
$\Delta_{t,\ t-1}$ Positive rainfall shock	0.029 (2.28)**	−0.004 (0.29)	−0.056 (1.78)*	−0.068 (2.12)**
$\Delta_{t,\ t-1}$ Negative rainfall shock	0.030 (0.45)	−0.120 (2.71)**	−0.079 (2.42)**	−0.091 (2.73)**
$\Delta_{t,\ t-1}$ Negative rainfall shock x any sale of oxen, cows or heifers			0.015 (1.37)	0.018 (1.71)*
Time varying individual characteristics				
$\Delta_{t-1,\ t-2}$ Lag log body mass index	−0.065 (0.59)	−0.016 (0.18)	0.023 (0.29)	0.024 (0.26)
Time varying household characteristics				
$\Delta_{t,\ t-1}$ Log value of livestock	−0.005 (0.17)	0.058 (2.31)**	0.065 (2.38)**	0.028 (1.00)
Specification tests				
Sargan over-identification test	15.62	21.15	21.02	30.29
Arellano-Bond test for AR(2) in first differences	1.26	0.31	0.37	−0.23

Notes:
1. Dependent variable is log of body mass index.
2. Male sample consists of men who are household heads, or sons with a child aged 6–60 months currently residing in the household. Female sample consists of women less than 50 years old who are household heads, wives of heads, daughters, or daughters-in-law with a child aged 6–60 months currently residing in the household.
3. $\Delta_{t,\ t-1}$ agricultural wage rate, $\Delta_{t,\ t-1}$ price of cooking oil, $\Delta_{t,\ t-1}$ price of sugar, $\Delta_{t,\ t-1}$ price of beef and $\Delta_{t,\ t-1}$ individual days to ill to work are included but not reported.
4. Absolute value of t statistics in parentheses. *Significant at the 10 per cent level, **significant at the 5 per cent level.
5. Sample size, 326 for men; 593 for women.
6. Final column excludes women living in households in the lowest pre-drought livestock quartile.

livestock – especially oxen – can substitute for a wide variety of labour tasks. Although ox-ploughing rather than manual hoeing comes most readily to mind, oxen can also be used to pull carts carrying firewood and water. These activities are regarded as women's responsibilities in these survey areas. Not only does animal haulage reduce human energy expenditures, they also allow greater quantities of wood and water to be collected during a single trip.

Lastly, the lagged dependent variable is not statistically significant for either women or men, suggesting that adult BMI follows a stationary process. This reinforces our contention that this drought shock had no effect on the health of adult men and a small, but transient effect on adult women.[12]

V. Drought Shocks and their Impact on Children

In the case of children, we focus on the growth in their heights, a good indicator of underlying health status. Because we have investigated the impact of droughts on child growth elsewhere (Hoddinott and Kinsey, 2001; Alderman, Hoddinott and Kinsey, 2004), we restrict discussion to summarising several key findings.

Using the same survey data as has been analysed here, Hoddinott and Kinsey (2001) examine the determinants of the growth of pre-schoolers' heights. They find that the 1994–95 drought lowered annual growth rates of very young children, those aged 12–24 months, by somewhere between 1.5 and 2 cm[13,14] – but did not have a statistically significant effect on the growth rates of older pre-schoolers. Not only is this reduction in growth equivalent to a loss of 15–20 per cent of growth velocity, but four years after the failure of the 1994–95 rains, these children remained shorter than identically aged children who had not experienced this drought between the ages of 12 and 24 months. The impact was greatest amongst children living in households with holdings of livestock below the median in 1995 – a group that includes virtually (78 per cent) all households with two or fewer oxen. Recall, it was these households that were *not* selling livestock in the aftermath of the 1994–95 drought, even though they had assets that they could have sold.

The significance of these results lies in a growing body of evidence showing that this loss of growth velocity carries long-term functional consequences. First, there is considerable epidemiological evidence that stature by age three is strongly correlated with attained body size at adulthood (Martorell, 1995; 1999). Alderman, Hoddinott and Kinsey (2004) show, using an older cohort of children residing in these localities and who were adversely affected by the 1982–84 drought in Zimbabwe, that drought shocks have permanent effects in terms of reductions in attained height in young adulthood. Additionally, there are four mechanisms through which lost growth in childhood is correlated with lower productivity and lifetime earnings as an adult.[15] Further, other studies have shown that: lower adult height is associated with reduced earnings as an adult (Foster and Rosenzweig, 1993; Glick and Sahn, 1998; and Thomas and Strauss 1997); children experiencing slow height growth are found to perform less well in school, score poorly on tests of cognitive function, have poorer psychomotor development and fine motor skills (Grantham-McGregor et al., 1999). In turn, poor cognitive function as a child is associated with poorer cognitive achievement as an adult, see Martorell (1995; 1999); and shorter stature as a child is associated with slower progress through schooling (Leslie and Jamison 1990) and completion of fewer grades of schooling, Alderman, Hoddinott and Kinsey (2004). Both reduced cognitive skills and fewer grades of schooling are causally associated with lower earnings (Behrman, Alderman and Hoddinott, 2004). Taken together, this implies that young children in households with small holdings of livestock are likely to suffer permanent losses of human capital and earnings as a result of the 1994–95 drought.

VI. Conclusions

In this paper, we have argued that drought shocks do cause *some* households to draw down assets. More than half the households owning more than two oxen sold at least one ox in the aftermath of the 1994–95 drought compared to 15 per cent of households owning only one or two oxen. Just over a quarter of households (27 per cent) owning two or more cows/heifers made at least one sale compared to 4.6 per cent of households owning one or two cows. These findings remain intact when we apply relatively sophisticated econometric techniques to these data. Adult men were not adversely affected by this shock; nor were older pre-schoolers. Adult women were adversely affected, but recovered relatively quickly. Very young pre-schoolers, those 12–24 months in the aftermath of the 1994–95 drought, were adversely affected. While those children who resided in relatively well-off households eventually recovered this lost growth velocity, children from poorer homes did not. What makes this last result so striking is that the drought itself, by African standards was mild. There were no famine deaths, there was no call for outpourings of emergency food aid. Yet this relatively moderate shock appears to have generated permanent consequences.

As such, these findings speak to a number of issues. First, as noted by Zimmerman and Carter (2003), different households may indeed respond differently to income shocks depending on the level of their asset holdings. Second, 'consumption smoothing' is too broad a phrase – it implies that all household members' consumption may, or may not, be smoothed given a shock. Women's but not men's BMI fell in the aftermath of the 1994–95 drought; younger but not older pre-schoolers experienced a loss of growth velocity. Third, consumption smoothing implies an attempt to preserve assets, but consumption is an input into the formation and maintenance of human capital. This implies that the distinction between consumption and asset smoothing, while useful as a descriptive tool, may be somewhat misleading. Rather, household responses to adverse shocks are effectively changes in their asset portfolio, with a critical issue being the extent to which the draw down of a given asset has permanent consequences. In the case considered here, the preservation of physical assets by these Zimbabwean households led to a temporary reduction in women's health and a (likely) permanent reduction in the human capital of children unlucky enough to be caught in the aftermath of the 1994–95 drought.

Acknowledgements

Funding for the survey work underpinning this paper was provided by the British Development Division in Central Africa, UNICEF, the former Ministry of Lands, Resettlement and Rural Development, Zimbabwe, FAO, the Nuffield Foundation, ODI, DfID, IFPRI, CSAE Oxford, the Free University, Amsterdam, and the Research Board of the University of Zimbabwe. Work on this paper was partially supported by USAID/OFDA (Grant LAG-4111-G-00-3042), and USAID's BASIS CRSP programme. Discussions with Chris Barrett, Michael Carter and Stefan Dercon, and comments from participants at the BASIS CRSP Policy Conference, Combating Persistent Poverty in Africa, Washington, DC, and an anonymous reviewer have helped the author immensely in thinking through the issues discussed here. Research support from Trudy Owens, Alison Slack and Sanjukta Mukerjee made writing this paper feasible. The author owes a particular debt to Bill Kinsey not only for many years of collaboration, but also for his dedication to constructing this unique data set. Any errors are the author's alone.

Notes

1. Pitt, Rosenzweig and Hassan (1990) explore this idea in the context of rural Bangladesh.
2. Further indirect evidence underlying this claim comes from the 1997 survey round. Households were asked if they knew of anyone whom they believed had died from AIDS and if they knew of anyone who was living with HIV/AIDS. Affirmative answers to these questions were followed with the questions, 'How many people altogether?' and 'How many from this area'. Mean values to these questions were: 3.22 deaths altogether; 0.92 deaths locally; 0.58 people living with HIV/AIDS; and 0.21 living locally.
3. It is possible to nest this estimated relationship within a more formal model of livestock sales that occur in environments characterised by market failures and irreversibilities, see Rosenzweig and Wolpin (1993) and Lybbert, Barrett, Desta and Coppock (2004).
4. Because the prices of many consumer goods were regulated over much of this period, there is considerable collinearity in prices when expressed in deviations from means or first differences. The consumer price of cooking oil is included as a regressor; including the prices of other goods does not produce meaningful changes in the results reported here.
5. Full results are available on request.
6. Note that in all cases, we find no evidence of second-order serial correlation. This is important in that these estimates would be inconsistent if such correlation existed, see Arellano and Bond (1991: 278 and especially 281). The Sargan test tends to reject the over-identification restrictions in the cows regressions; however, Arellano and Bond (1991: 291) provide simulation results showing that this test statistic has a tendency to over-reject in the presence of heteroscedasticity.
7. These are treated as endogenous.
8. It is possible that households were selling livestock not because they needed to smooth consumption, but rather because the value of the animals had fallen and were therefore no longer worth holding. While it is not possible to be certain about this, there is some evidence suggesting that asset prices were not falling dramatically. Using households' reports of sales, I find that in real terms, the sales price of oxen fell by about 15 per cent in the aftermath of the drought, a reduction but hardly a dramatic fall. Further, it is possible that households were selling off poorer quality animals. A shred of evidence supporting this contention is that the distribution of self-reported animal values tightens up after the drought – in particular, the lower tail of the distribution is considerably shorter in 1996 than it is in 1995. The author thanks Chris Barrett for suggesting some exploration of this issue.
9. Specifically, we estimate in first difference: $BMI_{iht+1} = \beta'_i \cong \mathbf{X_{iht}} + \beta'_H \cong \mathbf{X_{ht}}\ \beta'_C \cong \mathbf{X_{Ct}} + \varepsilon_i + \varepsilon_h + \varepsilon_C + \varepsilon_{iht}$, where BMI_{iht+1} is log of adult body mass index of person i residing in household h at time $t+1$, individual characteristics affecting BMI (including lagged BMI) are placed in the vector, $\mathbf{X_{iht}}$, $\mathbf{X_{ht}}$ is a vector of household characteristics at period t and $\mathbf{X_{Ct}}$ is a vector of locality characteristics. β'_C, β'_H, and β'_C are vectors of parameters to be estimated. ε_i, ε_h, and ε_C are unobserved characteristics of the adult, household and locality that are assumed to be time invariant and ε_{iht} is a white noise disturbance term.
10. Hoddinott and Kinsey (2003) provide an extended discussion as well as a large number of specification checks.
11. Unfortunately, we do not have the data to explore why this gender difference exists. One possibility is that women forgo more food in times of stress. Alternatively, while food consumption might fall for both men and women, men may also reduce their energy expenditures (because there is less farming to do) whereas women continue to undertake a variety of reproductive tasks. Some of these, such as the collection of water, might even become more energy intensive if women need to travel further to collect water.
12. These transitory shocks might have had longer term consequences where women's BMI fell below a threshold value at which low BMI is associated with other health complications or where the shocks to mothers are transmitted to their children. However, we find no evidence of this possibility in these data. The proportion of women with low BMI (below 18) rose by only a single percentage point after

the 1994–95 drought. To investigate the inter-generational transmission of the drought shock, we examined the determinants of children's birth weights but found that, controlling for a larger number of covariates, negative rainfall shocks did not affect these.

13. These results control for a large number of child, maternal and household characteristics. They are robust to a number of econometric concerns, including the treatment of heteroscedasticity, the specification of the sample, measurement error and endogeneity of initial height and unobserved household and maternal effects.
14. A limitation of the data available to us is that it is not possible to ascertain the precise causes of this growth faltering. In children of this age, linear growth is a consequence of food intake, disease exposure and the use of appropriate child care practices; it is not known how these changed in the aftermath of the 1994–95 drought. Speculatively, it is somewhat difficult to believe that a shortage of food was directly responsible, given the results we obtain for adults and the relatively limited caloric requirements of these very young children. However, given the reduction in household incomes, it is possible that households altered behaviours in subtle ways: for example, by re-serving leftover foods rather than discarding them (thus exposing children to pathogens), or that mothers spent more time obtaining water or searching for non-farm income, reducing time available for child care.
15. This material draws on a larger body of work summarised in Behrman, Alderman and Hoddinott (2004).

References

Alderman, H. and Paxson, C. (1992) Do the poor insure? A synthesis of the literature on risk and consumption in developing countries. Policy Research Working Papers, Agricultural Policies, WPS 1008, World Bank, Washington, DC.

Alderman, H., Hoddinott, J. and Kinsey, B. (2004) Long-term consequences of early childhood malnutrition. Mimeo, International Food Policy Research Institute, Washington, DC.

Alderman, H., Behrman, J., Lavy, V. and Menon, R. (2001) Child health and school enrollment: a longitudinal analysis, *Journal of Human Resources*, 36, pp. 185–205.

Alderman, H. Chiappori, P. A., Haddad, L., Hoddinott, J. and Kanbur, R. (1995) Unitary versus collective models of the household: Is it time to shift the burden of proof? *World Bank Research Observer*, 10, pp. 1–19.

Arellano, M. and Bond, S. (1991) Some tests of specification for panel data: Monte Carlo evidence and an application to employment equations, *Review of Economic Studies*, 58, pp. 277–97.

Barrett, C. and McPeak, J. (2005) Poverty traps and safety nets, in A. de Janvry and R. Kanbur (Eds) *Poverty, Inequality and Development: Essays in Honor of Erik Thorbecke*, (Kluwer), forthcoming.

Baulch, B. and Hoddinott, J. (2000) Economic mobility and poverty dynamics in developing countries, *Journal of Development Studies*, 36, pp. 1–24.

Behrman, J., Alderman, H. and Hoddinott, J. (2004) Hunger and malnutrition, in B. Lomborg (Ed.) *Copenhagen Consensus – Challenges and Opportunities* (Cambridge: Cambridge University Press), pp. 363–420.

Corbett, J. (1988) Famine and household coping strategies, *World Development*, 16, 1099–112.

Dasgupta, P. and Ray, D. (1986) Inequality as a determinant of malnutrition and unemployment: theory, *Economic Journal*, 96, pp. 1011–34.

Deaton, A. (1991) Savings and liquidity constraints, *Econometrica*, 59, 1221–48.

Deaton, A. (1992) Saving and income smoothing in Côte d'Ivoire, *Journal of African Economies*, 1, 1–24.

Dercon, S. and Hoddinott, J. (2004) Health, shocks and poverty persistence, in S. Dercon (Ed.) *Insurance Against Poverty* (Oxford: Oxford University Press), pp. 124–36.

Devereux, S. (1993) Goats before ploughs: dilemmas of household's response sequencing during food shortage. *IDS Bulletin*, 24, pp. 52–9.

Foster, A. and Rosenzweig, M. (1993) Information, learning and wage rates in low-income rural areas, *Journal of Human Resources*, 28, pp. 759–90.

Glewwe, P. and Jacoby, H. (1995) An economic analysis of delayed primary school enrollment and childhood malnutrition in a low income country, *Review of Economics and Statistics*, 77, pp. 156–69.

Glick, P. and Sahn, D. (1998) Health and productivity in a heterogeneous urban labour market, *Applied Economics*, 30, pp. 203–16.

Grantham-McGregor, S., Walker, C., Chang, S. and Powell, C. (1997) Effects of early childhood supplementation with and without stimulation on later development in stunted Jamaican children, *American Journal of Clinical Nutrition*, 66, pp. 247–53.

Grantham-McGregor, S., Fernald, L. and Sethuraman, K. (1999) Effects of health and nutrition on cognitive and behavioral development in children in the first three years of life: Part I.' *Food and Nutrition Bulletin*, 20, pp. 53–75.

Fafchamps, M. and Gavian, S. (1997) The determinants of livestock prices in Niger, *Journal of African Economies*, 6, 255–95.

Fafchamps, M., Udry, C. and Czukas, K. (1998) Drought and saving in west Africa: Are livestock a buffer stock? *Journal of Development Economics*, 55, pp. 273–308.

Haddad, L., Hoddinott, J., and Alderman, H. (Eds) (1997) *Intrahousehold Resource Allocation in Developing Countries: Models, Methods and Policy* (Baltimore: Johns Hopkins University Press).

Harrower, S. and Hoddinott, J. (2005) Consumption smoothing and vulnerability in the Zone Lacustre, Mali, *Journal of African Economies*, forthcoming.

Hoddinott, J. and Kinsey, B. (2003) Adult health in the time of drought, Mimeo, International Food Policy Research Institute, Washington, DC.

Hoddinott, J. and Kinsey, B. (2001) Child growth in the time of drought, *Oxford Bulletin of Economics and Statistics*, 63, pp. 409–36.

Jacoby, H. and Skoufias, E. (1998) Testing theories of consumption behaviour using information on aggregate shocks: income seasonality and rainfall in rural India, *American Journal of Agricultural Economics*, 80, pp. 1–14.

Kinsey, B. (1982) Forever gained: resettlement and land policy in the context of national development in Zimbabwe, *Africa*, 52, pp. 92–113.

Kochar, A. (1999) Smoothing consumption by smoothing income: hours-of-work responses to idiosyncratic agricultural shocks in rural India, *Review of Economics and Statistics*, 81, pp. 50–61.

Leslie, J. and Jamison, D. (1990) Health and nutrition considerations in education planning. 1. Educational consequences of health problems among school-age children, *Food and Nutrition Bulletin*, 12, pp. 191–203.

Lybbert, T., Barrett, C., Desta, S. and Coppock, D. (2004) Stochastic wealth dynamics and risk management among a poor population, *Economic Journal*, 114, pp. 750–77.

Martorell, R. (1995) Results and implications of the INCAP follow-up study, *Journal of Nutrition*, 125 (Suppl), 1127S–1138S.

Martorell, R. (1999) The nature of child malnutrition and its long-term implications, *Food and Nutrition Bulletin*, 20, pp. 288–92.

Morduch, J. (1995) Income smoothing and consumption smoothing, *Journal of Economic Perspectives*, 9, pp. 103–14.

Morduch, J. (1999) Between the market and state: Can informal insurance patch the safety net? *World Bank Research Observer*, 14, pp. 187–208.

Owens, T., Hoddinott, J. and Kinsey, B. (2003) The impact of agricultural extension on farm production in resettlement areas of Zimbabwe. *Economic Development and Cultural Change*, 51, pp. 337–58.

Pitt, M., Rosenzweig, M. and Hassan, M.D. (1990) Productivity, health and inequality in the intrahousehold distribution of food in low-income countries, *American Economic Review*, 80, pp. 1139–56.

Rose, E. (1999) Consumption smoothing and excess female mortality in rural India, *Review of Economics and Statistics*, 81, pp. 41–9.

Rosenzweig, M. and Wolpin, K. (1993) Credit market constraints, consumption smoothing and the accumulation of durable production assets in low-income countries: investments in bullocks in India, *Journal of Political Economy*, 101, pp. 223–44.

Rosenzweig, M. and Wolpin, K. (1988) Migration selectivity and the effects of public programs, *Journal of Public Economics*, 37, pp. 265–89.

Skoufias, E. and Quisumbing, A. (2002) Consumption insurance and vulnerability to poverty: a synthesis of the evidence from Bangladesh, Ethiopia, Mali, México, and Russia. Mimeo, International Food Policy Research Institute, Washington, DC.

Strauss, J. and Thomas, D. (1998) Health, nutrition, and economic development, *Journal of Economic Literature*, 36, pp. 766–817.

Thomas, D. and Strauss, J. (1997) Health and wages: evidence on men and women in urban Brazil. *Journal of Econometrics*, 77, pp. 159–86.

Townsend, R. (1995) Consumption insurance: an evaluation of risk-bearing systems in low-income countries, *Journal of Economic Perspectives*, 9, pp. 83–102.

Townsend, R. (1994) Risk and insurance in village India. *Econometrica*, 62, pp. 539–91.

Udry, C. (1994) Risk and insurance in a rural credit market: an empirical investigation in northern Nigeria, *Review of Economic Studies*, 61, pp. 495–526.

Zimmerman, F. and Carter, M. (2003) Asset smoothing, consumption smoothing and the reproduction of inequality under risk and subsistence constraints, *Journal of Development Economics*, 71, pp. 233–60.

Rural Income and Poverty in a Time of Radical Change in Malawi

PAULINE E. PETERS

I. Introduction

Malawi is a country where 'agriculture... offers the best prospects for stimulating broad based, poverty reducing growth in rural areas' (Dorward and Kydd, 2004: 355).[1] Current analyses recognise that markets are not the sole answer and emphasise the political economic and institutional dimensions of development. This is far from the 'pricism and state minimalism of the Washington consensus' that dominated the 1980s and, after a period of realism in the early to mid-1990s, again in the late 1990s (Harrigan, 2003).

In the context of this more realistic discussion of Malawi's development challenges, a detailed understanding of rural families' strategies and their outcomes over a decade can help sharpen the policy debate about reducing poverty and increasing rural incomes. The insights given by a longitudinal study – monitoring the same rural families over a decade – help reveal the ways in which common events and crises at national level are experienced by different categories of the population, how they provide opportunities that benefit some but maintain or increase obstacles for others. This paper reviews what categories of the rural sample move up or down the income/welfare distribution, and which remain either at the top or the bottom, and why. The first year's study in 1986–87, which becomes a 'baseline', took place in Zomba district, one of the most densely populated parts of southern Malawi, just before the major liberalisation policies affecting smallholders were put in place, while subsequent restudies were in 1990 and 1997.[2]

After sketching the key shifts in policies and in political economy more generally over the past two decades, I present the study families as they appeared in 1986 and the changes and continuities in their livelihoods and income up to 1997. These provide the basis for a discussion of what the changes in smallholder income and livelihood strategies imply for policy directed at reducing poverty and increasing food security.

II. Political Economic and Policy Context, 1980–2004

This significant period is marked by considerable policy and political change. Harrigan divides the World Bank-influenced policy reform into three phases: 1981–87 focused on 'pricist' policies, 1988–94 took a more 'flexible' stance that 'acknowledged the structuralist critique' of the first structural adjustment period, and 1994 to the present sees greater politicisation of the policy process (2003: 847).

The prevailing view in policy circles up to 1980, of Malawi being a successful 'free-market, non-interventionist, capitalist economy,'[3] was overturned by research showing that the 'dual' structure of Malawi's economy rested on a systematic process, achieved through agricultural, marketing and financial institutions, that privileged the estate sector at the cost of smallholder producers (Kydd and Christiansen, 1982). This dualist system ran into problems by the early 1980s consequent on 'exogenous shocks' of a collapse in the terms of trade, drought, and effects of the Mozambican civil war, that revealed the vulnerability of 'a highly import dependent estate sector, and marginalised smallholders leading to food and foreign exchange shortages' (Harrigan, 2003: 849).

The Banda government was forced to enter into negotiations with the IMF and the World Bank for Structural Adjustment Loans, the first in 1981. Raising the producer prices of non-maize crops (tobacco, groundnuts and cotton) led to increases in export crops but by displacing maize. The failure of ADMARC (the agricultural marketing board) to purchase hybrid maize at prices farmers expected, and some reduction in the fertiliser subsidy reduced the profitability of hybrid maize. Devaluation led a doubling in the consumer price of maize between 1983 and 1988 (Sahn et al., 1990: 107). This, with the closure of some ADMARC centres, resulted in consumers not being able to obtain staple maize in the deficit period,[4] and to a food crisis by 1987.[5] As a result, the Banda government unilaterally introduced a new set of smallholder prices at ADMARC, reversing the structural adjustment conditionality. The planned SAL IV was abandoned, and serious reappraisal of the World Bank policies in Malawi ensued.

The 1988–94 phase of the WB's 'structuralist revisionism toward the agricultural sector' (Harrigan, 2003: 847) typified the 1990 Agricultural Sector Adjustment Programme that stressed the prerequisite of improving food crop productivity and the need for targeted subsidies (Harrigan, 2003: 851). In addition, a moratorium was placed on conversion of land under customary tenure to leasehold estates, and estate land rents were raised. The most revolutionary move was to allow smallholders to grow burley tobacco that, until then, had been the prerogative of the estates. The World Bank accepted the need for ADMARC to maintain its 'developmental role' in maintaining markets in so-called remote areas and defending floor and ceiling prices, especially for maize. In response, smallholder agriculture grew by almost 16 per cent in 1991 due to a bumper maize harvest and rapid increase in burley tobacco production; by 1997–98, smallholder tobacco represented 70 per cent of the country's total tobacco production. However, smallholder growth proved unsustainable in light of policy and political shifts, as well as of adverse climatic conditions throughout the region.

From 1994 on, 'a schism developed between the Bank and the Government' (Harrigan, 2003: 847). The World Bank's 1997 Country Report rejected subsidies wholesale, stressed the marginal viability of hybrid maize production in the absence of input subsidies, and promoted the use of foreign exchange earnings from export crops, especially tobacco, as the route to food security. The Bank, with the IMF, also pressured the government to place more emphasis on financial reserves rather than physical reserves of maize. This stance ran counter to the evolving position of President Muluzi's 'democratic' government that had succeeded Banda's demise. Events within the new democracy also worsened the overall policy situation. As part of their electioneering, competing candidates made sweeping promises, including that debts to agricultural credit clubs would be forgiven because Banda and his cronies had 'stolen the country's money'. The existing credit system collapsed and, in combination with the reduction in input subsidies (allocated precisely through credit groups), a sharp devaluation in the kwacha and rise in input prices, produced a precipitous decline in smallholder production (Harrigan, 2003: 852).

A period of dissension between government and donors, and among donors, followed. The government insisted on the importance of improving food crop productivity as a prerequisite for expanded export crop production, a position supported by the Bank from 1990, but then rejected in 1997. Despite opposition by the Bank and USAID, in 1998 the government introduced the Starter Pack Programme that distributed small packages of fertiliser, hybrid maize seed and legumes to all smallholders. This was seen by the Design Task Force as a long-term development programme through which, over some years, improved yields and production would boost household food stores and sales of maize, so pushing many poor rural producers over a threshold where they would be able to purchase seed and fertiliser themselves.[6] The government objective was an improvement in national food security; some donors saw it as a social safety net, and most saw the need for actions to boost a seriously failing economy. The programme led to a marked rise in maize production and an overall increase in smallholder growth. Subsequently, becoming the Targeted Inputs Programme (TIP, funded mainly by the British), the programmes overall had a positive effect on maize harvests at national and household levels, though gains were reduced due to delays in distribution, and a replacement of hybrid seeds with lower-yielding composites.[7]

Objections by donors against such programmes included that they were equivalent to subsidies and thus antagonistic to the then prevailing liberalisation dogma. Recently, the recognised need for reasonable government interventions and support counter this objection. Another objection was that these programmes create 'dependency' in the rural recipients. There is no evidence to support this 'anti-welfare' view and research shows that recipients do not lessen their production and work efforts, and use the received packages to intensify their livelihood strategies. A third objection is that these programmes undercut the private market in fertiliser. This has been countered by the fact that the distributed amounts are so small that they do not deter those who can afford to buy fertiliser from doing so; that distributing fertiliser, even in small amounts, to the many smallholders who are unable to raise the cash or credit to buy sufficient fertiliser improves their production at the margin and, importantly, improves the overall level of economic production in rural areas; and that, even though a certain amount of 'leakage' to the better-off may occur, the resulting increase in maize production has positive effects on the overall supply of maize in the deficit period, especially in local markets, from which the main beneficiaries are the poorer consumers. The managing director of the one of the biggest fertiliser companies in the country made several of these points, including a rejection of a negative effect on the company's sales, in a recorded interview in 2001.[8] A different response to the concerns about leakage to the better-off and about private input markets is to link the distributed inputs to work programmes (see below).

The assessment of government programmes was also affected by the justifiable concerns about the Muluzi government's ability to follow appropriate policies and about the sharp rise in mismanagement and corruption from the highest levels down. The most egregious case was the famine that occurred in parts of the country in 2001–2002. While part of this was due to a very poor harvest due to problems with the rains, and to the pressure by the IMF to reduce the grain reserves held by the government, much was due to a sequence of events that have not yet been fully explained, but that involved both inept management and corruption.[9]

A recent assessment of the 'challenge for rural development' in Malawi repeats the overall story of a rural population with a 'narrow range of risky and low productivity activities ... exacerbated by poor infrastructure, services and communications ... low ... education and literacy ... and poor health exacerbated by the spread of HIV/AIDS' (Dorward and Kydd, 2004: 346). The authors see the main challenge as dealing with the 'systemic investment risks' to agricultural investment and conclude that, while there have been problems with the performance of parastatals, these, with related institutional structures, did manage to provide financial, input and marketing services to farmers,[10] and ensured the necessary coordination among these services. The structural adjustment cum liberalisation programmes dismantled these. The authors point out that liberalisation, while having some positive effects (such as trimming bloated and corrupt bureaucracies), has failed to replace these services and 'private sector investment has not replaced the parastatal system that aspired to support rural investment in maize production ... rural economies are now caught in a low equilibrium trap' (pp. 352–3). They call for more proactive actions by the state and see 'solutions' in 'regulated monopolies, regional commodity franchises, traders' associations, farmers' associations ... and some form of insurance for investors and consumers against price risk'. The latter include 'state grain reserves, price intervention and guarantees, and market information systems' as well as roads and other infrastructure (p. 357). This is a return to the 'structural' and 'gradualist' orientation of the early to mid-1990s before the resurgence of a market ideology. It is a call for a more proactive and more accountable state that seeks to provide livelihood and investment supports to agriculture that is most likely to stimulate broad-based growth and poverty reduction among the majority rural population (Kydd et al., 2004).[11]

III. Rural Households' Strategies before and after Market Liberalisation and Political Change

In this section, I summarise the main findings of the initial study in 1986–87 and the continuities and changes in subsequent studies of the same households in 1990–91 and 1997. The focus is on how rural families use their resources in seeking an acceptable level of living for themselves, and the changes and continuities observed over the period.

The long regime of Dr Banda was oppressive and enriched a small elite while keeping the majority in deep poverty, as evidenced by the high child mortality undiscussed until the mid-1980s. But tight control kept the consumer price of maize in ADMARC generally low and, though poverty resulted in chronic under-nutrition, it avoided the kind of famine seen in 2001–2002. The regime also funnelled agricultural inputs on credit to the better-off smallholders. In a sense, Banda's policies kept a lid on rapid socio-economic differentiation, which, after the economic and political changes in the early 1990s, has greatly increased. In 1986–87 the top income quartile of the Zomba sample households had a total income three times that of the bottom income quartile, whereas this difference increased to nine times in 1990–91 and to 11 times in 1997, suggesting a pattern of rapidly accelerating differentiation among rural families.

Unsurprisingly in a densely populated region, adequate land is one of the most critical differentiating factors among rural families, and there are significant correlations between size of landholding and maize harvests, income, and assets. Yet the income differentiation is produced largely out of very similar activities – there is nothing equivalent to a specific caste or group identified as the most poor. Families at the top and the bottom ends of the income and wealth distributions draw on the same resources and carry out the same productive activities, but in different proportions and with different outcomes. The resources are land, labour, cash for other inputs, management skills, discipline, hard work, and information; there is also luck and, the villagers would add, magic or witchcraft. One important point is that this sample, originally selected to study agricultural commercialisation, does not include the completely landless though it does include some families with small amounts of land (the smallest being 0.2 ha).

Things that rich and poor have in common in the villages include the definitions of lack of poverty as 'sufficient food, shelter, and clothing'. The study surveys showed that better-off households, on average, had more land, produced larger maize harvests and grew a larger diversity of crops, were far more likely to grow tobacco (dark-fired in 1986, burley in 1990–97), had higher levels of income from off-farm as well as farm sources, so giving them the wherewithal to purchase agricultural inputs, a sufficiency of foods, and some high-value consumption goods like better furniture, radios, watches, bicycles, tin roofs, and even motor-cycles for the richest. In contrast, the poorest households had, on average, smaller landholdings, produced very small maize harvests and had a lower and less productive range of crops, and, crucially, were extremely short of cash income despite their often working long hours at various types of poorly-remunerated casual work for the better-off families or local estates. The markers of poverty were those clearly designated by villagers: insufficient food especially in the deficit months of November–February when agricultural work demands peaked, but food was at its most scarce and most expensive, and morbidity levels high; poor housing, often a single-roomed, grass-thatched hut of unfired mud that was vulnerable to being literally washed away in heavy rains; and very few clothes – often only one set, and perhaps one thin blanket for all to share. The comfortable families were limited to only about one in five or fewer. The other families were all pressed for part to all of the year. Overall, this remains a poor population by most standards, despite my use here of such terms as richer or better-off for the top income group.[12]

Sample households revealed the typical rural diversification of income across farm and non-farm sources. In 1986–87, the proportions were 24 per cent of total income from off-farm sources, plus 15 per cent from transfers, 30 per cent from agricultural produce sales, and 30 per cent from the value of home-retained maize. The changes in 1990 were not huge, but the agricultural sales increased on average, while off-farm dropped slightly, and home consumption remained more or less the same. The variation across sample income groups seen in 1986, with the poorer earning more from temporary labour and the richer from agricultural sales, was also repeated in 1990. By 1997, this pattern intensified. The overwhelming source of cash income for the top quartile came from burley tobacco, with important contributions from sales of maize, legumes and vegetables. The poorest quartile households were finding it more difficult to obtain all the staple maize they needed and therefore reduced their (already small) maize sales, and they intensified their wage work, mostly temporary agricultural labour for local farmers.

Time allocation data indicated that temporary jobs taken up by members of poor, land-short households had extremely low returns to effort directed away from own farm production. In years of poor harvests, the number of jobs and the rates of compensation dropped even more, so forcing some of the poorest into desperate circumstances. These poor households are caught in a vicious cycle: they are unable to generate enough income and food from their own production, yet their off-farm work does not generate a large enough income to increase substantially their low maize and other food stores (Whiteside, 1999).

Such vicious cycles also help to perpetuate inequality. The better-off households who, on average, have more land, bigger maize harvests, more agricultural and non-agricultural income, disproportionately hired neighbours as well as temporary labourers coming from other areas. A primary use of the large surplus maize stores held by these better-off households was to hire workers in the peak agricultural season. The vicious cycle for the poor is tightly bound to the virtuous cycle of accumulation by the better-off.

A feature distinguishing household composition by relative wealth is the presence of an active man: over a half of the poorest quartile households, compared with less than a fifth in the top income quartile, were without an active man in 1986–87. This dropped to about 11 per cent among top quartile households in 1990–91, reflecting the need for an active couple (man *and* woman)[13] to engage in extensive burley production. Adult men add considerably to the agricultural labour available to a family, bring in cash income from other work, and usually have more influence in public arenas outside the village.[14]

Common to families at all levels of income is the desire to produce as much of their staple maize as possible. The apparently tautological reason I was given over and over by farmers, that '*chimanga ndi moyo*' (maize is life), states not merely that maize is 'the staff of life' but also implicitly refers to the pervasive uncertainty in supplies and prices of maize. Very few – less than 15 per cent – got anywhere near self-sufficiency in maize, but in 1986–87 the average proportion of total maize available contributed by own production was 70 per cent, and only 11 per cent of the maize harvest of the *entire* sample was sold. These were 86 per cent and 9 per cent respectively in 1990. In all three years (1986–87, 1990, 1997), the top quartile households produced larger harvests, sold larger proportions of their produce (food crops as well as non-food crops like tobacco), but also retained more maize for their own family needs (both absolutely and proportionally), while the poorer produced less, and what they retained provided a smaller proportion of their needs. These food-deficit families had to purchase or work for maize in the 'hunger' season.

The positive correlation between 'subsistence' and 'commercialisation' is an important empirical fact about rural families, but also an analytically important point. The larger quantities of crops sold and the higher cash income from sales of tobacco and other crops achieved by the top income quartile households mean that they had a lower 'subsistence ratio' as measured by the share of retained crops in total agricultural output, and in total income (including non-farm income). On the other hand, 'subsistence' understood as the value of the share of retained maize in total food expenditures was negatively correlated with income. Those with larger landholdings, larger maize harvests, and higher cash incomes did *not* reduce the proportion of own produced maize in their total maize/food needs. Subsistence and commercialisation are not two alternative orientations, but interdependent strategies followed by individuals and households, best understood in relative terms.[15] Moreover, this relationship also shows that the poor, indeed the poorest, are in no way 'outside the market' as some writers have erroneously assumed about Malawi (see Peters, 1996b). The amount of maize (or other foods such as root crops) given as compensation to poor families for their work is determined largely by the current price in local markets, though it may be modified by the type of relationship between the hirer and the hired.

The common aim of food self-sufficiency is more a dream than a reality since the ability to reach it lies beyond most families. This is a population dependent on purchases for much of their food supply. While 53 per cent in 1986–87 and 60 per cent in 1990–91 of sample households sold maize, mostly in small amounts, fully 99 per cent in 1986–87 and 95 per cent in 1990–91 purchased maize. The percentage of households selling maize dropped steadily from the early 1990s to 29 per cent in 1997 while the proportion buying maize has not changed significantly. There are good reasons for families trying to produce as much of their food as possible even while recognizing that they will also need to purchase some or a lot, especially in the food-deficit period of November–February. First, 'Consumers . . . face very uncertain maize prices . . .' (Dorward and Kydd, 2004: 354) and there is instability in sources of maize for purchase in the deficit season. An important source of maize is ADMARC, but the selling points are distant from many sample respondents who spend half or more of a day going to and fro, and there are often large numbers of people waiting in line, as well as periodic shortages of supply. The other sources of maize are local farmers willing to sell maize, sellers in local markets, and the few traders and shops with maize for sale. But the prices for maize from these sources are always higher than at ADMARC. The instability has increased since the early 1990s, which accounts for the declining rate of maize sales seen in my sample and in the national statistics.

Secondly, cash is generally scarce in the villages, but particularly so in the food-deficit and main cultivation season (November – January) when medical costs also rise since malaria and other illnesses peak in that period. A contributing reason is that maize stores are considered more socially protected than cash which people see as more fungible and more open to demands from others. Maize in a granary is considered to be under the authority of the primary woman of the house, who decides how much maize to be taken out and for what purposes. It is considered reprehensible for a husband to take maize from a granary or even look in it without permission from his wife: he will be teased as a thief and as being 'food-jealous'. Along with other customs about stored maize, such ideas serve as 'brakes' on its use. Money, in contrast, is seen as more subject to requests by kin and friends, and as liable to be frittered away, disappearing with little to show for it (in ways not peculiar to Malawi).

Unsurprisingly, it is the poorer people who are forced to buy from the more expensive local sources since they tend to obtain smaller amounts of money more sporadically and rarely manage to afford the larger quantities sold at the ADMARC centres (or the 'tips' they are often required to give the staff in times of short supply). Although only 11 per cent of the total sample maize harvest in 1986–87 was sold, the poorest income quartile sold twice that proportion of their harvests (22 per cent) because they had no other source of cash. Surveys in 1986 and 1990 revealed a U-shaped distribution of maize sales, with higher proportions of sellers in the top and bottom of landholding and income categories, and a parallel curve for proportion of maize harvest sold. This reflects surplus at the top end and desperation at the bottom.

The clearest indication of the pressure on the poorest is seen in the expenditures on staple maize (see Table 1). From the quite high percentage of 25 per cent of total expenditures in 1986–87 spent on maize, households in the poorest income quartile spent a sharply risen 36 per cent in 1990–91 and 30 per cent in 1997. The first period matches the very difficult years of the early structural adjustment when food prices rose much faster than revenues (Sahn, et al., 1990). The increase over the whole period in the amount of income that has to be spent on staple maize compared with what was already a below-poverty line level of living for the poorest households reveals an intensified pressure on them.

IV. Changes in Income and Relative Poverty 1986–97

For the sample as a whole, incomes (proxied on expenditures) have risen between 1986 and 1997 by 59 per cent. However, there was a drop of about 8 per cent between 1986 and 1990 and an increase of 72 per cent between 1990 and 1997 (see Table 2). The fall in the first period is explained by the detrimental effects of the first structural adjustment and liberalisation programmes, as discussed above. The rise in the second is overwhelmingly due to the sharp rise in growers of burley tobacco. The aggregate figures for the sample, however, mask an increasing gap between the families in the top income group and those at the bottom. In 1986–87, the mean

Table 1. Expenditure shares on foods and selected items

		Percent of budget spent					
	Year	Maize	Other foods	Goods & services	Health	Education	Fertiliser
Total sample	1986	20.0	26.0	32.0	2.0	0.4	1.9
	1991	22.0	22.0	31.0	1.1	2.0	3.7
	1997	19.5	19.6	35.1	1.0	0.6	5.6
Expenditures quartile 1 – (Lowest)	1986	25.0	20.0	32.0	2.2	0.2	0.7
	1991	36.0	23.0	29.0	1.3	2.0	1.3
	1997	29.5	22.0	35.3	0.7	0.6	0.2
Expenditure quartile 2	1986	23.0	34.0	33.0	2.5	0.6	0.3
	1991	24.0	23.0	31.0	1.2	1.7	3.2
	1997	22.0	22.8	32.5	1.3	0.4	4.6
Expenditure quartile 3	1986	19.0	25.0	32.0	1.6	0.5	2.2
	1991	19.0	23.0	30.0	1.1	1.7	4.3
	1997	19.8	19.6	32.5	1.4	0.8	5.2
Expenditure quartile 4 – (Highest)	1986	13.0	25.0	31.0	1.9	0.3	4.4
	1991	9.0	18.0	33.0	0.6	2.7	6.0
	1997	6.6	14.2	37	0.6	0.6	12.6

income of the top 25 per cent was three times that of the bottom quartile, whereas this had increased to nine by 1990–91 and to 11 by 1997. In the period between 1986 and 1990, benefits from the policy changes were concentrated among the top income quartile households with others registering a decline – a regressive pattern. This was reversed in the second, longer period between 1990 and 1997 with all quartiles experiencing some improvement in income (as measured by expenditures). Gains were much greater, however, for the top quartile. Over the total period, 1986–97, households in the bottom quartile have lost ground absolutely and, even more, relative to the top quartile, as seen in the increased share of expenditures spent on maize staples by the poorest quartile. They have also reduced the proportion of income derived from agricultural sales and increased that from wage labour, most of it temporary agricultural work for local farmers. In direct contrast, households in the top income quartile have significantly increased the share of agricultural income relative to other sources, reflecting the high burley incomes and, to a lesser extent, sales of maize and other crops.

Transition Matrices

What can we learn from seeing the movement or lack of it across expenditure groups?[16] Overall, between 1986 and 1997, almost exactly half of the households in both bottom and top quartiles remained there (see Figure 1). There was less movement in the first period, 1986 and 1990, than the second. Between 1986 and 1990, 54.8 per cent of those in the bottom quartile remained there and 57.8 per cent of the top quartile did so. The second period, 1990–97, saw more movement in all except the third quartile. Approximately 54 per cent of households in both the top

Table 2. Sample per capita household annualised expenditures: 1986–87, 1990–91 and 1997 Nominal and adjusted for inflation

	1986–87	1990–91	1997 (n = 215)	1990–91 Deflated**	1997 Deflated**
Total sample	62.06	109.89	573.91	57.14	98.48
Expenditure quartile 1 (Lowest)	34.43	32.52	137.07	16.91	23.52
Expenditure quartile 2	46.11	55.17	271.63	28.69	46.61
Expenditure quartile 3	64.25	78.61	456.37	40.88	78.31
Expenditure quartile 4 (Highest)	105.92	276.37	1,449.29	143.71	248.70
Tobacco producing*	63.86	157.05	621.41	81.67	106.63
Smallholders		116.55	585.58	60.61	100.49
Non-tobacco producing	61.30	78.80	369.70	40.98	63.44
Female de jure headed	46.46	109.76	474.85	57.08	81.48
Female de facto headed	65.04	57.13	387.58	29.71	66.51
Male headed	64.42	117.18	631.49	60.93	108.36

Notes: 1986–87 data were recorded monthly for a 10 month period and have been annualized. 1990–91 data were recorded monthly for 12 months 1997 data were recorded six times during a one year period.
*Tobacco producing equals both smallholders and leaseholders (no leaseholders in 1986/7).
**Low Income Zomba Consumer Price Indices were used to derive a Non-Food Index to Low Income Zomba Consumer Price Indices were used to derive a Non-Food Index to A deflator of .33 was used to deflate the 1997 data to a 1990 base and then a deflator of .52 was used to deflate to a 1986 base.

and the bottom quartiles moved compared with 42 per cent and 45 per cent in the first period, and more households in each of these quartiles moved up and down compared with 1986–90.

The use of quintiles in transition matrices modifies this picture only slightly, while that of deciles reveals rather more. The greatest stability is seen among the very richest in that 47 per cent of the top decile remained at the top between 1986 and 1997 compared with much smaller percentages for other deciles. On the other hand, only 16.7 per cent of the bottom decile remained in that position over the period while a half shifted up to the next two deciles. Thus, despite an overall worsening in income distribution overall and an increased stress on the bottom quartile households seen in the expenditure patterns, the matrices do not show a large percentage stuck at the level of the bottom 10 per cent. As the quintiles and quartiles show, however, 43 per cent and 50 per cent respectively, did remain in the bottom 20–25 per cent between 1986 and 1997.

Qtl 1= lowest

Quartiles 1986	1990 Q1	Q2	Q3	Q4
Q1	54.8%	23.8%	14.3%	7.1%
Q2	20.0%	37.5%	35.0%	7.5%
Q3	18.2%	29.5%	31.8%	20.5%
Q4	11.1%	8.9%	22.2%	57.8%

Quartiles 1990	1997 Q1	Q2	Q3	Q4
Q1	45.5%	25.0%	15.9%	13.6%
Q2	26.2%	31.0%	28.6%	14.3%
Q3	20.5%	25.0%	34.1%	20.5%
Q4	17.1%	19.5%	17.1%	46.3%

Quartiles 1986	1997 Q1	Q2	Q3	Q4
Q1	50.0%	26.2%	14.3%	9.5%
Q2	22.5%	32.5%	35.0%	10.0%
Q3	22.7%	27.3%	29.5%	20.5%
Q4	15.6%	15.6%	17.8%	51.1%

Quintile Percentages	1997				
1986	Q5	Q4	Q3	Q2	Q1
Q5	52.9%	14.7%	5.9%	20.6%	5.9%
Q4	20.6%	29.4%	29.4%	11.8%	8.8%
Q3	8.8%	29.4%	17.6%	23.5%	20.6%
Q2	8.8%	14.7%	26.5%	26.5%	23.5%
Q1	5.7%	11.4%	20.0%	20.0%	42.9%

Deciles	1997									
1986	D10	D9	D8	D7	D6	D5	D4	D3	D2	D1
D10	47.1%	17.6%	11.8%	5.9%	0.0%	0.0%	5.9%	5.9%	5.9%	0.0%
D9	23.5%	17.6%	11.8%	0.0%	11.8%	0.0%	11.8%	17.6%	5.9%	0.0%
D8	5.9%	17.6%	11.8%	11.8%	23.5%	17.6%	0.0%	0.0%	11.8%	0.0%
D7	11.8%	5.9%	5.9%	29.4%	5.9%	11.8%	11.8%	11.8%	0.0%	5.9%
D6	0.0%	5.9%	23.5%	11.8%	0.0%	11.8%	11.8%	17.6%	17.6%	0.0%
D5	5.9%	5.9%	11.8%	11.8%	0.0%	23.5%	11.8%	5.9%	5.9%	17.6%
D4	0.0%	17.6%	5.9%	0.0%	11.8%	17.6%	17.6%	5.9%	0.0%	23.5%
D3	0.0%	0.0%	0.0%	25.0%	25.0%	0.0%	6.3%	18.8%	0.0%	25.0%
D2	0.0%	11.8%	0.0%	5.9%	17.6%	5.9%	5.9%	17.6%	17.6%	17.6%
D1	0.0%	0.0%	16.7%	0.0%	5.6%	11.1%	0.0%	16.7%	33.3%	16.7%

Figure 1. Transition matrices

The greater mobility up and down after 1990 reflects the much greater changes in that period, especially the expansion of burley tobacco production as well as the broader set of political economic changes outlined earlier. For those placed to take advantage of burley, especially to join the clubs allowed to sell at the world price, these years saw advantage. Some also benefited from the expansion in trade of other crops, especially food crops, such as sweet potatoes, cassava, legumes, sold to the urban areas. But many lost ground, unable to find the income sources to combat a period of rising inflation and rising prices. A currently worsening situation due to HIV/AIDS is making life even more difficult and with ramifying effects through the social system in ways not yet fully understood.[17]

The period 1990–97 is marked by considerable movement for the burley tobacco growers in the sample, with only half of the top quartile growers remaining there, the rest dropping, and while no lowest quartile households had grown tobacco in the first period, 29 per cent of burley growers were in the bottom quartile in 1990 and remained there in 1997. This reflects the fact that many farmers had raced into burley production, but without sufficient resources, particularly seeds and fertilisers, and without access to the burley clubs, they were unable to make a consistently high income. Most of the households *not* growing tobacco in the second period are seen to be worse off over those years, but some remain in the top income group, revealing an increase in income disparity even among the non-tobacco growing households. Fully 73 per cent of the lowest quartile non-tobacco households remained in that position between 1990 and 1997 while over 40 per cent of those in the next to lowest quartile lost ground, falling into the bottom quartile. In contrast, two-thirds of those in the top quartile remained there, as did half of those in the next to top quartile. This comparison of burley growing households with non-tobacco growers shows that while burley tobacco production has been a key factor of differentiation among smallholders since 1990, it is not the only one. Other contributing factors to growing inequality include the reduced access to credit and hence new seeds and fertilisers, the increasing importance of access to sufficient land in face of the volatility of crop prices in more open markets, the decline in migrant labour opportunities and a flood of people into petty trading with low returns (Dorward and Kydd, 2004: 346, Ellis et al., 2003), and the tendency for droughts and other climatic problems as well as political economic crises to intensify pre-existing inequalities.

Some Portraits

While landholding is a key factor in the ability of rural families to achieve decent living standards, human resources are also critical in the type of labour and skill-intensive agriculture found in Malawi. Some portraits of families on different income (poverty and wealth) trajectories capture this. The three families remaining in the bottom decile between 1986 and 1997 were headed by women, two of them widowed over the period. Similarly, in another 12 families remaining in the bottom fifth over the period, nine were or became female-headed: three were so throughout, one had her husband die, three divorced (one of these was polygynous), and two had husbands working away from home within the district, but in low-paying jobs as watchmen. Of the three jointly-headed, two had very small landholdings, but a number of dependants, and one was an elderly couple with grandchildren coming and going. In these families, many of the youngest generation left school early and took labouring jobs in estates. In the cases where the families had the labour of a man and woman as well as land of around one hectare, the problems were too many dependants, insufficient management skills, inability to raise cash for inputs, and ill-luck.

In four families who dropped from the top quartile in 1986 to the lowest by 1997, the effects of life cycle changes are evident. In one, the death of the elderly but strong man who was a good farmer and a close adviser to the village chief, led to a precipitous drop in income as the elderly widow parcelled out most of the land among her children. The fact that several of her daughters lived around her probably meant that the sharp drop in the income of her own household did not mean she was bereft.[18] In two other households, divorce again removed a key worker and income earner: in one, the woman remarried after the husband left, but to a polygynous man who ‘comes rarely’ and who did not provide adequate income; in the other, the husband took a second wife, gradually reduced his presence and income support and finally divorced her. In the fourth family, which had been doing well on 2.6 ha of land growing maize and tobacco, serious quarrels developed between wife and husband by 1990 and the husband died in 1991, according to rumour poisoned by his wife, which caused a great deal of disruption among neighbouring and related families.

At the other end of the scale–those who remained in the top quartile over the period – all were 'intact' households with active wife and husband working together on the family production. Most also had above average landholdings. One family is perhaps the archetypical hard-working farm family. They have 1.3 ha of land, including very good wetland gardens (*dimba*), which belong to the wife's family, one of the 'original' settlers of the village. The husband was found – almost literally – always working in these gardens, growing a great deal of vegetables which he and his wife sold at local and town markets. They also grew maize and, from 1990, a fairly large amount of burley tobacco. By 1997, the husband had acquired another landholding in a neighbouring district where he had contacts. One of the other families with two and a half hectares did not grow burley, but specialised in maize, also keeping a few livestock. Of the three families with smaller landholdings, one was a successful stall-fed cattle farmer. He had learned about cattle in his job, over many years, as cattle guard in a local research station. He had started his own business before he retired in 1996 and was intensifying his efforts in 1997, selling considerable milk through the local collection system. In another family who had 1.3 ha of land on which they grew maize and burley, the husband had for many years been the manager of a local estate (growing maize and keeping livestock), but he and his wife also ran a small grocery in the village (abutting the estate). When he retired as manager, he increased his burley production and spent more time on the grocery. A third family with 1.4 ha (belonging to the wife, a sister of the local village head) grew a range of crops, including maize and burley. But the husband was also a builder who gained income from local contracts. They did well from burley, but when the prices started to drop in the mid-1990s, he switched more of his efforts to growing onions in his *dimba* and in 2001 (in a brief encounter) said he was making more profit selling these on a contract to an educational institution in the local town.

While these successful families are the envy of others in their ability to provide all the food, clothing, and other needs for themselves as well as, in some cases, motorbikes or other vehicles, they all face the problem of declining landholdings. Thus, for their advantage to be passed onto the next generation, one mode is to ensure their children are educated to higher levels than normal in the villages. This is true for only a minority of these families, so that the stability over the period may be stability for a generation, but their status will not necessarily be passed onto the next for many. At present, while there is net out-migration from the research area, many of those leaving are heading for districts where there is land available, again a dwindling number, or for the towns where reports suggest that poverty is growing much faster than wealth. Against this, the growth of the small market or trading centres in the research area is quite obvious and has generated economic activity so providing income and jobs for some.

V. Discussion: Key Issues for Reducing Rural Poverty in Malawi

The decade of the 1990s constituted an enormous challenge to the farmers of Malawi because of the climate-related disasters and the political and economic crises. The early years of the new millennium have continued to be difficult. The period is one of persisting patterns (as discerned from the 1980s) and key, potentially radical, changes. By 1997, the income distribution had worsened, with some households clearly benefiting, some worse off, and the rest continued 'churning.'

The persistent patterns include, first, diversification in agricultural production, especially cropping patterns, and in income strategies. There is tension between this 'grass-roots' reality and an often misguided national debate (in which international agents, especially aid donors, are prominent) about diversification, which have had negative effects on agricultural policies. Second, the centrality of maize production in food security by rural households has been maintained. Third, the skewed income distribution has persisted and deepened.

The changes include, first, a large increase in hybrid maize production in the late 1980s and early 1990s,[19] but then a highly uneven trend because of the policy and other shifts described above. Second, the opening of burley tobacco production to smallholders led to a veritable explosion of growers. Third, national statistics show increased proportions of burley tobacco and non-maize food crops in smallholder cultivation, though apparently not at the cost of maize. Fourth, policies of market liberalisation have brought an influx of crop traders into the villages at harvest time, and an increase in crop marketing among most farmers, but failed to replace the parastatal's crucial role as food supplier in the deficit season. Fifth, liberalisation has brought a great deal of institutional confusion in its wake, exacerbated by the tendency for donors and government to shift and backtrack on their positions, with negative effects on the production and food security strategies of farmers. Finally, certain trends that escape the attention of commentators on the national picture include the growth of small trading centres (mainly positive) and an increasing competition over land and landed resources (more problematic).

As pointed out above, the first disastrous structural adjustments revealed that the problems facing agricultural production and rural livelihoods in Malawi are not amenable to policies based *simply* on prices and markets. Current debate and suggestions for Malawi stress the problems of access to and use of factors of production by rural people, the need to increase the value of production, and the appropriate institutional organisation for finding solutions. Some of the key issues are addressed here.

Land, Labour and Agricultural Inputs

A major problem facing Malawi is the shortage of agricultural land relative to its rural population. The average smallholding is less than half a hectare with the smallest landholdings occurring in the southern region, which thus resembles Rwanda, Burundi and parts of Kenya and Nigeria. One result is a very intensive pattern of use on land under permanent cultivation. Farmers use complex intercropping and crop sequencing to obtain as much as possible from their smallholdings. In the study site, against the constant backdrop of maize and intercropped legumes,[20] farmers plant a wide variety of crops and crop varieties as these become available, judging which to plant according to crop characteristics including yield, taste and commercial value. Those with sufficient land seasonally shift crops around their land-holdings (many families have several fields, often spaced apart from one another) according to soil type, sun/shade, pests, and to changing conditions in availability of inputs, climate, policy effects, and market conditions. A particularly valuable type of land, found along streambeds and other seasonally wet lands, allows families to grow crops, some for consumption, some for sale, in the dry season. These gardens, which are largely irrigated by hand but some now by treadle pumps, are very unevenly distributed, subject to increasing demand, and rising rents.[21]

These labour-intensive patterns of use on tiny landholdings produce the situation, described earlier, of poorer families being forced to work as casual labourers, ending in a vicious cycle of low production, low income and low food supplies. Alwang and Siegel (1999) call this 'the paradox of on-farm labour shortages on small landholdings'. They attribute the paradox to 'land scarcity ... exacerbated by food security concerns' (p. 1472), and conclude that the central problem is lack of finance or credit to tide the poor over the deficit period.

This lack of credit and financial resources is also identified by Barrett and Carter (this issue) as needing redress if the poverty of rural Africans is to be reduced. Methods to fill this gap through cash, credit or in-kind transfers include programmes of credit, preferably linked with savings, and state-supported programmes for distributing cash, food and/or inputs in return for public works. Programmes of targeted subsidies and fertiliser and seed distribution, as well as the new (but small-scale) credit programmes in Malawi through the 1990s had clear positive effects on household and national production. Linking cash or inputs to work on rural roads and other key infrastructure also has well-documented benefits for the wider rural economy.

The need to increase the productivity of agriculture is critical. Agricultural research can help through developing better yielding and pest-resistant crops such as groundnuts, beans, tubers, and magoye soya beans (Orr, 2000: 359, citing Carr, 1993), and extension programmes are needed to get these out to villagers (as some NGOs are doing). A programme to help smallholder farmers form small business 'clubs' in order to achieve more leverage in obtaining inputs and in selling produce has been very successful.[22] Though, to date, most of the clubs, like the burley clubs (which were part of this programme when it first started), are made up of the better-off smallholders, the ideas are appropriate for rural producers on a wider scale (Dorward and Kydd, 2004).

The challenges in reorienting agricultural extension are particularly acute.[23] Up to now, extension field staff have concentrated on the top tier of smallholder producers, one well-documented shortcoming of the otherwise successful farmers' clubs up to the early 1990s. As part of the current decentralisation programme in Malawi, the Ministry of Agriculture has declared that extension staff will no longer deliver advice *to* farmers but that farmers will obtain advice from staff, probably through payment, but this remains in the future.

The Challenge of Diversification within and Outside Agriculture

On-farm diversification is typical among the smallholders of the southern highlands and, to judge from other studies, in other parts of the country, too. At present, burley tobacco remains the highest value crop available to smallholder farmers and despite its not being *the* single solution to rural poverty, it has had positive effects for some families, and, in normal or good years, it has positive effects on the wider rural economy in that much of the income is spent there (Orr and Mwale, 2001: 1327). There is also the rise in smallholder sales, in the Zomba sample as more generally, of root crops, especially sweet potatoes and cassava, legumes such as pigeon peas, chickpeas, soya, a wide variety of vegetables, as well as several 'new' crops such as chilli peppers and paprika. The impetus for this includes both household food security (re root crops) and new or expanding markets (for pigeon peas in India, and all foods for the expanding urban and peri-urban populations). Nevertheless, some of the new markets are 'niche markets' and easily saturated (such as chillies), or the quality criteria are beyond most smallholders (paprika and organic herbs), or other potential opportunities such as macadamia nuts, require levels of capital investment too high for most smallholders. The shortage of land is clearly a huge obstacle in the way of achieving sufficient output from any of these diversified crop directions. Increasing the productivity of cultivated land is crucial, and includes agricultural research for better yielding and pest-resistant crops, as well as effective extension, and, more support for farmers' associations to give them more leverage in the purchase of inputs and the marketing of produce. On-farm diversification is aimed at *both* food security *and* cash income, and is a strategy to deal with the 'systemic investment risks of poor rural areas' (Dorward and Kydd, 2004: 347).

The perceived risk factors have all increased since the late 1980s. In the Zomba site, by 1997 people were saying that shortages of maize in the ADMARC centres had become much more marked, that private traders were unable to make up the deficit, and they were further unnerved by the extreme seasonal shifts in local prices observed that year. Some of the large-scale producers who, during the mid-1990s, had increased burley production and reduced their surplus maize production and sales, on the then realistic assumption that it was more economic to earn more from burley and buy any extra maize needed, were reversing themselves and once more increasing the relative proportion of their surplus maize.[24] For most people, these events have led them to produce and retain as much maize as they can, and to purchase as much of what they need beyond their own production as near the harvest as possible.

In light of the considerable diversification seen 'from the fields', the national debate emerging over the past ten or so years that calls for greater diversification in Malawi's agriculture is perplexing. This may make some sense for the place of export crops in Malawi's foreign exchange earnings – these come overwhelmingly from tobacco, followed by sugar, tea and a range of other crops.[25] But it makes less sense when applied to the vast majority of smallholder farmers in Malawi. It is particularly inappropriate when the 'lack of diversity' is linked with views that the land is 'mono-cropped' in maize and that Malawian people are unwilling to eat anything but maize. The vision of 'mono-cropping' is misleading because it completely erases the vast number of intercrops and sequenced crops that are grown in most 'maize fields' (at least in the southern highlands).[26] The notion that Malawians refuse to eat other foods than maize is egregiously wrong.

These misrepresentations have been made possible by several factors. The official crop statistics for many years made limited attempts to count intercrops and even now, under-estimate them, and too many commentators 'eye-ball' fields during the cultivation season without examining fields carefully, and in different parts of the country. In recent years, more effort has been made in official statistics to account for non-maize crops. New statistics have revealed a national trend downwards in the proportion of maize planted compared with other grains and root crops, and declining shares of maize in smallholder fields. These have been interpreted by some as indicating a welcome shift towards non-maize food crops by farmers anxious to improve their food security. However, several points of caution have to be made about the perceived trends and their interpretation. Data for non-maize crops are often flawed, given the complex inter-cropping and crop-sequencing. There was no systematic collection of data for many of the 'minor' crops until the last few decades.[27] Most seriously, the statistics for cassava production were based on highly exaggerated yield estimates that were 'two to three times the average for the best growing areas in Africa', namely, parts of Nigeria (Carr, 1998; Dorward and Kydd, 2004: 345).

Several serious consequences have flowed from this. The failure to recognise the pending famine following on the 1992 drought and disastrous maize harvest was exacerbated by the 'very biased and inaccurate cassava figures (produced by the Ministry of Agriculture which) were taken as evidence that there was no food crisis' (Devereux, 2002: 7). In addition, some donors have made the absurd assumptions that maize could be replaced by cassava as a staple food. Not only were their yield estimates wildly inaccurate, but they also ignore 'the deleterious impact of continuous cassava cultivation on the soil', and the impact of cassava that contains 'cyanide on the health of a population with problems of early child survival and widespread iodine deficiency' (Carr, 1998). Moreover, cassava, sweet potato and other non-maize crops have long been incorporated into diets whenever people had access to them, as shown below. A final point is that donors and other observers have ignored another important reason for the increase in production of non-maize food crops: namely, the demand from rising urban and peri-urban populations.

With respect to the eating habits of Malawians,[28] detailed study, such as that in Zomba, reveals that in the late rains (February–April) when many crops are maturing in the fields, the maize *nsima* that is the 'normal' staple food is replaced for at least one of the two main meals and sometimes at both by dishes of boiled sweet potatoes, groundnuts, various legumes (peas and beans), and vegetables (cucumbers, pumpkins). In addition, throughout the year, cassava in various forms provides supplementary meals to maize *nsima*. It is correct that most Malawian farmers (and not just they) will respond to questions about 'food' with reference to maize, especially in the form of *nsima*. But careful observation and surveys have shown that they eat a much wider range of foods. In addition, this study shows a distinct increase in the consumption of all these 'supplementary' foods since the mid- to late-1980s, as does another study in the Southern Region (Orr and Mwale, 2001). The reasons appear to include concern about food security and a new market opportunity, as well as the efforts by government, donors and NGOs to promote and sometimes to provide information and seeds/cuttings of these crops.

While crop diversification represents a central strategy for Malawian smallholders, one that has enabled many to avoid the worst crises in food security and to obtain needed cash income, it depends on having sufficient land on which to grow different crops, labour to work them, and access to seeds and other inputs. The strategy is thus beyond the poorest who, on average, are also those with the smallest landholdings: they grow fewer crops in their fields, and have greater difficulties obtaining seeds and cuttings for the planting season. They frequently depend on charitable handouts by relatives and neighbours and, inevitably, tend to receive second-best or even rejected seed and cuttings. They also are the least able to buy fertiliser and, when they do, it is in minute proportions. Hence, there is a particular need for the kind of distribution, public works, and credit programmes mentioned above for the poorer rural families, as the following illustration – one out of several – conveys.

In 1993, people received free distribution of seeds and maize food after the severe 1991–92 drought: this was very effective in reducing the level of want. I was intrigued, however, by the complaints of the minority of bigger producers of maize and burley about their difficulties in obtaining 'enough casual labourers'. I came to realise that the issue was less a lack of available workers than the workers' being unwilling to work for the low levels of remuneration being offered by the employers. The latter, in fact, had to increase their usual low rates to get workers. A number of these bigger farmers spontaneously attributed this unusual situation to the fact that local families 'were satisfied with the drought relief food'. The relief gave the poorest families a welcome margin of supplies that increased their bargaining power, a complementary view to the need for such transfer programmes to replace missing capital markets (Alwang and Siegel, 1999; Dorward and Kydd, 2004).

Burley tobacco production shows the most dramatic change in crop diversification. The Zomba research was done in an area selected in 1990–91 as one of the pilot sites for the historic opening of burley to smallholders. Other types of tobacco had long been grown there. My sample had been purposively selected in 1986 to have growers of tobacco (then the dark-fired type) as approximately 30 per cent of the sample. In 1990–91, there was a rapid turn away from dark-fired tobacco towards burley tobacco, resulting in approximately 30 per cent burley growers. In subsequent years, the numbers have increased, though rising and falling depending on climate, price, and other conditions. By 1997, an amazing 80 per cent of sample households were growing burley, though at variable scale. These figures do not represent the national picture because of the sample, and because burley growing is possible only in certain areas. However, the explosion in production is a national phenomenon, as discussed in the first part of the paper. Two features explain the sharply discrepant benefits to a smaller proportion of the tobacco growers. First, the bulk of the burley is produced by a smaller number of growers with the requisite land, seed, fertiliser and labour. Second, access to the world price on the auction floors is available only to smallholders in burley clubs. The numbers of growers who managed to become club members was much lower than the total growing (though the proportion in my sample had increased from around 30 per cent in 1990 to 57 per cent in 1997). The high revenues of these larger-scale growers explain the much higher average income of growers of burley as contrasted with non-growers in the sample (see Table 2).

The reasons for burley tobacco not being the single answer to reducing poverty among smallholders include the need for land and labour in an already severely constrained cultivation system, adequate amounts of the correct fertilisers whose prices have risen, pesticides, and nurseries that, depending on the scarce *dimba* (wetland or stream-bank gardens), are often difficult to access and/or require high rents. In addition, the rapid expansion in numbers growing burley resulted in a large increase in the amount of burley produced, but the few international companies buying burley on the Malawian auction floors (about four) have not increased their purchases proportionately and the price has drifted downwards. The variable quality said to have occurred in the burley being brought to the floors has also contributed to an overall fall in price since the mid-1990s. The further question of whether the world market demand is sufficient for expansion of Malawi burley is also being debated.[29] For all these reasons, burley tobacco definitely represents a huge opportunity for some smallholders, but by no means all (Orr, 2000).

Nevertheless, if burley is a feasible option for only a relatively small proportion of the smallholder population, one must not myopically consider the poorest when addressing the reduction of poverty. Hence, one must ask whether there are wider benefits to burley income in its spreading beyond the grower households themselves. The Zomba research suggests that there are such benefits in years when there are no major problems in harvests or crop prices. In the 1992–93 agricultural year, for example, which had enjoyed exceptionally good rains, the burley farmers spent some of their crop income in the local villages on their increased demand for labour throughout the season, and for other services and goods (building, carpentry, bricks, poles, grass, bicycle repairs, clothes, and so on). Since some, and perhaps much, of the burley income is spent in and around the growers' villages, the effects appear positive for more than the growers themselves.

A second issue concerning the effects of burley production on smallholder livelihood is whether there are negative effects for maize production and, in turn, what are the implications for household food supply. The high variance of per capita maize harvests among tobacco growers compared with other households requires considering the relation disaggregated by income. This shows no significant difference in harvests of poorer households who grow tobacco compared with those who do not. The lower mean per capita maize harvest in 1997 among the lowest income quartile tobacco-growing households compared with non-growers was not statistically significant. Moreover, in the lowest income quartile, non-growers of burley ran out of maize stores earlier than growers, and there is virtually no difference in the average share of expenditures on maize for tobacco and non-tobacco households in the bottom quartile, both being around 21 per cent.

I review these points because observers often raise the potential problem of burley production systematically lowering the maize production and, thereby, the food security for growers who have very little land and income. This is not to deny, of course, that individual families do indeed end up with less maize harvested than they might have had if they did not grow burley, or that, if the harvests of both maize and burley are poor, then their overall lower cash income as well as maize stores can result in lower maize supplies for consumption. People themselves express concern about this risk and it is not surprising that the smaller the landholding (and related resources) the more tentative the scale of burley growing. The point here is that the survey data do not show any *consistent* pattern of either lower levels of maize production or lower levels of maize consumption for those families in the bottom income quartile who grow some burley tobacco.

The question remains of how an expanded smallholder production of burley tobacco affects total maize production. The national statistics show a dramatic increase in tobacco hectarage. This, combined with increased production of non-maize food crops, has led to declining shares of maize in smallholder fields, as discussed above. This changing pattern presumably pleases those who see an over-concentration on maize in Malawi's agriculture but, as Harrigan points out, it raises concern among those, including the Malawi government, who see national maize production as central to national food security.

Non-farm diversification is well recognised to be a key part, along with increasing agricultural productivity and agricultural diversification, to improving the livelihoods of rural Malawians (Ellis et al., 2003: 1495). The problem is *how* to achieve these ends. The previous section discussed above, how farmers have long been following diversified crop patterns and the new challenges they face. The calls for more non-farm employment (Alwang and Siegel, 1999: 1472; Ellis et al., 2003) present their own difficulties, given the dynamics of socio-economic differentiation described earlier, although some observers do see increases in off-farm options (Orr, 2000; Orr and Mwale, 2003). Similarly, efforts to develop more agro-processing and other manufacturing in the rural areas remain more on paper than in practice. However, the massive absence of electricity in most rural areas would be one means to boost such developments, as would the greater development of rural roads. Programmes that have had some success in pumping assets into rural areas are those where work on roads and other basic infrastructure (bridges, dams, etc) are compensated in cash or in-kind (most recently in Malawi, in fertiliser vouchers). Institutional obstacles to rural enterprise have also been identified to include 'gatekeepers and blockages' that discourage risk-taking, and the newer burdens of local revenue collection in decentralisation programmes (Ellis et al., 2003).

Role of Government in Achieving Food Security for Poor Rural Families

One crystal-clear conclusion emerging from both village-level studies and from interpretation of national data is the essential role of government in assuring adequate supplies of staple foods, here maize, available for consumers in the deficit season. In countries like Malawi where the majority of its rural population (in addition to the urban population) is food deficit, ensuring adequate, affordable food is surely a primary task for combating poverty, let alone averting famine. The single most disastrous effect of the first round of structural adjustment and liberalisation programme was to assume that the parastatal's function of providing affordable consumer maize in the deficit season could be taken up – virtually overnight – by private traders. The results, as indicated above, were ruinous. Private traders who moved into the new market were – and still are, 15 years later – overwhelmingly small-scale and opportunistic. The situation seems little changed since the experience in the late 1990s when '(t)he underdeveloped private sector, facing numerous constraints and unwilling to tie money up in maize as opposed to the more lucrative tobacco trade, failed to deliver' (Harrigan, 2003: 858). When short-term speculation by highly-placed officials is added, as in the famine of 2002, it is even more important to stress the need for a guaranteed supply by an accountable government. One means of ensuring accountability is the presence of active civil organisations and 'non governmental organisations'. Decentralisation, which is actively promoted across Africa, promises greater empowerment to sub-national levels of organisation, but recent research raises serious questions about the resulting bureaucratic and tax burdens on rural households in Uganda and Tanzania (Ellis and Freeman, 2004).

Earlier, I cited the call by Dorward and Kydd for more proactive actions by the state and civil organisations, involving parastatals, 'regulated monopolies, regional commodity franchises, traders' associations, farmers' associations . . . and some form of insurance for investors and consumers against price risk . . . state grain reserves, price intervention and guarantees, and market information systems' as well as roads and other infrastructure (2004: 357). Here, one has come full circle to the more sensible 'structuralist' and 'gradualist' approach of policy of the early- to mid-1990s. The challenge for Malawi in raising the standard of living of its population (largely rural, but increasingly urban) is to support the present and emerging markets but to find ways of improving the access of rural families to assets and resources through well-conceived and implemented programmes while avoiding bureaucratic rigidities, overload and corruption.

Acknowledgements

For the research, the author's thanks go to the villagers who have put up with her questions over many years, and to her research assistants, Chancellor College and the Centre for Social Research in the University of Malawi, her own university, and the sources of research funds. Thanks for help in preparing this paper go to Todd Benson, Stephen Carr, Michael Carter, Salimah Samji, and reviewers for *Journal of Development Studies*. Remaining shortcomings are the author's alone.

Notes

1. Malawi is poor: the gross national income per capita was $US160 in 2002, down from $US200 in 1990, dependent on aid, and a low rate of investment (Dorward and Kydd, 2004: 344).
2. The first year-long study took place in 1986–87, the second in 1990–91, and the final in 1997. Between 1993 and 1996, I conducted short studies, based on a sub-sample. The research grants came from USAID/W, USAID/Malawi, with a small addition from the World Bank in 1990–91. Since 1998, I have visited Malawi most years for other purposes, supported by the BASIS programme, as well as by a faculty research grant from the Kennedy School of Government. Thanks are due to these institutions for the grants, but they are not responsible for my analyses and interpretations.
3. Harrigan (2001: 25), citing several World Bank reports and papers.
4. Lele (1989), Mkwezalamba (1989), Peters (1992), Chilowa (1998).
5. Sahn et al. (1990), Harrigan (1988, 1997).
6. Personal information below from Charles Mann; he was one of the SP programme design task force, in his capacity as Food Security Adviser to the Malawi Government.
7. There is disagreement on the question of which seeds to distribute: composites have the advantage of being open-pollinated, more like the 'local' varieties, and not requiring new seed ever year as with hybrids. The advantage of the latter is their higher yields. This has also been a point of dissatisfaction among many smallholders who are keen to get higher-yielding varieties.
8. Victoria Keelan, Managing Director, Norsk Hydro/Malawi in a videotaped interview in January 2001 with Charles Mann (DVD about the Starter Pack programme, in preparation).
9. In his evidence to the UK Parliamentary Inquiry into the Humanitarian Crisis in Southern Africa, December, 2002, Stephen Devereux spoke of confusions over 'the locus of accountability' concerning 'the sale of the Strategic Grain Reserve in Malawi. On the one hand, the government of Malawi blames the IMF for giving the very strong "advice" that they should sell their grain. On the other hand, the IMF is saying, "The government disposed of their grain without telling us. We don't know

where the grain has gone'" (p. 3). In August 2004, the government under newly elected President Bingu wa Mutharika released the Strategic Grain Reserves Report which begins to provide public information on this.

10. In practice, these were farmers in the top 25 per cent of landholding and wealth. The challenge is how to expand the reach of credit systems.
11. The newest direction for agricultural policy in Malawi is to increase small-scale irrigation; this is not addressed here.
12. Compare the definition of well-being by villagers along the lake shore in northern Malawi c 2001: '... someone who is doing well has a house that doesn't leak, bedding, shoes, fishing nets, and a plate-drying rack ... and drinks tea with milk' (Kadzandira et al., 2002).
13. There is considerable debate about 'female-headed' households, but next to none about the fact that *all* successful tobacco households and a majority of the better-off households are jointly headed households where the role of a wife/adult woman is crucial. I found virtually no households without an active woman present and none among the most economically and socially prominent.
14. People in Zomba follow a matrilineal and matrilocal system: land passes overwhelmingly to female heirs and sons are expected to use land in their wives' villages (Peters, 1997; compare Kambewa, 2004 on a neighbouring area of the Chilwa Basin). A woman with adequate land is more able to attract and keep a husband.
15. This is noted by others, but unfortunately continues to need emphasis. See, for example, Hill 1970, Little and Horowitz, 1987, de Janvry et al., 1991.
16. Expenditure quartiles, quintiles and deciles were used rather than absolute poverty lines to form transition matrices because attempts by a team of poverty researchers in Malawi to compare the poverty indicators in the 1997/8 IHS (Integrated Household Survey) with absolute poverty lines used in previous assessments (by World Bank and Government of Malawi) failed. The comparison revealed widely differing poverty head counts because the welfare indicators were not directly comparable for a range of reasons, including the differing quality of administration of the surveys and the measures used. As a result, to compare the IHS data with those from a 2003 survey, the researchers used the welfare indicators to form welfare quintiles that were then used to form transition matrices (personal communication Todd Benson; Sharma et al., 2002; GOM, 2000).
17. The effects of HIV/AIDS in my sample started to emerge in the mid-1990s and by 1997, the last full year's study I conducted, were revealed in increased illness and deaths among adults. This has surely increased. I plan on conducting another study of the sample in 2005/6 to see more fully the effects on household structure, landholdings, etc.
18. This raises the issue of how 'households' can be identified over time. Some, like this widow's, eventually disappear or members are merged into other households. The strategy I used in the Zomba study was to add new households where daughters married and set up in or near their mother's compound, and to identify a daughter inheriting compound and field from a deceased mother as the new 'key woman' of that numbered household. Households were 'lost' when all members moved far from the research site.
19. Smale et al., 1991 found the same pattern across the country.
20. These are particularly cowpeas and pigeon peas; the latter are beneficial in that they last well into the dry season, are nitrogen-fixing, and are effective users of the scarce phosphorous in the soil (information from Dr S. Snapp, Michigan State University), and in addition to being a key food crop, they have become a sought-after cash crop over the past 15 years.
21. Recent research conducted under the BASIS programme (by Mulwafu, Ferguson, Peters, and Kambewa) shows increasing competition over both dryland fields and irrigable land in response to the impending land reform policy and to the government promotion of irrigation.
22. National Smallholder Farmers' Association of Malawi, for which USAID/Mw has been a major funder, though a report in a local paper in September 2004, said,'ASFAM is transitioning from being donor-funded to being self-sustaining.'
23. See Peters (2003) for some examples.
24. 'Surplus' maize because they continued to produce all the maize needed for family consumption.
25. On the other hand, it runs against another development mantra of 'comparative advantage' in global markets. More importantly, it fails to point to the problems faced by cotton, sugar and tobacco from the huge subsidies and lobbies in the US and the EU, and the related monopsony of tobacco buyers in Malawi.

26. As a JDS reviewer reminded me, intercropping varies across the country, with the highest rates in the Shire Highlands and the lowest in Kasungu area. One study shows a decline in intercropping between the late 1960s and late 1980s, based on aggregate data (Heisey and Smale, 1995).
27. Cf. Orr and Mwale 2001: 1341, n.10 on the lack of data on the field pea, a crop whose cultivation for sale in the nearby urban areas had greatly increased in the research villages.
28. The majority staple is maize, but for lake-shore populations it is cassava, supplemented by banana in the north, and for Lower Shire, sorghum plays an important role.
29. A related issue that has not received as much attention as it deserves is the US protection of its remaining tobacco farmers through subsidies and preferential pricing and quotas. These also affect the purchasing behaviour of the companies buying on the Malawi Auction Floors.

References

Alwang, J. and Siegel, P. B. (1999) Labor shortages on small landholdings in Malawi: implications for policy reforms, *World Development*, 27(8), pp. 1461–75.

Carr, S. (1998) Sustainability, liberalisation and survival: are they compatible in the Malawian smallholder sector? Paper presented to the Inaugural Ceremony of the IDEAA Fellows Program, Lilongwe, Malawi.

Chilowa, W. (1998) The impact of agricultural liberalisation on food security in Malawi, *Food Policy*, 23(6), pp. 553–69.

De Janvry, A, Sadoulet, E. and Fafchamps, M. (1991) Peasant household behaviour with missing markets: some paradoxes explained, *Economic Journal*, 101, pp. 1400–17.

Dorward, A. and Kydd, J. (2004) The Malawi 2002 food crisis: the rural development challenge, *Journal of Modern African Studies*, 42(3), pp. 343–61.

Ellis, F., Kutengule, M. and Nyasulu, A. (2003) Livelihoods and rural poverty reduction in Malawi, *World Development*, 31(9), pp. 1495–510.

Ellis, F. and Freeman, H. A. (2004) Rural livelihoods and poverty reduction strategies in four African countries, *Journal of Development Studies*, 40(4), pp. 1–30.

Government of Malawi (GOM) (2000) Using earlier poverty lines for Malawi with household welfare information from the Malawi Integrated Household Survey, 1997–98, *Working paper 5, Poverty Analysis of the Malawi IHS*, Lilongwe: Poverty Monitoring System, Malawi.

Harrigan, J. (1988) Malawi: the impact of pricing on smallholder agriculture 1971–88, *Development Policy Review*, 6, pp. 415–33.

Harrigan, J. (1997) Modeling the impact of World Bank policy-based lending: the case of Malawi's agricultural sector, *The Journal of Development Studies*, 33(6), pp. 848–73.

Harrigan, J. (2001) *From Dictatorship to Democracy: Economic Policy in Malawi 1964–2000* (London: Ashgate).

Harrigan, J. (2003) U-turns and full circles: two decades of agricultural reform in Malawi 1981–2000, *World Development*, 31(5), pp. 847–63.

Heisey, P. and Smale, M. (1995) Maize technology in Malawi: a green revolution in the making? *CIMMYT Research Report No.4* Mexico.

Hill, P. (1970) *Studies in Rural Capitalism in West Africa* (Cambridge: Cambridge University Press).

Kadzandira, J., Khaila, S. and Mvula, P. M. (2002) Malawi: tangled web, in D. Narayan and P. Petesch (Ed.) *Voices of the Poor: From Many Lands* (Washington, DC: OUP and World Bank), pp. 51–84.

Kambewa, D. (2004) Patterns of access and use in wetlands: the lake Chilwa Basin, BASIS Research Report, Oct., Zomba: Malawi.

Kandawire, R. K. and Ferguson, A. (1990) Smallholder agriculture, food security, and estate expansion in Malawi: a case study of the Salima ADD, Bunda College of Agriculture, Lilongwe, Malawi. Mimeo.

Kydd, J. and Christiansen, R. E. (1982) Structural change in Malawi since independence: consequences of a development strategy based on large-scale agriculture, *World Development*, 10(5), pp. 355–75.

Kydd, J., Dorward, A., Morrison, J. and Cadisch, G. (2004) Agricultural development and pro-poor economic growth in sub-Saharan Africa: potential and policy, *Oxford Development Studies*, 32(1), pp. 37–57.

Lele, U. (1989) *Agricultural Growth, Domestic Policies, the External Environment and Assistance to Africa: Lessons of a Quarter Century* (Washington, DC: World Bank).

Little, P. D. and Horowitz, M. M. (1987) Subsistence crops are cash crops: some comments with reference to Eastern Africa, *Human Organization*, 46, pp. 254–8.

Mkwezalamba, M. (1989) *The Impact of Liberalization of Smallholder Agricultural Produce Pricing and Marketing in Malawi* Lilongwe, Malawi: Ministry of Agriculture.

Orr, A. (2000) 'Green gold'? Burley tobacco, smallholder agriculture, and poverty alleviation in Malawi', *World Development*, 28(2), pp. 347–63.

Orr, A. and Mwale, B. (2003) Adapting to adjustment: smallholder livelihood strategies in Southern Malawi, *World Development*, 29, pp. 1325–43.

Peters, P. E. (1992) *Monitoring the Effects of grain Market Liberalization on the Income, Food Security and Nutrition of Rural Households in Zomba South, Malawi* Final Report to USAID/Malawi, and to the World Bank, AF6 Department.

Peter, P. E. (1996a) *Failed Magic or Social Context? Market Liberalization and the Rural Poor in Malawi* Development Discussion Paper No. 562, Harvard Institute for International Development, Cambridge, Mass.

Peters, P. E. (1996b) Conceptual quagmires, old problems and new questions: rethinking policy assumptions about Malawi's rural economy. Mimeo.

Peters, P. E. (1997) Against the odds: matriliny, land and gender in the Shire Highlands of Malawi, *Critique of Anthropology*17, 2: pp. 189–210.

Peters, P. E. (1999) *Agricultural Commercialization, Rural Economy and Household Livelihoods, 1990–1997*. Final Report to USAID/Mw.

Peters, P. E. (2002) The limits of knowledge: securing rural livelihoods in a situation of resource scarcity, in C. B. Barrett, F. Place, A. A. Aboud (Eds) *Natural Resources Management in African Agriculture: Understanding and Improving Current Practices* (Oxford and New York: CABI Publishing), pp. 35–50.

Sahn, D. E., Arulpragasam, J. and Merrid, L. (1990) *Policy Reform and Poverty in Malawi: A Survey of a Decade of Experience* Cornell Food and Nutrition Policy Program, Monograph 7.

Sharma, M., Tsoka, M., Payongayong, E. and Benson, T. (2002) Analysis of poverty dynamics in Malawi, Draft Report to World Bank, Washington: IFPRI.

Smale, M, with Kaunda, Z. H. W., Makina, H. L., Mkandawire, M. M. M. K., Msowoya, M. N. S., Mwale, D. J. E. K. and Heisey, P. W. (1991) Chimanga cha Makolo, hybrids, and composites: an analysis of farmers' adoption of maize technology in Malawi, 1989–1991 (Lilongwe: CIMMYT).

Whiteside, M. (1999) *Ganyu* Labour in Malawi and its implications for livelihood security interventions. An analysis of recent literature and implications for poverty alleviation, Final Version, July 1999, Oxfam International Programme in Malawi, Blantyre, Malawi.

Escaping Poverty and Becoming Poor in 36 Villages of Central and Western Uganda

ANIRUDH KRISHNA, DANIEL LUMONYA, MILISSA MARKIEWICZ, FIRMINUS MUGUMYA, AGATHA KAFUKO, & JONAH WEGOYE

I. Introduction

According to the most commonly cited estimates, poverty in Uganda declined from 56 per cent in 1992 to 35 per cent in 2000, and a combination of economic growth and recovery from civil war damage are widely regarded to be responsible for this accomplishment (Appleton, 2001a; Collier and Reinikka, 2001; GoU, 2001). However, reduced poverty in the 1990s may have gone hand-in hand with increased inequality (Appleton, 2001b; Deininger and Okidi, 2003; Hickey, 2005) and the degree to which different segments of the population can take advantage of and benefit from further growth-induced opportunities is in doubt (Okidi and Mugambe, 2002; Mijumbi and Okidi, 2001; Ssewanyana et al., 2004). Poverty reduction may have slowed down after 2000 (Kappel, Lay and Steiner, 2005) and the extent to which 'sustained growth can facilitate an escape from poverty – even in the longer term – for those left behind is debatable' (CPRC, 2004: 67).

What needs to be done now for the one-third of the population left behind in poverty? A different set of strategies will most likely be required (Brock et al., 2002; Lwanga-Ntale and McClean, 2003), but it is not entirely clear what these strategies should be. Some insights have been provided by household surveys and participatory poverty assessments carried out in the past (GoU, 2002a; Lawson et al., 2003). Additional knowledge of a disaggregated nature is required, however, for identifying poverty-reducing and poverty-creating processes at work within different regions of the country (Jayne et al., 2003; Johnson, 2002; Woodhouse, 2003).

The present study was designed in order to identify these processes and fill some of the remaining gaps in poverty knowledge in Uganda. It utilises the Stages-of-Progress methodology that was developed and applied earlier in two parts of India and one region of Kenya (Krishna, 2004; Krishna et al., 2004; Krishna, 2005). Everything worth knowing about poverty cannot be learned using only one particular methodology. Different methodologies complement rather than compete with one another (McGee, 2004). The Stages-of-Progress methodology complements and enriches findings from household surveys and participatory assessments, and it adds significant new knowledge about processes and reasons.

Before applying this methodology extensively in two regions of Uganda, a feasibility study and pilot test was first carried out in February 2004 in Rakai district. Following refinements and adaptations, the Stages-of-Progress methodology (described in Section II) was implemented in 36 village communities of Western and Central regions.

Data presented in Section III show that poverty in these 36 villages has fallen overall from 47 per cent 25 years ago, to 37 per cent ten years ago, to 35 per cent at the present time. A significant gender gap persists, however: while 31 per cent of male-headed households are poor at the present time, 46 per cent of female-headed households are poor.

Escaping poverty and falling into poverty have gone hand in hand in these villages. A total of 24 per cent of village households have escaped from poverty over the past 25 years. Simultaneously, however, another 15 per cent of households have fallen into poverty in these villages.

While escaping poverty in these communities is associated with one set of factors, falling into poverty is associated with another and different set of factors. Two different sets of policy responses are required, therefore: one set to help promote households' escape from poverty, and another set to prevent descent into poverty. Factors associated with escaping poverty and falling into poverty are not similar between the two regions. Therefore, regionally differentiated policies are required for more effective poverty reduction.

Section IV discusses reasons associated with escaping poverty and falling into poverty, respectively. While ill health and high healthcare expenses are commonly and increasingly associated with descents in both the Western and Central regions, some other poverty-causing factors – including crop disease, land exhaustion, large family size, marriage expenses, and land division – vary significantly between the two regions.

Growth in industry and the urban sectors have not been the major removers of poverty in these villages. Commonly in both regions, land-related factors have been associated with a much larger number of escapes from poverty, and finding regular employment has been associated with many fewer escapes. Because jobs have not been more significant, education also does not have a strong association with escaping poverty. The direct impact on poverty of these factors relative to others has also declined over time.

Section V concludes by discussing the policy implications of these results. Notably, descents into poverty have become more frequent in recent times, and even as growth has accelerated, poverty reduction has slowed down. Regular monitoring of factors associated with descent and with escape in each region will be required in order to keep policy interventions more current and relevant in future. A methodology for performing such exercises on a continuous basis is presented in the next section.

II. Methodology: Stages of Progress

A total of 36 villages were studied: six villages in each of three districts in the Western and Central regions of Uganda. A total of 2,631 households are resident in these villages, and following the participatory, community-based methodology described below, the poverty status of each household was ascertained for the present time, for 25 years ago, and for an interim period, ten years ago. The trajectory of each household was compiled in this manner, and reasons associated with these trajectories were examined for a random sample of 40 per cent of all households. Members of 1,068 households were individually interviewed to verify and elaborate upon information collected at a community meeting.

We selected three districts within each region, Central and Western, with the intent of covering a range of diversity. In the Central region, we selected Mukono, Luwero, and Ssembabule, while in the Western region, we selected Bushenyi, Kabale, and Ntungamo.[1] We conducted initial visits to the six district headquarters. We met and solicited support from the administrative and political leaders, and we selected 25 experienced Research Assistants (RAs) from among staffs of the community development departments of these districts.

Villages for study were also selected at this time in consultation with district officials. In each district, six villages were selected, two located near the district town centre, two located near a main road but not near the district town centre, and two located relatively far away from either a main road or the district town centre and are therefore relatively remote and hard to access. The selected villages represent quite well the considerable diversity that exists within the two selected regions; they are not, however, 'representative' in the statistical sense of this term.

The 25 selected RAs took part in a ten-day training exercise during which the methodology was explained and practised in detail. Training included two complete rehearsals of all steps of the methodology. Villages located close to the training centre were selected for these rehearsals. The RAs were then divided into four teams, with two teams assigned to each of the two regions. Members of each team were fluent in the local language of the region (Luganda for Central and Ruyankole and Rukiga for Western) and also in English. With the four teams working simultaneously and supervised closely by the authors, data was collected over a total period of 28 days.

The study in each village commenced with a community meeting. Dates for these meetings were determined in advance through prior consultations with the Local Council (LC1) chairperson of each village. Members of each village community attended in large numbers. Males and females were equally represented in most cases, and older villagers were also present in significant numbers. As the issues to be discussed were sometimes sensitive, deliberate efforts were made to encourage free, frank and open discussions.

A key aspect of introducing the study to community members was making clear that project staff did not represent any government or NGO programme, and emphasising that no 'beneficiaries' were to be selected; that is, no immediate material benefits (or losses) would be brought into the community as a result of the study. Members therefore were less likely to deliberately misrepresent any household's poverty status with the hope of attaining material gains.

The community meetings began with the research teams asking community groups to define the local terms that people apply to those whose conditions construed a clear and commonly understood state of poverty. In this study, the term *Omworo* came up most often in the west, while in the Central region the terms *Omwavu Lunkupe* or *Omwavu Lukyolo* were most often used.

Once community members' attention was focused on discussing poverty and its local characteristics, they were asked to delineate the locally applicable Stages of Progress that poor households typically followed while making their ways out of poverty. What does a household in your village usually do, we asked the assembled villagers, when it climbs out gradually from a state of acute poverty? Which expenditures are the very first ones to be made? 'Food,' was invariably the answer. Which expenditures follow immediately after? 'Some clothes,' we were invariably told. As more money flows in, what does this household do in the third stage, in the fourth stage, and so on? This process was continued until the community meeting had defined a progression of stages up to a point where a household was clearly very well off in the community's estimation. No more than 12 stages were defined in any village.

Lively discussions were held as villagers identified these stages, but the answers they provided, particularly about the first *four* Stages of Progress, were invariant across all villages in both regions. Table 1 presents the typical Stages of Progress reported in these 36 villages. The first four stages are exactly the same in all 36 villages.

It is hardly surprising that communities sharing common economic and cultural spaces should, in fact, report a common set of aspirations, represented in the locally applicable Stages of Progress that poor households typically follow on their pathways out of poverty. Poverty, like any other relational concept, is socially constructed and collectively defined, and the Stages of Progress provide a convenient and well-tested device to get closer to these communal definitions.[2]

Community groups were asked to identify two cut-off points on the progression of stages. The first cut-off denotes the stage after achieving which a household is no longer regarded as poor. It is equivalent to the concept of the poverty line commonly used in poverty studies in the sense that it enabled villagers to classify who was poor and who was not. Instead of being defined by outsiders, however, the poverty cut-off in this case was determined by villagers themselves. As Table 1 shows, the first cut-off was made in all villages after stage four. Basic needs had been met, including food, clothing, shelter and basic education, and the household could now begin to make small investments in housing, in small animals, or in a tiny plot of land.[3]

Table 1. Stages of progress

	Stage	
1.	Food for the family	
2.	Some clothes for the family	
3.	Send children to school	
4.	Repair the existing shelter (Roof with iron sheets)	*Poverty cut-off*
5.	Buy small animals like goat, chicken, sheep, rabbits	
6.	Buy a small piece of land	
7.	Buy a bicycle for transportation	
8.	Buy more land	*Prosperity cut-off*
9.	Build permanent house	
10.	Start operating a business of few farm products	
11.	Buy a car/ build commercial property	

The second cut-off point, which was drawn after stage eight, denotes the prosperity line. Once a household has crossed beyond this cut-off, it is regarded as having left poverty quite far behind. In villages of the Central region it was quite common for the community to say that at this stage the household could be characterised as *oyo avudeyo,* meaning that it was now quite a distance away from poverty and could make significant investments.

The next step of the Stages-of-Progress methodology was to develop a complete list of all households in the village. This list was generated during the community meeting in some villages, while in other villages it was obtained beforehand through consultations with the LCI chairperson.

Next, researchers worked with the community assembly to identify a clearly understood and commonly remembered milestone to denote the time period of 25 years ago, and another such milestone to denote ten years ago. Establishing these milestones provided community members with a specific reference point, which they remember clearly, rather than referring to some particular year, which may have little meaning for many. During the pilot test and training exercises, communities had identified the coming to power of Obote II (in 1980) as the milestone for 25 years ago, while they regarded the Constituent Assembly elections (held in 1994) as the appropriate milestone for ten years ago.

Community groups were asked to identify each household's specific location along the Stages of Progress for each of the two milestones and also for the present time. Referring constantly to the Stages of Progress and to the household lists, community members were asked, for example, 'At what stage on the Stages of Progress was Nsubuga's household at the time the Obote II regime came into power (that is, 25 years ago)? What stage did these household members occupy at the time of the Constituent Assembly elections (that is, ten years ago)? At what stage are they now?' Community members participated enthusiastically in the discussions, and there was often considerable debate about the status of some particular household. The discussion continued until this information had been obtained for every household presently resident in the village.[4]

Based on this information, the research team categorised each household in the following manner:

Category A: Poor 25 years ago and poor today (Remained poor)
Category B: Poor 25 years ago but not poor today (Escaped poverty)
Category C: Not poor 25 years ago but poor today (Became poor)
Category D: Not poor 25 years ago and not poor today (Remained not poor)

Present-day households constituted the unit of analysis for this exercise. When asking about conditions at the present time we inquired about present-day households' members, and when asking about conditions in the previous time period we asked about conditions faced by these same members 25 years ago. In case of younger households, we asked about conditions in their parents' household 25 years ago.[5]

Once the categorisation was complete, a random sample of 40 per cent of households in each category was selected, and in-depth discussions were held with the community group regarding the reasons associated with each household in the sample – for moving into or out of poverty, as the case may be, or for staying poor or not poor. A comparative framework was adopted for these inquiries. After completing this step, the community meeting was concluded.

Interviews with individual members of the selected households followed the next day. These interviews were conducted to verify, validate and complement the information provided by the community group. Household members were interviewed in the privacy of their homes. The stages and reasons provided by the community group were verified separately with each household in the sample. Additional household-level information was also obtained at this time, including information on demographic features and assets owned. Rarely was a single reason responsible for descent or escape, and multiple reasons were usually associated with each household's trajectory. Up to five reasons were recorded for each selected household.

III. Trends in Escape and Descent

On average in these 36 villages, 45 per cent of all households lived in poverty 25 years ago, 37 per cent were poor ten years ago, and 35 per cent are poor at the present time. Overall, poverty has fallen consistently over this period, and the average figure at present for these 36 villages – 35 per cent in poverty – is the same as the average figure for the entire country (Deininger and Okidi, 2003; Lawson et al., 2003), suggesting that these villages are not dissimilar in terms of poverty from other areas in the country.

Table 2 shows that of the total of 2,631 households resident in these 36 villages, 20.4 per cent were poor 25 years ago and they are also poor today, and 40.6 per cent were not poor 25 years ago and they are not poor today. Twenty-four per cent of households escaped poverty during this time, and another 15 per cent simultaneously fell into poverty, making for a net poverty reduction of 9 per cent over the 25-year period. While the large numbers escaping poverty, 24 per cent, are heartening to observe, the substantial numbers who fell into poverty during the same period give cause for concern.

It is useful to examine the relationship that the four categories utilised in this methodology have with some other indicators of poverty, more often utilised within

Table 2. Trends in household poverty in 36 villages

Region	(A_{25}) Remained poor over the past 25 years	(B_{25}) Escaped poverty over the past 25 years	(C_{25}) Became poor over the past 25 years	(D_{25}) Remained not poor over the past 25 years	Poor 25 years ago	Poor today
All 36 villages	20.4	24.0	15.0	40.6	44.4	35.4
Central (18 villages)	12.8	28.6	14.5	44.0	41.4	27.3
Western (18 Villages)	28.9	18.8	15.5	36.8	47.7	44.4

academic discourse. Land ownership is quite often considered an index of wealth in rural settings, and land ownership is closely associated with the categories of poverty utilised here. Households classified under Category A (remained poor over 25 years) possess, on average, just 1.19 acres of land. Households of Category B (escaped poverty) and Category D (remained not poor) possess more land: 2.09 and 2.48 acres, respectively, while households of Category C (became poor) possess 1.58 acres on average.

Ownership of other assets is also similarly distributed among these four separate categories. Household were asked about ownership in respect of ten different types of assets, including animals, radios, household furniture, and so on. Households of Category A possess, on average, 3.3 of these ten assets, while households of Categories B, C, and D possess, respectively, 5.4, 3.8 and 5.8 assets on average.

There is, in fact, a monotonically increasing relationship between a household's present stage and its average number of assets. Notice that average number of assets increases quite sharply when households move beyond the first and also the second poverty cut-offs.[6] Other visible characteristics – housing type, cattle ownership, education levels – also align neatly with a household's position on the Stages of Progress. How well any household is doing in terms of material achievement is thus reflected quite by well by its recorded stage.

Community members in these villages were quite certain that those households that they had identified as poor in terms of the Stages of Progress were indeed the ones who are poor in their villages. Such households consider themselves to be poor, and they are also considered as such by other people in their village. Their strategies for a better life are built around these everyday understandings of poverty that they share with fellow villagers, and it is these understandings and the strategies to which they give rise that underpin households' efforts to deal with poverty as they know it (Chambers, 1995).

The stages also serve as a useful heuristic device. Communities are able to assign households to particular stages quite easily and without confusion or stigma, and communities that have lived together for reasonable periods of time are also able to recount the stages different households had achieved at a previous point in time. Recall can be quite imperfect for an earlier period, thus the methodology relies on retracing large steps that are better remembered, rather than finer distinctions, which

Table 3. Stages of progress and asset ownership

Household's stage at the present time	Average number of household assets (out of 10)
1	2.46
2	3.08
3	3.58
4	4.08
5	4.94
6	5.24
7	5.55
8	5.71
9	6.42
10	6.72
11	7.31
12	8.01

are more easily forgotten. Each movement upward along the Stages of Progress represents a significant improvement in material and social status. People remember, for instance, whether their household possessed a bicycle or a radio set at the time when the Constituent Assembly elections were held, whether they lived in a house that had iron sheets or plain thatch, and whether they could afford to send their children to school or not. By seeking recall data in terms of these clear, conspicuous and sizeable referents, the Stages-of-Progress method adds reliability to recall.

Table 4 considers two separate time periods, with the *first period* running from 25 years ago to ten years ago, and the *second period* from ten years ago to the present time. A total of 13 per cent of households escaped from poverty during the first time period (11.9 per cent + 1.1 per cent), while a total of 12.2 per cent escaped poverty during the second time period, that is, an almost equal proportion of households have escaped from poverty during these two separate time periods.

On the other hand, many more households *fell into* poverty during the second compared to the first time period. Only 5.6 per cent of households fell into poverty in the first time period (Row 2 + Row 4 of Table 4, or 3.7 per cent + 1.9 per cent), however, as many as 10.9 per cent have fallen into poverty during the second time period (Row 3).

The pace of economic growth in Uganda was faster in the second time period compared to the first time period (for example, Collier and Reinikka, 2001), and we had expected that poverty reduction would also have been faster in the second time period. However, because descents have been almost twice as frequent in the second time period compared to the first time period, the pace of poverty reduction has slowed down in recent times.

Trends in other villages and regions of Uganda might be similar. Using data from the Uganda National Household Surveys, Kappel, Lay and Steiner (2005: 28, 49) detect 'an increase in poverty between 1999–2000 and 2002–2003,' that is, 'from 7 million to 9 million in only three years' for the entire country. Results of participatory poverty assessments also suggest that movements into poverty have increased in recent years (McGee, 2004). It seems worthwhile to examine in future

Table 4. Escape and descent over two time periods

	CAT.25	CAT.10	Poverty status in three time periods	Percent of households: Central (18 villages)	Western (18 villages)	Total (36 villages)	Implication
1	A_{25}	A_{10}	Poor in all three periods	11.7	27.9	19.4	Chronic poor
2	C_{25}	A_{10}	Fell into poverty in the earlier period, and remained poor	3.4	4.0	3.7	*Relatively few descents occurred in the earlier period. Most descents occurred in the later period.*
3	C_{25}	C_{10}	Fell into poverty in the later period	11.2	10.6	10.9	
4	D_{25}	B_{10}	Fell into poverty in the earlier period, and rose back in the later period	3.0	0.6	1.9	*About one-third of those who fell into poverty in the first period came back up again in the later period*
5	B_{25}	D_{10}	Escaped poverty in the earlier period, and remained not poor later	14.4	9.0	11.9	*Escapes have occurred equally in both periods*
6	B_{25}	B_{10}	Escaped poverty in the later period	14.2	9.8	12.2	
7	A_{25}	C_{10}	Escaped poverty in the earlier period, and fell back into poverty later	1.2	1.0	1.1	*Relatively few who escaped poverty fell back into poverty in the later period*
8	D_{25}	D_{10}	Not poor at any time	40.9	36.2	38.8	Chronic non-poor

studies why higher volatility has gone together with greater liberalisation and commercialisation, especially since the late 1990s.

Gender disparity has also worsened during the second period. While 10.4 per cent of male-headed households fell into poverty during this period, 17.6 per cent of female-headed households joined the ranks of the poor.

Some comfort can be taken from observing that of all households that fell into poverty during the first period (5.6 per cent) about one-third (1.9 per cent) were able to overcome poverty during the second time period. The majority of these households, two-thirds, remained poor at the end of the second time period, however, indicating that falling into poverty is not merely a temporary inconvenience.

Some households that escaped from poverty during the first period have also fallen back into poverty in the second time period. Fortunately, relatively few households experienced such reversals. Of 13.3 per cent of households that escaped from poverty in the first time period, less than one-tenth (1.1 per cent) fell back into poverty during the second time period.

These averages for all 36 villages conceal the very substantial differences, however, that exist from village to village. In as many as 16 of the 36 villages that we studied, net poverty has increased over the 25-year period.[7] Villages such as Kitinda (Ntumgamo district) where household poverty increased by 53 per cent, Yandwe (Luwero district) where it increased by 38 per cent, and Katooma Central (Bushenyi district) where it increased by 29 per cent, are particularly worrying in this respect.[8]

Providing more effective assistance for those who have been left behind in poverty – and for those who have actually become poor over the past ten or 25 years – will require addressing separately the reasons for escape and for descent. These reasons are discussed in the next section.

IV. Factors Associated with Escape and with Descent

Previous studies of poverty dynamics provide important clues about some factors associated with decline and ascent in Uganda. Participatory poverty assessments conducted in 36 sites in 1998 and in 60 additional sites in 2002 suggest that alcoholism, large family size, ill health, and expenses on dowries and funerals can be important reasons for descending into poverty. Separately, Deininger and Okidi (2003) and Lawson (2004) also found ill health to be significantly associated with descent into poverty. Bird and Shinyekwa (2003) found multiple correlated reasons associated with descent, including ill health and drunkenness. Respondents to surveys have also indicated several other factors that are associated in their view with ascent out of poverty, including multiple income sources, access to employment, land and start-up capital, and higher education and skills (GoU, 2002a; Lawson, et al. 2003; Lwanga-Ntale and McClean, 2003).

Reasons for escape and descent identified by these studies served as a starting point for our investigations. Many among these reasons were confirmed by the random sample of 1,068 households whom we interviewed. However, some among these reasons were not validated by the experiences and trajectories that we examined. On the other hand, some other reasons were also identified that have not been recognised by previous studies.

While previous studies have relied upon the collective opinion of villagers regarding factors associated with escape and descent, this study matches factors and causes to the actual experiences of specific households. Reasons for escape and descent were identified through community meetings in each village and they were verified and cross-checked with members of each selected household. The methodology used here provides an opportunity to examine the relative frequency, magnitude, and statistical significance of these factors, while at the same time identifying additional factors and processes of change, thereby complementing knowledge obtained through other methods.

Eight factors are associated with decline in a household's material circumstances. These eight factors form three separate clusters. Ill health, healthcare expenses, and death of income earners form the first and numerically most important cluster. The second cluster is related to social and behavioural factors, including family size, funeral and marriage expenses, alcoholism and laziness. The third cluster includes all land-related factors, especially land division, crop disease, and land exhaustion.

Health and health-related expenses are the single most important reason associated with descending into poverty. More than 70 per cent of households that fell into poverty (Category C) cited ill health and healthcare expenses as the most important part of the process leading to their descent. Deaths of income earners, which have occurred mostly on account of disease, are important in the case of another 35 per cent of such households. As examined later, the impact of these health-related factors on descent has become even more deleterious during the second period (the last ten years) compared to the first period (ten to 25 years ago).[9]

> Twenty-five years ago my welfare was good. My husband was still alive and we had enough land and animals. My husband was sick for ten years before he died and all the money we had was spent on medical charges. We even sold some animals and land to raise money for treatment. Our welfare became worse because we were left with small land and few animals. My children had dropped out of school because we could not pay school fees. Then my husband died and the small land we had left was shared among my sons. My welfare became even worse because I was left with a very small piece of land and I can't even get enough food to eat. Now I work as a casual labourer on other people's farms. (Female respondent, Kikoni village, Ntungamo district, Western Region) I lost my husband who had a government job as a pharmacist to sickness. I used to grow some crops for cash but now I am ever sick and the little I get from my garden I use for buying drugs. Some of my grandchildren are sickly and I may tell you some of my children died of AIDS. (Female respondent, Katega village, Mukono district, Central Region)

Social and behavioural factors, including family size, age of household head, funeral and marriage expenses, alcoholism and laziness, constitute the second cluster. These factors were examined because they are frequently brought up in poverty analyses. Large family size was quite important for descent in these 36 villages. In all, 39 per cent of households that have fallen into poverty over the

25-year period mentioned large family size as a critical factor associated with this decline. This factor was also significant in regression analysis, presented below.

None of the other factors in the second cluster are significantly associated with descent. Funeral and marriage expenses are not significant for this analysis. Drunkenness is also not significant, as seen below in regression analysis. Alcoholism is, no doubt, a serious social ill, and we came across evidence of considerable drunkenness in many villages that we visited. It does not appear to be associated preponderantly with households that have suffered a decline in their circumstances, and households that have improved their status provide evidence of drunkenness as much as households that have declined. Drunkenness does not emerge consequently as a factor particularly associated with descent. Laziness is similarly not important for this analysis, and it is unfortunate that people should ever consider it to be so.[10]

The third cluster of significant factors are all land related. Crop disease, land exhaustion, and land division are all importantly associated with descent into poverty.

> My father died and I had to drop out of school because of lack of school fees. My father's land was divided among my brothers and myself, and the piece I inherited is too small for me to earn enough income from crops or animals. Furthermore, coffee has been affected by the wilt and further reduced my income. Now my family depends on casual labour and hiring land from other people to grow crops. (Male respondent, Kikoni village, Ntumgamo district, Western Region)

Crop disease was an important factor in the case of 19 per cent of all households that have fallen into poverty. Another 8 per cent of all Category C households mentioned land exhaustion as a factor critically associated with their experiences of falling into poverty. Division of land is also associated with households' decline. Regionally disaggregated analysis (presented later) shows that this factor is more relevant to the Western experience, and not very relevant to households of Central villages.

Business loss is another factor associated with descent. It was particularly relevant to the experience of households in the Central region, as we will see below in disaggregated analysis. The term, business losses, as used here is related most often with loss of income from commercial crops, and these losses arise, in turn, from price changes or due to crop disease and/or land exhaustion.[11]

Logistic regression analysis helped to further confirm these findings. The analysis in Table 5 is restricted only to Category C and Category D households, that is, all those who were not poor 25 years ago. The intent is to discern why some previously non-poor households fell into poverty, while other non-poor households continued to remain not poor.[12]

Odds ratios reported in Table 5 should be interpreted in the following manner. For variables that are significant, an odds ratio greater than one indicates that the related factor tends to accelerate descent, while an odds ratio lower than 1 indicates that the related factor tends to avert or deter descents into poverty.

Consider, for instance, the odds ratios associated with each of the three health-related variables belonging to the first cluster, namely, ill health, healthcare

Table 5. Results of binary logistic regression for falling into poverty (Households that were not poor 25 years ago, i.e., Category C and Category D households)

	Coefficients	Odds ratios (95% Wald Confidence Limits)
Intercept	−1.14**	
Ill health	0.34**	1.40 (1.31–2.70)
Healthcare expenses	0.95**	2.60 (1.43–4.72)
Death of income earner	0.63*	1.87 (1.02–3.43)
Age of household head	−0.16*	0.98 (0.97–0.99)
Large family size	0.96**	2.61 (1.48–4.58)
Marriage expense	0.99*	2.71 (1.10–6.62)
Drunkenness	1.23	*n.s.*
Laziness	0.33	*n.s.*
Business loss	1.61*	4.99 (1.66–15.05)
Land division	0.72*	2.07 (1.13–4.61)
Land exhaustion	1.21**	3.32 (1.20–5.21)
Crop disease	0.34**	1.35 (1.13–3.80)
Land improvement	−1.61*	0.20 (0.05–0.76)
Diversification	−3.39***	0.04 (0.01–0.13)
Business gain	−1.03*	0.36 (0.13–0.94)
Job (government)	−0.44	*n.s.*
Job (private)	−1.18*	0.31 (0.10–0.91)
Education	−0.03	*n.s.*
Distance to market	−0.03	*n.s.*
Distance to health centre	0.20***	1.22 (1.10–1.36)
−2 Log likelihood	739.03	
Likelihood ratio Chi-square	340.94	
P>Chi-Square	<0.0001	
N	553	

*: statistically significant at 0.05 level.
**: statistically significant at 0.01 level or better.
**: statistically significant at 0.0001 level or better.
n.s.: not significant.

expenses and death of income earner. These odds ratios are, respectively, 1.40, 2.60 and 1.87. These odds ratios imply that, everything else remaining equal, the odds of descent were enhanced by 40 per cent (1.40 minus 1.00), on average, for households that experienced one or more episodes of ill health. Correspondingly, the odds of descent were 160 per cent greater when high healthcare expenses were experienced, and they increased by 87 per cent when the death of major income earner occurred. Notice that the variable, distance to health centre, is also significant in the analysis. For residents of villages located more than five kilometres distant from a health centre the likelihood of falling into poverty is greater by 22 per cent on average.

Among the factors in the second cluster, only age, large family size, and marriage expenses are significantly associated with descent into poverty. None of the other factors in the second cluster is significantly associated with descent. Drunkenness is not significant. Laziness is also not significant for this analysis.

Age of household head is significant, and higher age goes together with a slightly diminished likelihood of falling into poverty, indicating that lifecycle effects do matter somewhat. The impact of age is quite slight, however; other variables continue to matter when life cycle effects are considered, and many among them matter considerably more.

Four factors included within our third cluster are all significantly associated with descent. The likelihood of a household falling into poverty is enhanced by, on average, 399 per cent, 232 per cent, 107 per cent, and 35 per cent, respectively, when the household concerned experienced business loss, land exhaustion, land division, or crop disease.

Table 5 also shows that some factors have worked in the opposite direction. Five significant factors – including age, diversification, business gain, land improvement, and private sector job attainment – have odds ratios lower than one, which indicates that the presence of these factors reduces the likelihood of falling into poverty. For instance, the likelihood of falling into poverty was lower by 96 per cent (0.04 minus 1.00), on average, for a household that undertook diversification of income sources. Similarly, the likelihood of falling into poverty was reduced, on average, by 80 per cent, 64 per cent, and 69 per cent, respectively, when land improvement, business gain, and private sector job attainment formed part of a household's reported trajectory. By preventing or offsetting the effects of factors that exert a downward pull, these positive factors enabled Category D households to retain their non-poor status.

Factors responsible for households' falling into poverty have to be considered alongside other factors that help households escape from or stave off poverty. While these two sets of factors are quite different from each other, individual households are simultaneously susceptible to factors belonging to both sets. Where any households land up eventually is the net result, therefore, of both sets of factors.

Examining the experiences of households that escaped from poverty shows that the same set of four positive factors – including land improvement, diversification of income sources, gain from business (mainly commercial crops), and obtaining a private sector job – is significantly associated with movements upward, out of poverty.

Among all households of Category B, that is, those who escaped from poverty over the 25-year period, 27 per cent cited diversification of income sources as a principally important factor. Households that were able to vary their sources of income were more likely to escape poverty than those who could not.

> My husband died in the war in Luwero. I started brewing waragi and got a reasonable amount of money from it and was able to start up a small piggery project. The project is still paying me very much. I also generate some money from making and selling mats and baskets. (Female respondent, Katega village, Mukono district, Central Region)

Land-related factors, especially improving productivity and diversifying into commercial crops, were comparatively much more important in both these regions of Uganda. Business gains were often associated with such land-related activities (as also found by Kappel, Lay and Steiner, 2005). These two factors were significantly associated with escape for 38 per cent of Category B households.

> After the war I worked so hard in agriculture. I grew a lot of coffee, which had a market then and sold it. Now the most selling item is bananas, which make local brew and I am seriously doing that. The difference between other banana growers and me is that I make the beer myself instead of selling the bananas. Therefore, I earn more. (Male respondent, Lwanda village, Luwero district, Central Region)

Jobs in the private sector were a factor for ascent for many fewer Category B households – only 9 per cent in all. These findings indicate that contrary to conventional wisdom on this subject, employment creation is not always the major pathway out of poverty.

Table 6 reports the odds ratios from logistic regressions that compare the experiences of Category A households (those which have remained poor) and Category B households (those which have escaped from poverty). The focus here is to examine why some previously poor households escaped from poverty, while other poor households continued to remain poor.

Table 6. Results of binary logistic regression for escaping from poverty (Households that were poor 25 years ago, i.e., Category A and Category B households)

	Coefficients	Odds ratios (95% Wald Confidence Limits)
Intercept	0.02**	
Ill health	−2.03**	0.13 (0.03–0.62)
Healthcare expenses	−3.40***	0.03 (0.01–0.17)
Death of income earner	−3.21***	0.04 (0.01–0.21)
Age of household head	0.02	*n.s.*
Large family size	−1.62**	0.20 (0.06–0.61)
Marriage expense	−2.49**	0.08 (0.02–0.40)
Drunkenness	−0.83	*n.s.*
Laziness	−1.91	*n.s.*
Land exhaustion	−0.39*	0.57 (0.42–0.87)
Crop disease	−1.76*	0.17 (0.04–0.77)
Land improvement	1.54**	4.67 (1.81–12.06)
Diversification	4.04***	56.79 (10.75–299)
Business gain	2.24***	9.49 (3.19–27.85)
Job (government)	1.71*	5.51 (1.12–27.11)
Job (private)	1.26*	3.58 (1.03–12.32)
Education	0.63	*n.s.*
Distance to market	−0.06	*n.s.*
Distance to health centre	0.08	*n.s.*
−2 Log likelihood	671.15	
Likelihood ratio Chi-square	457.12	
Pr > Chi-Square	< 0.0001	
N	494	

*: statistically significant at 0.05 level.
**: statistically significant at 0.01 level or better.
**: statistically significant at 0.0001 level or better.
n.s.: not significant.

Notice that the likelihood of escaping from poverty is substantially higher, on average, for households that have experienced land improvement, diversification, business gains, or obtained jobs in the government or private sector. These odds ratios imply, for instance, that for a household which was poor in the previous period the likelihood of escaping poverty increased by 5.5 times in cases where a household member obtained a job in the government. However, members of only 33 households in all were lucky enough to obtain a government job. Even though the likelihood of escaping poverty increased a great deal when this factor was present, this factor was present overall for only a small number of households. Private sector jobs similarly represent a substantially increased likelihood of escaping from poverty. However, relatively few poor households (only 9 per cent in all) have been able to find this pathway to escape.

Notice also that the factors previously found to be significantly associated with descent – including ill health, healthcare expenses, death of income earners, large family size, marriage expenses, land exhaustion and crop disease – are also significant in this analysis of escaping poverty.[13] The presence of these factors has acted as a dampening effect upon the prospects for escape. Households of Category A (remained poor) have experienced these negative factors more often than have households of Category B (escaped poverty), and their non-escape is accounted for as much by the absence of positive factors as by the presence of negative ones.

More disaggregated analysis shows that factors of escape and descent are significantly different across the two separate regions. They have also changed somewhat from the first time period (ten to 25 years go) to the second time period (present time to ten years ago).

More reasons for descent have begun to operate during the second time period, and the overall pace of poverty reduction has slowed down. Household poverty fell by 9 per cent during entire 25-year period. Reduction over the past ten years has been just 1.6 per cent in all.

Table 7 presents the disaggregated picture for the two regions and the two separate time periods. Separate regression analyses were carried out for each separate region and time period. To facilitate brevity and enable comparison, only odds ratios for statistically significant variables are reported.

Factors that were significant for descent in the first time period have continued to remain significant during the second time period. However, several additional factors have also become significant for descent in the second time period. It should come as no surprise, therefore, that almost twice as many households fell into poverty during the second period as compared to the first.

None of the three factors in the first cluster – ill health, healthcare expenses, and death of income earner – was significant for descent in Western villages during the first period, and only one of these three factors, healthcare expenses, was significant during the earlier period in Central villages. During the past decade, all three of these factors have become significant for descent in both regions.

The second cluster of descent-related factors included large family size and marriage expenses. The figures in Table 7 show that none of these factors was significantly associated with descent in the first time period in either the Central or the Western region. During the second time period, however, large family size

Table 7. Disaggregated regression analysis: two regions and two time periods

	Odds ratios (95% Wald confidence intervals in brackets)	
	Central Region (18 villages)	Western Region (18 villages)
First period (25 years ago to ten years ago)		
Factors with negative effect		
Ill health	Not significant	Not significant
Healthcare expenses	0.79 (0.48–0.93)	Not significant
Death of income earner	Not significant	Not significant
Large family size	Not significant	Not significant
Marriage expense	Not significant	Not significant
Land division	Not significant	0.38 (0.21–0.66)
Land exhaustion	Not significant	Not significant
Crop disease	0.37 (0.22–0.61)	Not significant
Business loss	0.44 (0.22–0.87)	Not significant
Distance to health centre	0.92 (0.85–0.97)	Not significant
Factors with positive effect		
Diversification	Not significant	Not significant
Job (private sector)	2.23 (1.30–3.84)	2.20 (1.21–4.03)
Land Improvement	Not significant	2.35 (1.39–4.00)
Business gain	2.00 (1.34–2.98)	Not significant
Second period (ten years ago to present time)		
Factors with negative effect		
Ill health	0.40 (0.25–0.65)	0.57 (0.34–0.77)
Healthcare expenses	0.49 (0.29–0.63)	0.41 (0.26–0.65)
Death of income earner	0.45 (0.28–0.74)	0.56 (0.35–0.89)
Large family size	Not significant	0.35 (0.22–0.56)
Marriage expense	0.46 (0.21–0.84)	Not significant
Land division	Not significant	0.38 (0.23–0.63)
Land exhaustion	Not significant	0.30 (0.13–0.68)
Crop disease	0.48 (0.29–0.77)	0.26 (0.12–0.56)
Business loss	0.48 (0.25–0.91)	Not significant
Distance to health centre	0.89 (0.84–0.95)	Not significant
Factors with positive effect		
Diversification	2.19 (1.46–3.14)	Not significant
Job (private sector)	Not significant	3.13 (1.75–5.58)
Land Improvement	1.58 (1.09–2.50)	1.72 (1.06–2.78)
Business gain	Not significant	Not significant

became a significant factor of descent in Western villages, while marriage expenses were significantly associated with descent in villages of Central region.

The third cluster includes land-related factors: land division, land exhaustion, crop disease, and business losses (mostly from commercial crops). Here the story is more mixed. Land division played a key role in decline in the Western region in both time periods, but was not significant for Central villages at either time. Land exhaustion became significant in the Western region in the last decade, but has not been an issue in the Central region in either time period. Crop disease has remained a significant factor of descent during both time periods in Central villages. In Western villages, however, this factor only became significant in the past decade. Business loss was a significant factor of descent during both time periods in Central villages, but it was not significant during any period in Western villages.

Factors related to ascent also differ across the two regions. In the Central region, these factors have changed considerably between the two time periods, whereas in the Western region, the same two factors were significant in both time periods.

In villages of Western region, jobs in the private sector and land improvement were associated with ascent during both time periods. Private sector jobs and business gains were significant for ascent in Central villages during the first time period. In the second time period, private sector jobs lost significance, while diversification of income sources gained significance in the Central region. In most cases, diversification in these villages has involved additional activities related to commercial crops, animals and retail trade. In relatively few cases, diversification has also involved taking up a position or a trade within the informal economy.[14]

Private sector jobs have lost the earlier significance that they had in Central villages. Even in general, the contribution made by private sector jobs has declined overall. Among all households in both regions that escaped from poverty over the entire 25-year period, private sector jobs were mentioned as an important factor in the case of only 58 households. Forty-two of these 58 households, 73 per cent, escaped poverty during the first period, while only 27 per cent did so during the second time period.

Business gains and business losses were most often related to land and commercial agriculture. Business loss, which was a factor of decline in Central but not in Western villages, reflects the risks and volatility that accompany such commercial enterprises, especially commercial crops such as coffee. Many families in Central villages have fallen into poverty on account of failed ventures, while others have struck lucky from undertaking ventures of essentially the same kind.

Two other factors need to be discussed in relation to ascent. First, it is important to note that government anti-poverty programmes were not significant in any of the 36 villages studied. In fact, only a handful of households of all categories identified government assistance as significant within their trajectories of the past 25 years.

Second, the role of education is also noteworthy. Even though it does not achieve significance in statistical analysis, education was, in fact, associated with quite a few cases of ascent from poverty. Nearly 9 per cent of all ascending households mentioned education as an important factor. In almost all of these cases, however, a job in the private sector or in government was another important factor. Education has contributed successfully to poverty reduction, but only in those cases where the educated have also found jobs. Others who got education but did not find jobs have remained poor, indicating that increasing education without enlarging opportunities does not constitute a reliable pathway out of poverty (Deininger and Okidi, 2003: 505).

V. Conclusion

Progress in poverty reduction is not a one-way street, with households only coming out of poverty. Measures to help lift households out of poverty address only one side of the problem. Future poverty policies will need to consider not only those who have been 'left behind' by growth, but must also pay deliberate attention to the significant numbers of households that continue to fall into poverty.

Escapes from poverty occurred at roughly the same rate in the two time periods. However, nearly twice as many households fell into poverty in the last decade as compared to the earlier period. While 5.6 per cent of households fell into poverty in the first period, 10.9 per cent fell into poverty during the second period. As a result of this increased pace of descents, poverty reduction in these two regions of Uganda has slowed over the past ten years, even as national economic growth has accelerated.

Different sets of factors are associated, respectively, with movements upward, out of poverty, and movements downward, into poverty. Therefore, different policy measures will be required for dealing with these two separate sets of factors. In addition to cargo nets, which help carry households out of poverty, stronger safety nets will also be required that can prevent or slow down descents into poverty (Barrett, 2005; Devereux, 2002; Lipton, 1997).

Policies aimed at controlling descent will – and should – have some common aspects across both regions. However, more region-specific policies are also needed that address specific factors associated with the distinct geographic, cultural and socio-economic conditions of each separate region.

Slowing descent that has accelerated in recent years will require dealing urgently with three sets of negative factors. Ill health, high healthcare expenses, and the associated deaths of major income earners constitute the first of these three sets. These factors have contributed principally to households' descent into poverty in both regions – and they have become more significant for descent within the last ten years. Providing better and more affordable healthcare will therefore constitute a major part of the response to poverty-causing factors in both regions.

Other studies point similarly to the role played by health-related factors. Lawson (2004) and Deininger and Okidi (2003) similarly found ill health to be significantly associated with descent, with the latter study also indicating how sickness has increased in all regions of the country between 1992 and 1999. Infant mortality remains high and has not improved over the past five years (GoU, 2002b). Sickness is a very important reason for children dropping out of school and frequent school absences (Mijumbi and Okidi, 2001), and a close relationship exists between poverty and disability (Lwanga-Ntale, 2003).[15] Distance to health centres plays an important role in a household's ability to fend off sickness and poverty. While the location of the facility is not the only means of reducing vulnerability to poverty on account of ill health, it does have a significant impact (Okwi, 1999).

It is quite likely that AIDS has an important part to play in the increased significance of ill health between the first period and the second. We do not have any direct evidence about AIDS and its effects in these villages. Our method does not permit an examination of which particular illness is associated with each particular case of descent into poverty. It would be important, however, to examine better in future the associations that particular diseases have in different regions with pathways leading into poverty.

We examined the likely impact of HIV/AIDS indirectly, however, by constructing an interactive variable multiplying together the variables for large family size and death of income earner. This interactive variable was significantly associated with descent in both regions during the second time period (though not in the first time period). Okidi and Mugambe (2002) find evidence of a similar interaction between AIDS incidence and large family size. As many as 1.4 million children have been orphaned by AIDS in Uganda, and the households that have taken in these children have grown in size and become more vulnerable to poverty.

AIDS is not, however, the only cause of death or debility. Malaria continues to account for more deaths than AIDS (Hutchinson, 2001), so dealing with ill health as a reason for deepening poverty will require doing more than controlling AIDS and alleviating its effects in terms of increased dependence ratios.

Land and socially related factors must also be considered when formulating policies to control descent into poverty. Dealing with these two other clusters of negative factors will require more regionally differentiated responses. For example, while land exhaustion was salient for descent in Western villages, it was not significant in Central villages. Reducing future descents will require focusing on mitigating this factor in the Western region, while working to prevent its occurrence in Central villages. Analysis by Pender et al. (2004) suggests that soil fertility appears to have degraded throughout most of Uganda, while Olson and Berry (2003) indicate that large percentages of land in each region face acute degradation, with this percentage going as high as 90 per cent in Kabale district.

Cultural practices also vary between the two regions, giving rise to different factors associated with decline. Division of land and large family size are more salient for decline in Western compared to Central villages. Marriage expenses have the opposite effect, however, being significantly associated with material decline in Central but not in Western villages. Region- and even district-specific policies will be required to address these factors better.

A different set of policies will be needed to assist households in their efforts to escape from poverty. More focus on land-based policies for supporting escape will also be of considerable utility. Nearly 70 per cent of all households escaping poverty over the past 25 years were assisted in this transition by increased incomes derived from commercial cropping and diversification on agricultural land. However, concerns related to crop disease and land exhaustion must be addressed if this avenue out of poverty is to remain viable.

Less than 10 per cent of households escaping poverty over the past 25 years were assisted in this achievement by obtaining a job in the private sector. Indeed, the importance of private sector employment has diminished from the earlier period (ten to 25 years ago) to the more recent period (the past ten years).

Policies must stay current with these changes in order to remain relevant and to be more effective. Policies must also be differentiated significantly for different regions and districts, suggesting that causes associated with escape and descent will need to be studied more regularly on a decentralised and localised basis.

The Stages-of-Progress methodology is helpful for these purposes. In addition to examining the status and various characteristics of different households, it also enables an examination of the *processes* that accompany households' escape or descent. Positive reasons – those which help pull households upward – can be identified along with negative reasons, which push households downward, and policies can be formulated to address both sets of reasons as they operate within any specific region.

The application of this method within these 36 villages in Uganda shows that poverty policies will have to concentrate better upon expanded and more easily accessed rural health services, improved agricultural research and extension, and better incentives for private sector development. Preventing descents more effectively by focusing on the negative factors will be as important as promoting escapes through attending to the positive factors.

Why people fall into poverty needs to be known much better, and why only some people (and not others) are able to benefit from opportunities generated by growth also needs to be investigated more closely. Suitable methodologies need to be developed for figuring out better the processes that are associated with escape and descent at the micro level. The Stages-of-Progress methodology was developed with this purpose in mind, and it is currently being adapted and implemented in different parts of the developing world. Not only analysts, but also communities, can utilise these methods on their own to track poverty in their midst, to isolate reasons for escape and for descent, and to develop strategies to deal with these reasons.

Some limitations will need to be addressed, however, as this methodology is extended further. First, it will need to deal better with intra-household differences, particularly those based on gender. In its present form, the methodology does not disaggregate further below the household level.[16]

Second, the methodology will need to be adapted for dealing better with newly formed communities, particularly those in large cities. Because it relies upon commonly shared community memories, this methodology works better among more longstanding and close-knit communities. Such communities are easier to find in rural areas, and they are less prevalent in metropolitan areas, which limits the reach of the methodology in its present form.

Third, in order to understand poverty comprehensively in any region it is important to use multiple methods, including household surveys, panel studies, and participatory appraisals. Each method enables us to learn better about different aspects of poverty, and none can entirely replace the learning that accrues from another method.

Combining multiple methods in a single study will also help to validate results derived from each of them. Thus, single-period poverty statistics from the Stages-of-Progress method can and should be checked against results from conventional household surveys. At the same time, changes in poverty over time as indicated by repeat household surveys should be verified in terms of processes and reasons identified by a Stages-of-Progress study.

Because studies using different methods are undertaken in dissimilar spaces, it is not possible at the present time to compare results and obtain more comprehensive information on poverty and its causes.[17] We end, therefore, with a plea for a new set of more eclectic studies, concerned simultaneously with issues of 'how much' (poverty there is at some point in time) and issues of 'why' (households fall into or come out of poverty in some region). Studies combining different methods will contain in-built cross-checks on data and methods, they will be richer in terms of information provided, and more relevant for policy formation than any single-method study can ever be.

Acknowledgement

Krishna is Assistant Professor of Public Policy and Political Science at Duke University; Lumonya is Lecturer, Department of Social Work and Social Administration, Makerere University; Markiewicz is Program Director, Cross Sectoral Public Policy, Duke University; Kafuko and Magumya are Assistant Lecturers in the Department of Social Work and Social Administration at Makerere University; Wegoye provided data management expertise. Research support from the Cross Sectoral Public Policy programme at Duke University and I@mak at Makerere University is acknowledged with gratitude. Chris Barrett, Sam Hickey, John Hoddinott, David Hulme, Patti Kristjanson, Francis Lethem, Ole Therkildsen, Norman Uphoff, Steven Younger, participants at a workshop held in Kampala on 6 December 2004, and anonymous reviewers provided helpful comments. Special thanks to lead trainer, Dr. Mahesh Kapila and to the 25 research assistants and village community members who shared their knowledge with us. All of the usual disclaimers apply. Corresponding author: krishna@pps.duke.edu

Notes

1. Initial interviews with key informants suggested the inclusion of these particular districts for the following reasons: In Central region, Mukono is often regarded as a model district in terms of growth and poverty reduction, and it is also located close to the capital city, Kampala. Ssembabule is most remotely located in this region. Luwero has a history of insurgency; it was the epicentre of the prolonged bush war. In Western region, Bushenyi has a concentration of plantation agriculture, particularly coffee and bananas. Kabale has relatively high population density, mountainous terrain, and diverse agriculture, while cattle farming dominates the economy of Ntungamo district. Districts in these regions are considerably diverse, and selecting districts for diversity seemed appropriate in this context.
2. Later Stages of Progress beyond the first four were also very similar in these 36 villages. Some discrepancies arose, but they relate to the ordering of these later stages and not so much to their identification. Commonly shared Stages of Progress were also similarly reported when similar investigations were carried out in village communities of India and Kenya (Krishna, 2004, 2005; Krishna et al., 2004).
3. In five villages of Central region, community groups added 'household utilities,' that is, a basic few pots and pans, as an additional stage after Send Children to School and before Repair the Existing Shelter. The poverty cut-off in these five villages was drawn after stage five consequently. This additional stage did hardly anything to change the identity of households identified as poor: adjusting for it affected the classification of only three out of 494 households in these villages.
4. Villagers were usually not reticent about either their own or other households' situations along the Stages of Progress. Poverty is not stigmatised in these villages, as it is, for instance, in the West, and it is regarded as resulting from misfortune more than personal failure. The researchers did not label or otherwise segregate those who were found to occupy a stage below the poverty cut-off, and making clear that no material benefits would follow from this exercise removed the incentive for deliberate misrepresentation. The researchers also stressed that the respondents' names and material status would be held in confidence.
5. Some studies consider households of the previous time period as their unit of analysis, the Stages-of-Progress method does the reverse, considering households of the present time as its unit of analysis. This method fails to capture households of 25 years ago from which no single member survives in the community, and some bias is likely to arise on this account. Local inquiries revealed that this 'survivorship bias' affected both ends of the household distribution. A few households that no longer remained in these villages had done extremely well by migrating to cities. Some others that had done extremely poorly had also entirely vanished leaving no trace behind. Permanent migration out of these villages has been relatively small, however, affecting less than 3 per cent of all households.

6. There is an interesting correspondence, thus, between the Stages-of-Progress methodology and the asset-based framework of Barrett and Carter (2004).
7. We met with Uganda Bureau of Statistics (UBoS) officials to find whether other researchers had also come across similarly large downward trends in these or other villages. While we could not obtain any comparable village-level data from them, recent research by Kappel, Lay and Steiner (2005) and McGee (2004) provides similar evidence of a downward trend.
8. We examined a host of village-level features, including distance to market, population size, type of school facility, and so forth, but apart from distance to health centre none of the others was significantly associated with higher or lower poverty reduction.
9. An analysis of household panel data for 1992–99 similarly found ill health and death of income earners on account of illness to be particularly associated with descent into poverty (Lawson, 2004).
10. For an interesting examination of 'laziness' as a factor that is uncritically associated by some analysts with abiding poverty in rural Africa, see Whitehead (2000).
11. Coffee is particularly important in this respect. Place, Ssenteza and Otsuka (2001: 229) notes that 'while the average profit is higher for coffee, its variance is also higher'. Many respondents associated coffee cultivation with greater risk of loss and enhanced volatility.
12. Table 6 presents the complementary analysis of escaping from poverty. Category A and Category B households are considered here, to examine why some (but not other) previously poor households were able to escape from poverty. Independent variables were selected for both sets of analyses based on the previous analysis of interview and frequency data. Some variables (for example, ill health) can be alternately both causes and effects of poverty, thus these results should be interpreted with caution, especially to the extent they are not otherwise validated by household interviews and other data.
13. Age, or lifecycle effect, which was marginally significant (at the 5 per cent level though not at the 1 per cent level) while examining falling into poverty in Table 5, is not significant for the analysis of escaping poverty presented in Table 6.
14. Okidi and McKay (2003) also identify diversification as an important factor of ascent. Investigations conducted in other parts of the developing world similarly reveal the role that diversifying income sources has played for assisting households' escapes from poverty. See, for example, Ellis (2000) and Krishna (2004, 2005).
15. Uganda is hardly unique in this respect. In eight other African countries, studied by Christiaensen et al. (2002), ill health is also significantly associated with descent. Fabricant et al. (1999: 181–4) present evidence from a range of countries, which demonstrates how poorer households spend a much greater proportion of their incomes on healthcare. Sinha and Lipton (1999: 39) indicate how, in general, poorer households are exposed to different and more serious illness, injury and consequent costs. Macinko, Shi and Starfield (2004) demonstrate how the same is true within wealthy industrialised countries.
16. Intra-household differences based on gender can be investigated perhaps through incorporating an adapted version of the method used by Ravnborg, Boesen and Sorensen (2004).
17. For instance, only a very small number of households are studied in any village that is selected in national sample frames used for conventional household surveys. On the other hand, the Stages-of-Progress method considers all households in each studied village, and it ranks their poverty status in comparison with one another. This mismatch between study sites and study design makes it difficult at present to compare, combine and validate results from different studies.

References

Appleton, S. (2001a) Changes in poverty and inequality, in Ritva Reinikka and Paul Collier (Eds) *Uganda's Recovery: The Role of Farms, Firms, and Government* (Washington, DC: World Bank), pp. 83–102.

Appleton, Simon (2001b) *Poverty in Uganda, 1999/2000: Preliminary Estimates from the UNHS* (Nottingham: University of Nottingham).

Barrett, C., Reardon T. and Webb P. (2001) Nonfarm diversification and household livelihood strategies in rural Africa: concepts, dynamics, and policy implications. *Food Policy*, 26, pp. 315–31.

Barrett, C. (2005) Rural poverty dynamics: development policy implications. *Agricultural Economics*, forthcoming.

Bird, K. and Shinkeya, I. (2003) Multiple shocks and downward mobility: learning from the life histories of rural Ugandans. CPRC working paper 36, Chronic Poverty Research Centre, Manchester, UK.

Brock, K., McGee, R. and Ssewakiryanga, R. (2002) Poverty knowledge and policy processes: a case study of Ugandan national poverty reduction policy. Research report 53, Institute of Development Studies, Brighton, UK.

Carter, M. and Barrett, C. (2004) The economics of poverty traps and persistent poverty: an asset-based approach. Presented at the BASIS-CRSP Policy Conference, Washington DC, 15–16 November 2004, available at www.basis.wisc.edu/persistentpoverty.html.

Chambers, R. (1995) Poverty and livelihoods: whose reality counts. Discussion paper 347. Institute of Development Studies, Brighton, UK.

Christiaensen, L., Demery, L. and Paternostro, S. (2002) *Growth, Distribution and Poverty in Africa: Messages from the 1990s* (Washington, DC: World Bank).

Collier, P. and Reinikka, R. (2001) Introduction, in R. Reinikka and C. Collier (Eds) *Uganda's Recovery: The Role of Farms, Firms, and Government* (Washington, DC: World Bank), pp. 1–12.

CPRC (2004) *The Chronic Poverty Report 2004–05* (Manchester, UK: Chronic Poverty Research Centre).

Deininger, K. and Okidi, J. (2003) Growth and poverty reduction in Uganda, 1992–2000: panel data evidence. *Development Policy Review*, 21(4), pp. 481–509.

Devereux, S. (2002) Can social safety nets reduce chronic poverty? *Development Policy Review*, 20(5), pp. 657–75.

Ellis, F. (2000) *Rural Livelihoods and Diversity in Developing Countries* (New York: Oxford University Press).

Fabricant, S., Kamara, C, and Mills A. (1999) Why the poor pay more: household curative expenditures in rural Sierra Leone. *International Journal of Health Planning and Management*, 14, pp. 179–99.

GoU (2001) *Poverty Status Report* (Kampala: Ministry of Finance, Planning and Economic Development, Government of Uganda).

GoU (2002a) *Second Participatory Poverty Assessment Report: Deepening the Understanding of Poverty* (Kampala: Ministry of Finance, Planning and Economic Development, Government of Uganda).

GoU (2002b) *Infant Mortality in Uganda, 1995–2000: Why the Non-Improvement?* (Kampala: Ministry of Finance, Planning and Economic Development, Government of Uganda).

Hickey, S. (2005) The politics of staying poor in Uganda: exploring the political space for poverty reduction in Uganda. *World Development*, forthcoming.

Hutchinson, P. (2001) Combating illness, in Ritva Reinikka and Paul Collier (Eds) *Uganda's Recovery: The Role of Farms, Firms, and Government* (Washington, DC: World Bank), pp. 407–9.

Jayne, T.S., Yamano, T., Weber, M., Tschirley, D., Benfica, R., Chapoto, A. and Zulu, B. (2003) Smallholder income and land distribution in Africa: implications for poverty reduction strategies. *Food Policy*, 28, pp. 253–73.

Kappel, R., Lay, J. and Steiner, S. (2005) Uganda: no more pro-poor growth? *Development Policy Review*, 23(1), pp. 27–53.

Krishna, A. (2004) Escaping poverty and becoming poor: who gains, who loses, and why? *World Development*, 32(1), pp. 121–36.

Krishna, A. (2005) Why growth is not enough: household poverty dynamics in northeast Gujarat, India. *Journal of Development Studies*, forthcoming.

Krishna, A., Kristjanson, P., Radeny, M. and Nindo, W. (2004) Escaping poverty and becoming poor in 20 Kenyan villages. *Journal of Human Development*, 5(2), pp. 211–26.

Lawson, D. (2004) Uganda: the influence of health on chronic and transitory poverty. CPRC working paper 41, Chronic Poverty Research Centre, Manchester, UK, available at www.chronicpoverty.org.

Lawson, D., McKay, A. and Okidi, J. (2003) Poverty persistence and transitions in Uganda: a combined qualitative and quantitative analysis. CPRC working paper 38, Chronic Poverty Research Centre, Manchester, UK.

Lipton, M. (1997) Editorial: poverty – are there holes in the consensus? *World Development*, 25(7), 1003–7.

Lwanga-Ntale, C. (2003) Chronic poverty and disability in Uganda. CPRC working paper, Chronic Poverty Research Centre, Manchester, UK.

Lwanga-Ntale, C. and McClean, K. (2003) The face of chronic poverty in Uganda as seen by the poor themselves. CPRC working paper, Chronic Poverty Research Centre, Manchester, UK.

Macinko, J., Shi, L. and Starfield, B. (2004) Wage inequality, the health system, and infant mortality in wealthy industrialised countries, 1970–1996. *Social Science and Medicine*, (58), 279–92.

McGee, R. (2004) Constructing poverty trends in Uganda: a multidisciplinary perspective. *Development and Change*, 35(3), pp. 499–523.

Mijumbi, P. and Okidi, J. (2001) Analysis of poor and vulnerable groups in Uganda. Occasional paper No.16, Economic Policy Research Centre, Kampala.

Okidi, J. and McKay, A. (2003) Poverty dynamics in Uganda: 1992 to 2000. CPRC working paper 27, Chronic Poverty Research Centre, Manchester, UK.

Okidi, J. and Mugambe, G. (2003) An overview of chronic poverty and development policy in Uganda. CPRC working paper 11, Chronic Poverty Research Centre, Manchester, UK.

Okwi, P. (1999) Poverty in Uganda: a multivariate analysis. EPRC research series No.22, Economic Policy Research Centre, Kampala.

Olson, J. and Berry, L. (2003) Land degradation in Uganda: its extent and impact, available at lada.virtualcentre.org/eims/download.asp?pub_id = 92082.

Pender, J., Jagger, P., Nkonya, E. and Sserunkuuma, D. (2004) Development pathways and land management in Uganda. *World Development*, 32(5), pp. 767–92.

Place, F., Ssenteza, J. and Otsuka, K. (2001) Customary and private land management in Uganda, in Otsuka and Place (Eds) *Land Tenure and Natural Resource Management* (Baltimore: Johns Hopkins University Press), pp. 195–233.

Ravnborg, H. M., Boesen, J. and Sorensen, A. (2004) Gendered district poverty profiles and poverty monitoring: Kabarole, Masaka, Pallisa, Rakai and Tororo Districts, Uganda. DIIS working paper 2004: 1, Danish Institute for International Studies, Copenhagen.

Sinha, S. and Lipton, M. (1999) Damaging fluctuations, risk and poverty: an overview. Background paper for the World Development Report 2000/2001. Poverty Research Unit, University of Sussex.

Ssewanyana, S., Okidi, J., Angemi, D. and Barungi, V. (2004) *Understanding the Determinants of Income Inequality in Uganda* (Kampala: Economic Policy Research Institute).

Whitehead, A. (2000) Continuities and discontinuities in political constructions of the working man in sub-saharan Africa: the 'lazy man' in African agriculture. *European Journal of Development Research*, 12 (2), pp. 23–52.

Woodhouse, P. (2003) Local identities of poverty: poverty narratives in decentralised government and the role of poverty research in Uganda. Working paper, IDPM, University of Manchester.

INDEX